THE GULF OF NAPLES

Archaeology and History of an Ancient Land

UMBERTO PAPPALARDO

THE GULF OF NAPLES

Archaeology and History of an Ancient Land

Photographs by Luciano Pedicini

arsenale editrice

Umberto Pappalardo

The Gulf of Naples
Archaeology and History of an Ancient Land

Contributors:
Mario Grimaldi: Pre-history, Naples and
Naples National Archaeological Museum.
Rosaria Ciardiello: Capri, Ischia, Cuma,
Sorrento, Benevento, Capua, Phlegrean Fields.
Annapaola Capuano: Paestum and Velia.
Ivan Varriale: iconographic research.

Photographs by
Luciano Pedicini

English translation by
Peter Eustace

Editorial co-ordination
Paola Gobbi

Editor
Fabrizio Tolu

Printed by
EBS Editoriale Bortolazzi-Stei,
Verona

First edition
May 2006

Arsenale Editrice
A division of EBS
Via Monte Comun, 40
I-37057 San Giovanni Lupatoto (Vr)
www.arsenale.it
arsenale@arsenale.it

© 2006 Arsenale-EBS

ISBN 88-7743-316-7

Summary

NAPLES, A GREEK-ROMAN CAPITAL IN THE MEDITERRANEAN

"*We are the sons of an ancient people*" wrote Luciano De Crescenzo in his famous book *Thus Spoke Bellavista*. In short, this awareness of Antiquity is deeply rooted in the heart of the Neapolitan people, a phlegmatic and know-all people who know that time is always a third, invisible actor in all human relationships. Such antiquity is continually reminded to people even by the ancient remains standing all over the city that – two thousand years later – lives its ancient architectural substratum as if time has stood still. This millennial stratification and this "spirit of time", accumulated in the alleys and hearts of Neapolitans, is perhaps what most fascinates tourists. This is why the renaissance of Naples will always resume from the recovery of its particular historic, artistic and human heritage.

The history of Campania, over thousands of years of development, demonstrates certain constants that have determined many of its present-day characteristics.

The physical configuration and fertility of these places always attracted "foreigners" – ancient Myceneans and 1700s tourists taking the "Grand Tour" – and encouraged settlements by colonists and conquerors. Mycenean and Phoenician merchants – the first to travel to this more western part of the Mediterranean – found in the scenario of the Gulf a welcoming and reassuring haven thanks to the beauty of its places, the mild climate, the fertile land and the plentiful ports.

The creation of Greek and Phoenician emporiums was followed by the first colonists, from all over Greece: from Rhodes (to Naples), from Eubea (to Ischia and Cuma), from Samos (Pozzuoli) and from Focea (Velia). The Greeks colonists resident in Campania exported as far as Etruria, north of the Tiber, the products of the land (olive oil, wine and wheat) receiving in exchange the iron processed in Ischia, where ferrous slag from the island of Elba has been found.

While the Greeks settled along the coast, the Etruscans occupied the hinterland, with their capital in Campania at Capua, extending behind Vesuvius as far as Fratte and Pontecagnano (Salerno). At times, they made incursions as far as the coast (Pompeii and Punta della Campanella).

The cultural and technological heritage of the Myceneans and the Greek colonists was much more advanced than among local peoples. This awareness is stated by Virgil in Book VI of the Aeneid, where he tells how Dedalus had to travel from Crete to carve the bronze doors of the Temple of Apollo at Cumae (the origin of metallurgy). It was through the Greeks in Cumae that the Etruscans and Italic peoples learned the alphabet. Campania and Magna Graecia saw the foundation of two of the great schools of philosophy in Antiquity: the Pythagorean (mathematics) and Heleatic (medicine) schools.

The co-existence in this region of Greeks, Etruscans, Opics and Samnites gave civilisation in Campania a polymorph aspect, generating certain typical features of the local people still today vital and characteristic, such as: tolerance in daily life, imagination, acceptance of innovations and warm hospitality.

The city of Naples is the only one in the world that has grown seamlessly from its ancient urban fabric. The ancient Greek and Roman roads are still reflected in the layout of the current historic centre characterised by the Hippodamean ground plan designed in V century B.C. Via Spaccanapoli, for instance, perfectly follows the Roman "decumanus". The city has stratified its building history, since later expansion and reconstruction have overlapped pre-existing structures. The city is also the only one that is "nurtured" by its underground resources, made up of enormous beds of tuff. Continual excavations first and foremost for building reasons – since tuff is an excellent construction material – has created by today a full-scale "underground city": a network of tunnels merely 30 metres below ground level extending for over 400 kilometres!

These tunnels were always and continually utilised for all kinds of purposes: Hellenistic necropolis, Christian catacombs, cemeteries in the 1600s and 1800s following frequent pestilences, water channels, road traffic and pedestrian underpasses, air-raid shelters during the last war and – as the latest crime news suggests – even as a secret road network used by smugglers and bank raiders.

Opposite: Map of Campania by G.A. Rizzi Zannoni (1797). Naples, National Library.

THE GREEKS AND GREEK COLONISATION

Greek colonisation of southern Italy.

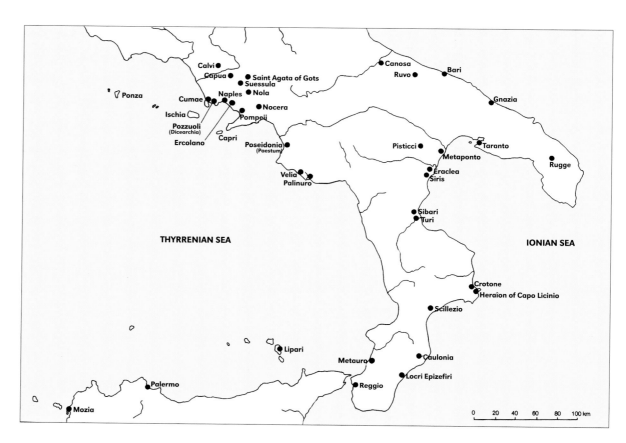

Mycenean pre-colonisation

The colonisation of Magna Graecia began precisely in Campania VIII century B.C., but was preceded by "pre-colonisation" under the Myceneans. In short, ancient sources – especially Strabo – narrate that numerous Greek heroes, on their return from the Trojan war, travelled here to found a city and fought against native peoples. Inasmuch, the coasts of Sicily, the Aeolian islands and the Tyrrhenian coastline almost as far as the Sarno estuary are rich in explicit archaeological evidence witnessing the arrival of the Myceneans in the II

millennium – the period corresponding to mythical colonisation. Evidently, in epic narratives, the Greeks were inspired to plough the seas in their mythical adventures, founding cities and setting up sanctuaries. In reality, mythical narration in the archaic age was a means of interpreting history; inasmuch, we must learn how to recognise true events in such myths. In short, Mycenean sailors were actually stimulated by the need to verify new sea routes for commerce in metals; they therefore challenged the dangerous currents of the Strait of Messina (personified by the mermaids Scilla and

Charybdis) and then sailed up along the Tyrrhenian coasts; after passing the currents of Cape Palinuro, they came upon delightful plains and rivers offering safe haven. The insidious currents and unfriendly lands were fixed in the mind of Palinuro, Aeneas' unhappy helmsman, who fell into the sea asleep while rounding the cape, as well as at Punta Licosa, where the hazards of navigation were transfigured into the myth of the mermaid Leucosia, whose body was deposited here by the billowing waves. Even Odysseus himself possibly passed through the Strait of Messina as far as the Circeo promontory and, travelling through Cam-

While "heroic colonisation" was more or less contemporary with the Iliad and the Odyssey, it was narrated in literature much later (VII-VI century B.C.). Evidently, all Greek peoples, when founding their cities, commemorated a particular epic hero in order to legitimise the occupation of a given territory in Italy; inasmuch, they were not expropriating native peoples but only reclaiming what already belonged to them.

Historical colonisation
Historical colonisation took place in VIII-V century B.C. Without doubt, traces of prior Mycenean

pania, apparently founded a sanctuary in honour of Athena at Punta della Campanella, near Sorrento. From Filottetes to Epeius, the carpenter of the Trojan Horse; from the subjects of Nestor, King of Pylos, to Diomedes – they all proved their valour in their travels and stays in the West.
Finds of Myceanean ceramics demonstrate the validity of these traditions, even if such items can be traced to a period much earlier than the destruction of Troy – that Erastothenes dated in 1184 B.C. – such as Vivara, even as early as XIV century B.C.

sailing expeditions remained in the memory of those Greeks who, from VIII century, travelled these westward routes. Our information about colonial foundations comes from literary sources and archaeological excavations, that often even suggest the exact year when a colony was set up.
Emigration from Greece was stimulated by growth in population and the development of trade. It was essentially a search for new lands, yet there was also the need to create a network of commercial relationships to supply the workshops in the mothercountry with raw materials.

These colonies therefore met the need of new space for a growing population. City institutions decided who should emigrate, the leader of the expedition (the "ecista") and the representatives of the dominant social classes responsible for supervising the enterprise. In some cases, this involved banishment – as for the Samii of *Dicearchia* – or escape – as was the case for the Phocaeans of *Elea*.

Native settlements and the first cities

When the colonists arrived, there were no cities. Native settlements focused on villages with huts built with wooden poles and mud walls; their bases comprised dry stone walls; there was a fireplace in the interior. Ceramics were not yet worked with a lathe and even figurative decorations were extremely primitive compared to the levels already attained by Greek art in the geometric age.

Yet the first colonial generation did not have time enough to create urban structures. Evidently, the early years saw only the establishment of urban perimeters, while cities as such were only finalised by later generations. The new cities therefore developed in the course of two generations. The Italic peoples were violently driven to the new cities as a labour force for the colonists. The various colonial cities did not embody an harmonised model yet nevertheless required homes, places for meetings and worship, and agricultural land. In short, individual colonists received land in the city to build a home and land in the country for agriculture. The civic area in the Greek world was the *agorà* or market, which the Romans later re-named as the *forum*.

Places of worship

Places of worship were already defined by the first colonists but their conversion into monuments only took place as of VII century B.C.

In VI-V century B.C., the public and holy areas of the cities of Magna Graecia took on a monumental appearance in the wake of new wealth.

The best-conserved temple architecture is to be found in *Poseidonia*; the most ancient of the three temples is the so-called Basilica, dedicated to Hera, as well as the nearby "Temple of Neptune": it can be dated after mid-VI century (about 550 B.C.) about a century older than its neighbour (about 450 B.C.); end-VI century (about 500 B.C.) is the so-called "Temple of Ceres", dedicated to Athena.

The Doric was the most frequent architectural order. Exceptions are the rare Ionic temples, such as the one in the acropolis at Velia.

Places of worship frequently come to light at crossroads, such as those dedicated to Hera on the Sele estuary or to Poseidon, handed down by sources, between Velia and *Poseidonia*.

All these sanctuaries were located on promontories or river estuaries – ideal sites for safe navigation – such as Heraion on the Sele estuary near Paestum, Palinuro south of Velia, and perhaps Sirene at Punta della Campanella. In particular, the sanctuary of Hera is eight kilometres from the city, close to the Sele estuary. The main building, founded by hero Jason, dates from end-VI century B.C. This building was preceded about a century earlier by one decorated with metopes, slabs and figurative reliefs. The sanctuary dates back to no earlier than mid-VII century B.C., since the area was probably an ancient landing-place for sailors.

Places of worship were also founded outside colonial settlements. It should never be forgotten that exchanges between different peoples often take place within the scope of religion. In any case, certain country fairs are still held today during religious festivals and in places outside towns – especially at crossroads – encouraging meetings and exchanges between different peoples.

Literacy

Writing was still in its early days in VIII century. The necropolis at *Pithecusa* revealed an engraved goblet imitating Homeric verses – evident proof of the spread of such poetics to the West. In addition, the signature of an artist in Ischia "*-inos m'epoiese*" bears witness to another major innovation introduced by the Greeks into Italy: literacy.

The most ancient imports

The most ancient imports in Italy were ceramics manufactured on the large island of Eubea, in the Aegean.

Pithecusa by the second half of VIII century B.C. already had its own production of ceramics: the same period also saw imports of Phoenician goods – not only ceramics but also objects in bronze and decorative elements. Phoenician merchants almost certainly traded in *Pithecusa*.

Most imports came from Corinth from mid-VIII to mid-VI century B.C. Judging from quantities, it could well be said that Corinthian commerce was essential in Magna Graecia, even if Corinth only had one colony (Syracuse). Trade involved small jars used to hold ointments and perfumes. There were also larger recipients, such as jugs, bowls and jars for the symposium. Local imitations were also produced.

The discovery of ovens and processing waste confirms widespread local manufacture of ceramics in the archaic period. The most common products were "Ionic goblets" decorated with narrow bands on a black enamelled base. Etruscan and so-called "boccaro" versions were also very frequent. Another type of ceramic production that was very common in VI-V century B.C. involved Attic figurative arts. While there is no proof of exports from Campania to Greece, the cause may perhaps lie in the fact that such exports especially involved raw materials and foodstuffs.

Agricultural production

As regards agricultural production, the system set up suggests that local peoples were forced to supply their produce to the colonists.

On the other hand, the main new foods introduced into Italy by the Greeks were grapes and olives. Literary sources for *Poseidonia* suggest that cereals were grown and horses reared in the plains, while the hills were exploited for livestock grazing, forestry and quarries. This was the onset of rational exploitation of the territory that culminated under the Romans.

Sculpture

Since there was no marble available, sculpture was essentially in limestone. In short, local stone was used for architectural decorations in *Poseidonia*, where there are two series of reliefs carved fifty years apart: the oldest dates from mid-VI century B.C., and depicts the Feats of Hercules and Odysseus on the turtle; the more recent, dating from the end of the same century, has repetitive pairs of female figures like dancing nymphs.

Inasmuch, figurative production was essentially in terracotta, such as the numerous figurative votary statuettes. There was also a larger painted terracotta sculpture – a seated male figure, probably a god – from *Poseidonia*.

The spread of marble sculptures increased, on the other hand, in V century B.C., as well as local processing.

Goldware and bronze artefacts

Strabo indicates gold-work as one of the reasons for the prosperity of *Pithecusa*. Inasmuch, it is assumed that some of the stupendous Etruscan fibulae may have been made in Ischia.

There are a great many gold and silver ornaments in Campania and their typology is similar to finds made in Greece.

As for bronze-work, on the other hand, ancient sources indicate Capua as a major production centre. The huge bronze works found at *Poseidonia*, on the other hand, may have been imported from Sibari.

Coinage

Sibari is attributed with the introduction of coins into Italy around mid-VI century B.C. The use of coins, despite the intrinsic value of the metal, always has a nominal value and assumes the warranty of an authority or institutional organisation.

The various cities adopted different weights and measures but they all represented a recognisable type together with the name of the city. The *Poseidonia* type depicts its patron divinity: Poseidon bearing his trident; *Neapolis*, influenced by Syracuse, used the nymph Parthenope, resembling Arethusa; Cuma adopted the mussel, and lastly Elea, in IV century, Athena and the lion.

Conclusion

In synthesis, Greek colonisation involved – for Italy in general and Campania in particular – a radical cultural and technological renewal. The introduction of the alphabet, the potter's lathe, grape and olive growing, urbanisation principles, domestic and religious architecture in stone and artistic culture were some of the elements that helped bring about "modernisation", involving Italy – as compared with countries north of the Alps – in the circuits of the great civilisation of the Mediterranean.

ISCHIA

Opposite page. Top: ground plan of the port of Ischia. Bottom: view of Forio d'Ischia in a painting by Philipp Hackert (XVIII century). Caserta, Royal Palace.

"In front of Cape Miseno there is the island of Prochyta, a fragment detached from Pithecusa. Pithecusa was colonised by the Eretraeans and Chalcidaeans, yet – despite living in prosperity thanks to the fertility of the earth and its gold mines – they abandoned the island following warfare, as well as earthquakes and eruptions of fire, boiling sea and water: the island, in short, suffered from volcanic exhalations which also prompted the envoys sent by Ieron, the tyrant of Syracuse, to leave the fortress and the island (after the battle of Cuma in 474 B.C., when Ieron defeated the Etruscans); *lastly, it was occupied by certain inhabitants of Neapolis on arriving here. These phenomena also gave rise to the myth whereby Typhon* (a monster with one hundred dragon heads who fought against Zeus and stole his thunderbolts) *lay under the island itself; his movements provoked flames and high seas and, at times, even small islands with jets of boiling water. Pindarus was more credible: his observations of these phenomena lead him to say that this region, from Cumae as far as Sicily, is volcanic with several deep, interlinked cavities stretching as far as the continent. Inasmuch, Etna presents these phenomena mentioned in all descriptions, just as for the Lipari islands and various places in the area around Dicearchia, Neapolis, Baia and, lastly, the island of Pithecusa. With these phenomena in mind, Pindarus claimed that Typhon lay beneath all this place: "Now the sea shores surrounding Cumae and Sicily stand on his great hairy chest"* (Pindarus, Pythica 1, 18 and following).

As for Pithecusa in particular, Timeus (IV century B.C.) *said that the ancients narrated many extraordinary things and that shortly before him the Epopeo Hill* (present-day Mount Epomeo), *in the middle of the island, was shaken by earthquakes, vomiting fire and flinging outwards all the land between it and the sea. A portion of the earth reduced to ash was first raised, then fell again upon the island as if in a typhoon, while the sea retreated by 3 stadiums; then, after withdrawing, the sea flowed violently back, submerging the island and dousing the fire; the tremendous noise prompted the people on the continent to escape inland from the coast of Campania.*

It seems that the spa waters found here are a cure for people suffering from gall-stones".

Strabo, *Geographia* V, 4, 9

History

The island of Ischia, the ancient *Pithecusa*, played a primary role as a trading point for Phoenician, Euboaean and Cypriot sailors travelling the ancient routes previously followed by the Mycenaeans. It was a safe port, where ships could dock to take on supplies of food and water and trade their wares; it soon became the centre for wide-ranging traffic of peoples and raw materials. It traded the metal from Elba and the ore-bearing sites of Tolfa. It was precisely from *Pithecusa* that a group of Greeks, Euboaeans and Chalcidaeans around 725 B.C., then decided to cross the narrow stretch of sea separating them from *Cumae*. Perhaps they only intended to set up a settlement colony or perhaps, more simply, conquer one of the outposts for supremacy over sea trading routes. The crossing was short yet the enterprise was immense. It is likely that harsh action was taken against the local peoples. Nonetheless, the expedition signalled the onset of one of the historic moments destined to leave an indelible mark on the entire future development of western civilisation: the Greek colonisation of the West.

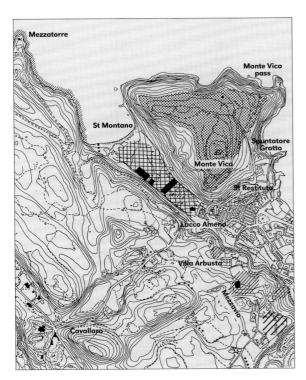

Ischia shares its volcanic origin with nearby Procida and the Phlegrean Fields. Still today, the island of Ischia has numerous spas with exhalations of vapours and emissions of hot water. The ancients explained this phenomenon by saying that Typhon, the rebel giant killed by Jove, was buried beneath the island and that his decomposing body issued flames and the sulphurous odours.

The Greek name *Pithekoussai* is traditionally translated as "the island of monkeys", although the other, preferable interpretation is "the island of the *pithoi*" (jars and vases), given the exceptional quality of its clay.

Believed by historians to be the first Greek colony in the West, the *emporion* was built around 770 B.C. as the centre for international trade, as witnessed by archaeological finds: pottery in the geometrical style from Chalcidice and Corinth, Phoenician vases, Attic amphoras, jars and vases in the Daunian geometrical style and Etruscan pottery. The island was densely populated from the very first settlements.

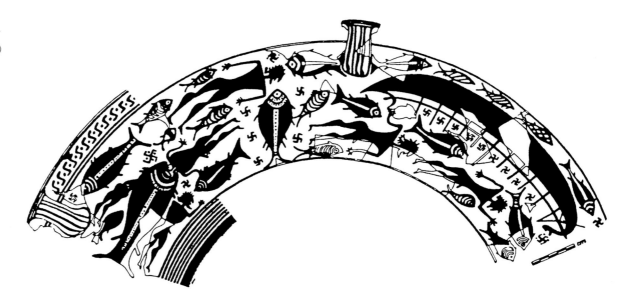

*"Crater of the Shipwreck"
and graphic reconstruction of
the decoration (725-700 B.C.)
– necropolis of* Pithecusa.
*Lacco Ameno, Ischia,
Archaeological Museum,
Villa Arbusto.*

The main settlement stood on the summit of Monte Vico, in the north-west of the island, today unfortunately partly destroyed by landslides. The excavation of the town revealed ceramics dating continuously from VIII century B.C. through to the Roman age. Monte Vico was the acropolis and very easy to defend, since it as delineated on two sides by inlets in the coastline, used as ports, and protected inland within the San Montano Valley where the necropolis was built.

Study of the necropolis highlights social distinctions: every family had its own burial place; adults were buried with a crematory rite, while those less than 18-20 years old were entombed.

The Mezzavia hill and the Mazzola village have revealed settlements dating from VIII-VI century B.C. with testimony of metal working. Strabo (V 4, 9) mentions gold (*chruseia*) on the island; perhaps rather than gold mines as such, we should assume local processing of imported precious metal in the workshops of goldsmiths; it is even supposed that the rich gold-work found in Etruria and commonly known as "Etruscan in the ancient oriental style" was in part produced in *Pithecussai*. Production waste highlights that craftsmen also exported, in the form of finished goods, other metal materials – although the raw material itself was imported from Etruria.

Great importance can be given to the archaic, apse-like homes and ovens found at Lacco Ameno beneath the Church of Santa Restituta.

Remains of a farm dating back to the period when the emporium was built were recently excavated in the Chiarito Cape area. Preserved intact with all its artefacts, the hut was then rebuilt in the National Archaeological Museum in Naples. Paleobotanical analysis confirms cultivation of olives and vines.

The contingent of Chalcidaeans and Eretrians left from the island of Ischia to found the first true Greek colony on firm land: *Cumae*. The island remained under its dominion until VI century B.C. *Cumae* then donated it to the Syracusans in exchange for their aid in 474 B.C. in the battle against the Etruscans, although the Syracusan military contingent sent here withdrew because of a violent earthquake.

It passed under the control of Naples and was then requisitioned, together with the city's fleet, by Sulla, after defeating Marius, supported by the city of Naples. Augustus returned Ischia to the Neapoli-

tans in exchange for Capri. The island then came to be known as *Aenaria*. In view of the numerous volcanic eruptions, the Romans never stationed here in force as in the Phlegrean Fields.

The Museum

Villa Arbusto, at Lacco Ameno, is home to the *Pithecusa* Archaeological Museum, with finds from the middle Neolithic Age through to the Roman Age, thereby witnessing the intense trading relationships developed between *Pithecusa* and the main emporia in the Mediterranean. Many of these objects were collected thanks to the archaeological research conducted by Giorgio Buchner from 1952.

The Museum has thousands of objects from the burial treasures found in the necropolis of San Montano (Lacco Ameno). The most important artefacts include the so-called "Cup of Nestor" and a fragment of a basin produced locally with late geometrical decorations and a signature with gaps "*... inos m'epoiese*" ("*... inos made me*") – the most ancient potter's signature ever found in the Greek world. Another highly interesting item is the locally made basin dating from end-VII century B.C. painted with a shipwreck scene. Testimony of

Cup of Nestor with graphic reconstruction of the inscription (725-700 B.C.) – necropolis of Pithecusa*. Lacco Ameno, Ischia, Archaeological Museum, Villa Arbusto.*

intense trade emerges in the Egyptian scarabs, one of which is inscribed on the scroll with the name of the pharaoh *Bocchoris* and oriental seals of the "Lyre Player Group". The main testimony of the Roman age involves marble votary reliefs from the sanctuary of the Nymphs at Nitrodi (Barano) and the lead and tin ingots from a foundry, today submerged, at Carta Romana.

The "Cup of Nestor" is undoubtedly the most prestigious item in the collection; it was found in 1954-1955 in the necropolis of San Montano, in tomb 168 for a young boy aged about ten years. The Cup of Nestor, King of Pilos in Messenia, was a major reliquary of Antiquity, a kind of Holy Grail of the Homerian epopea. In short, the Iliad (XI 632-637) describes this famous bronze vase with four handles, decorated with gold bosses and two pecking gold doves on each handle, from which Nestor and Macaon sipped a restorative drink of Pramnos wine mixed with goat's cheese and flour. Possession of the mythical goblet over later centuries became a matter of honour for many sanctuaries, testifying to their antiquity and venerability. In the Roman age, possession was claimed – among many other sites – by the Temple of Diana Tifatina at Capua. One may inasmuch imagine the surprise and emotion of the archaeologists on reading the inscriptions of fragments of a *kotyle* imported from Rhodes in VIII century B.C. the following epigram comprising three verses engraved backwards (that is, from right to left), with characters in the Euboaean alphabet: "*I am the good goblet where Nestor drank / whosoever drinks from the goblet / shall be immediately taken by the desire of Aphrodite of the fine crown*". Without doubt, the item in Ischia is not the legendary goblet of Nestor but only a convivial and playful citation. The owner, a skilled versifier parodying Homer, boasts the virtues of his goblet that, albeit not in precious bronze, evidently did not have lesser aphrodisiac properties.

In any case, this remains a very important discovery even from a literary point of view, since these verses are the oldest known of the Greek poetry and, while written on a humble clay jar, are the only verses written at the same time as the *Iliad*.

Opposite page.
View of San Montano at Ischia.

This page, fragment of geometrical vase with artist' signature. Lacco Ameno, Ischia, Archaeological Museum, Villa Arbusto.

CUMA

Map of Cumae and its territory.

Opposite: remains of the
Temple of Apollo – Acropolis
of Cumae.

"These cities are followed by Cumae, a very ancient settlement of the Chalcidaeans and Cumaeans and the most ancient of all colonies in Sicily and Italy.

Hippocles of Cumae (from Euboaean Cumae or Aeolian Cumae, in Asia Minor) and Megastenes of Chalcis, the leaders of the colonial expedition, agreed that the city should be a colony of the Chalcidaeans but should be named Cumae: this is why it is still called Cumae despite – as it seems – having been colonised by the Chalcidaeans. The city was initially prosperous, just like the so-called Phlegrean Plain, home to the legend of the Giants – if only since this fertile land was a constant bone of contention.

Later (421 B.C.), the Campanian people, having conquered the city, unleashed all kinds of violence on the local inhabitants and, in short, even lived with their women. In any case, there are still many traces of the Greek order involving holy ceremonies and legislative standards.

Some experts suggest that Cumae took its name from "kumata" (waves): in short, the nearby beach is rocky and exposed to the winds. There are also excellent fishing grounds nearby for large fish. The gulf itself also has a wood with small trees covering a rather larger area, lacking water and sandy, known as 'Silva Gallinaria'. Here, the leaders of Sextus Pompeus's fleet brought together the pirate crews during his rebellion in Sicily against Rome (43 B.C.)".

Strabo, *Geographia* V 4, 4-7

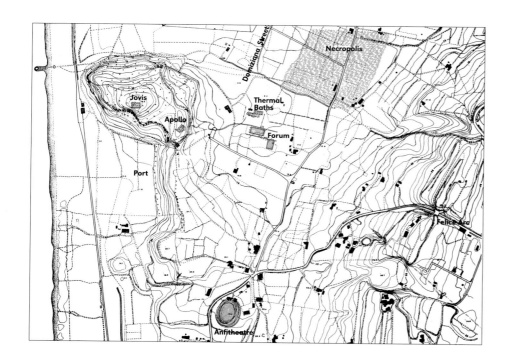

History

Cuma was one of the most important colonies in Magna Graecia. Its domain extended from Cape Miseno as far as Punta Campanella. It was founded in the second half of VIII century B.C. by Chalcidaean colonists originally from the island of Euboea, under Hippocles and Megastenes. These colonists suppressed the local peoples – with whom they had initially traded – and settled on the high part of the promontory (where they then built an acropolis) and, subsequently, even in the lower areas. Between VII and VI century B.C., the territorial domain of the city extended throughout the Phlegrean region, as witnessed by the spread of its cults, the distribution of artefacts characteristic of Hellenistic civilisation and the introduction of the alphabet.

The growth of Cumae's power provoked an alliance between the Daunians and Auruncians, the Italic peoples in Campania, under the command of the

Etruscans of Capua. In 524 B.C., the Cumaeans managed to defeat their much more numerous rivals, thanks to the tactical skill of their commander, Aristodemus, who became immensely famous after this victory. When, in 505 B.C., a Latin coalition requested the help of the Cumaeans against the Etruscans, the oligarchs of Cumae decided to send to Aricia a military contingent headed by Aristodemus, in the hope that the general would not return from the battle field. On the other hand, another victory signalled his definitive ascent to power: Aristodemus remained the tyrant of Cumae at least until 492 B.C. It was only between 492 and 490 B.C. that a conspiracy incited by the Cumaean oligarchs – having found refuge in Etruscan Capua – brought about a revolution and the deposition of Aristodemus, who was killed together with his family. The new government, however, marked the decline of the city.

In 474 B.C., in defence against the Etruscans, by now allies of the Punics, the old city formed an alliance with Syracuse, then the leading metropolis in the Greek West. The sea battle was fought in the waters of Cumae. The Etruscan fleet was sunk and with it the Etruscan civilisation also came to an end. An Etruscan helmet in bronze was dedicated in the sanctuary of Olympia.

This was how the poet Pindarus sang the victory of the Syracusan tyrant Ieron at Cumae: "*and so the war shouts of the Tyrrhennians* (that is to say, the Etruscans) *were silenced by the Syracusans who, from the tops of their ships threw the best youth into the sea … saving Greece from dire slavery*". Syracuse, by now in control of the Gulf of Naples, took the initiative and founded *Neapolis*, where their influence was evident in the ground plan, cults and coinage. Half a century later, in 421-420 B.C., the Samnites, succeeding the Etruscans in domain of Campania, also occupied Cumae. Subjected to Rome, Cumae achieved the *civitas sine suffragio* in 338 B.C.; the city remained faithful to Rome during Hannibal's invasion. In 180 B.C., Rome gave the city the status of *municipium* and, with full entitlement to political rights, its citizens began to use Latin as the official language. Under the Empire, the city was unaffected by the far-reaching urban renewal that changed Pozzuoli and Baia and was almost abandoned.

On becoming one of the first Christian centres in Campania, its temples were converted into Christian basilicas. It was the theatre of bitter warfare between the Goths and the Byzantines in VI century. Devastated in X century by the Saracens, it declined to a mere castle, where pirates and corsairs sought refuge. In 1207, the citadel was razed by the inhabitants of Naples and Aversa to quash piracy and the city, not the least following the silting of the River Clanis, was definitively abandoned. The first excavations of the necropolis, excepting clandestine activities, began 1853-1857 under Prince Leopold, the brother of King Ferdinand II and Count of Syracuse, followed by campaigns 1878-1893 under Emilio Stevens. Exploration of the acropolis began in 1912 with the discovery of the Temple of Apollo and continued until 1953. Today, systematic excavations are being carried out by archaeologists from "Federico II" University in Naples, the Oriental University Institute and the Jean Bérard Centre.

The high city

Mount Cumae is a natural fortress dominating the coastal plain. The Greeks built their acropolis here, exploiting its natural defences but also strengthening the site with walls. Many remains are still visible today. On the east side, where the entrance to the excavations is located today, the rocky wall is faced with squared blocks of trachyte, set into a solid brick structure. This barrier dates back to the years of the second triumvirate. Other defence installations include: a Samnitic wall in blocks of tuff – to the south, east and north – and Greek walls (VI-V century B.C.) on the lower terrace outlining the Temple of Apollo to the north and east.

A tunnel 180 metres long, the so-called *Crypta Ro-*

Opposite: remains of the Temple of Zeus – Acropolis of Cumae. In foreground, the baptismal font installed when the temple was converted into a paleo-Christian Basilica.

This page: the antrum of the Sibyl of Cumae.

mana, crosses Mount Cumae. It was built in the Augustan age to connect the low city and the port and has been identified as a military work by Roman architect Cocceius. It was liberated 1925-1930 of the detritus hiding it and was initially identified as the antrum of the Sibyl. It was only after completion of the excavation that Amedeo Maiuri, a great Neapolitan archaeologist, realised it was a military installation. The tunnel opening has a monumental vestibule decorated with four large niches. Illuminated by light-wells at the side and in the vault, the first section is clad in brick and leads to a vestibule with a rectangular ground plan and then proceeds in a straight line; this section opens out on to settings lit by circular wells, perhaps excavated to build cisterns.

The lower terrace of the Temple of Apollo hillside was excavated in 1912; it was believed to be a very important sanctuary in Rome itself. In short, Virgil in Book VI of the Aeneid narrates that Dedalus, the father of Icarus, escaping from the labyrinth of Knossos, found shelter on the acropolis of Cumae and there built a temple to Apollo, symbol of the Sun; Dedalus himself engraved the golden doors with the Cretan legends of the labyrinth, the Minotaur and Ariadne. Velleius Patercolus (I 4, 1) and Statius (*Silvae*, III 5, 79) suggest that it was precisely the god, in the form of a white dove or distant clashing of cymbals, who indicated the route to the colonists.

Sources also witness that the wooden statue of the god wept, especially in the event of Greek defeats by the Romans, whereby the Romans, interpreting this prodigy as a hostile sign, threw the statue into the sea, although it was saved by the intervention of the elders (*senes*).

At the end of I century B.C, new impulse was given to the cult of Apollo, who was at the centre of the Augustan programme of religious renewal and political propaganda. In short, after the Battle of Azium, Octavian promised to initiate that new era of peace foretold by the oracle since victory was precisely brought about by the intervention of the god. Inasmuch, the Temple of Apollo Aziacus was restored and a sanctuary was consecrated to the god on the Palatine in Rome, to where the ancient Cumae oracles lying at the feet of a large and famous statue of Apollo Citaredus were transferred. The Temple of Cumae faced north-south and may originally have also been dedicated to *Hera* in view of the oracular inscription engraved with the name of *Hera* on the bronze discus dating from second-half VII century B.C. Only the platea of the stereobate remains today of the most ancient section. In the Samnitic age, the temple also had a colonnade. In the Augustan age, the building was completely renovated with the addition of a pronaos that divided the cell into three parts and changed the initial orientation. It was converted into a Christian Basilica around V century A.D.: in short, the paving revealed around ninety tombs and the octagonal basin used as the baptistery also dates from this period. In the area of the sanctuary of Apollo, the so-called "Greek cistern" is probably the most ancient structure still preserved. Used to hold the water for rites of worship, it has an underground environment with a rectangular ground plan (4.35 × 9 metres) built using large blocks of yellow tuff placed using the isodome technique. The building technique suggests dating in VI-V century B.C.

The main sanctuary of the acropolis was attributed for some considerable time and without valid reasons to Zeus, so that the present name is still "Temple of Zeus"; in any case, it seems more likely that it was consecrated to Demetra, the ancient patron divinity of the Cumaeans held in high veneration in the city. The remains were brought to light between 1924 and 1932. The sanctuary was probably built towards end-VI century B.C.; over time, it underwent numerous conversions, that nevertheless always retained the original east-west orientation. The remains visible today date from the Roman and Byzantine ages, when the temple was converted (V-VI century A.D.) into a Basilica dedicated to San Massimo Martire. Access to the monument today is from the right side, along modern steps. These steps lead to the platea (39.60 × 24.60 metres) with blocks of tuff, standing on a cement foundations, still revealing Roman structures from the first imperial age. A better understanding of the overall site is gained from the original entrance. Here, one may observe, along the two sides of the sanctuary, the remains of a reticulated Roman perimeter wall; some collapsed portions of the wall today lie on the left side. The centre of the platea has the cell, whose inner walls are marked by brick semicolumns, between which there were once niches (later walled up). As well as the cell, there are four visible rows of pillars on the south side in brick once supporting low arches. Some of the inter-columns still have portions of the ancient "signinum" paving, with regular insertions of marble tesserae. It can be deduced that, towards end-I century B.C., the temple was pseudo-peripteral, surrounded by porticos with brick pillars dividing it into five naves; access was from the east front, through one main and two lateral entrances. The Roman and Christian paving almost entirely cover the original ground plan. With the coming of Christianity, the temple underwent progressive modifications. For example, the conversion into a Basilica saw the cell become the presbytery; an altar and a circular baptismal basin were added.

The lower city

The Forum of the Roman city occupied the flatter area at the feet of the mountain. The square (50 × 120 metres) had porticos along the sides, while the western side was delimited by the *Capitolium*. The eastern end had an imposing building of the imperial age known as the "Farm of the Giant" following the discovery in 1758 of a colossal torso of Zeus, today in the Archaeological Museum, Naples. The Forum area is currently being researched by "Federico II" University, Naples; the most ancient stages have already been documented, ascertaining that the structure incorporated into the so-called "Farm of the Giant" belonged to a temple on a podium that itself opened on to a monumental portico. The *Capitolium*, originally dedicated to the cult of Jupiter Flazios, was a peripteral temple with a pronaos and a cell with three naves standing on a podium. The building was erected in two stages. The first from IV century to II century B.C., when the building was dedicated to the cult of the Capitoline Triad (Jupiter, Juno and Minerva). The second stage, dating from I century B.C., saw the temple converted from peripteral to prostyle, the podium was shortened on the west side and extended on the east side and a terrace with a central staircase was added; moreover, the cell was enlarged to house three sections with the insertion of two rows of columns. The sculptural decoration in this stage includes the colossal acrolyte statues of the Capitoline Triad whose busts, today in the National Museum, Naples, can be dated between the end of the I century and the first half of the II century A.D. The bust of Jupiter was founded near Masseria del Gigante, the bust of Juno in the north-west corner of the cell and that of Minerva in the area surrounding the temple. The National Archaeological Museum in Naples also has a cladding slab with a rampant gryphon. The building was sacked several times in V-VI century A.D. The baths were built in the north-west part of the forum area. The building – comprising *frigidarium, tepidarium, calidarium, sudatio* and *prefurnium* – was erected a few decades after the opening of the Via Domitiana in 95 A.D. Only a few remains of marbles and floor mosaics remain of the original rich decoration.

Antrum of the Sibyl

Cumae is linked – in world culture – with the presence of the Sibyl, one of the most complex and fascinating figures of the ancient world. The antrum was recognised in 1932 by Amedeo Maiuri – on the basis of Virgil's description in the *Aeneid* (book VI, verses 42 onwards) – as a long trapezoidal and straight corridor (131.20 m) cut into the tuff and scanned by the light filtering through six lateral apertures. The trapezoidal cut perhaps dates from the second half of IV century B.C.; on the other hand, the floor was lowered at a later stage, so that the tunnel is now 5 metres high; it was illuminated by six open galleries on the western side, while the corridor (*dromos*) had, on the east side, three minor branches that were converted in the Roman age into tanks and then re-utilised in the Christian age as a burial place. The corridor, lastly, leads to a rectangular hall; each of the three walls has a large niche surmounted by a round arch. Here, a vestibule on the left, closed in ancient times by a gate – as shown by the holes in the jambs – leads to a small room divided into three cells. This is the room thought to be the *oikos endotatos*, where the Sibyl, enthroned, probably pronounced the oracles. This interpretation, however, was recently opened to new debate, since it is assumed that it may only be a tunnel having a military purpose.

The Cumaean Sibyl

The Sibyl of Cumae depicted by Michelangelo in the vault of the Sistine Chapel, Vatican.

In the ancient world, seers and prophets pronounced, in the name of a god, oracles and predictions. There was a widespread belief at the oracular sites that there were certain female "interpreters" of the divine word, not subject to the passing of time, isolated from the world and little inclined to let themselves be seen; they were the "Sibyls".

The Pizian Sibyl of Delphos is the most famous example but Varro listed ten: the Persian, Eretrian (from Eretrea, in Lidia), Hellespontian, Frigian, Cimmerian, Lybian, Delphi, Samian, Cumaean and Tiburtine sibyls, some of whom were depicted by Michelangelo in the Sistine Chapel between 1508 and 1512. Others even thought that in reality there was only one, immortal Sibyl who moved around these different places.

The Cumaean Sibyl is one of the most complex and fascinating figures emerging from Latin literature and the volcanic character of the region may explain the presence of the Sibyl who foretold the future by questioning the gods of the Underworld.

The first mention occurs in Licophron, a Greek author of III century B.C., yet the Sibyl was already known in VI century B.C. when – in accordance with tradition – King Tarquinius Priscus purchased a large collection of oracles, the *Sibylline Books*, written on palm leaves in Greek hexameters. These books were the most important texts of archaic Roman religion, so much so that they were consulted only in the event of dire necessity. These oracles could only be consulted by a particular college of priests, the so-called *Quindecemviri*. The books, kept in the Temple of Capitoline Jupiter, were burnt in the fire in the Campidoglio in 83 B.C.; they were then recomposed – thanks to the collection of oracles preserved throughout Greece and Asia Minor – and then placed by Augustus in the Temple of Apollo on the Palatine next to his own mansion. They remained here until IV century A.D., when they were destroyed by General Stilico.

The most ancient references to the antrum of the Cumaean Sibyl are to be found in a pseudo-Aristotelian text (*De mirabilium auscultationibus*, IV-III century B.C.) and in Licophron (III century B.C). The most famous evocation is that of Virgil who, in book VI of the Aeneid, described the antrum and the awesome figure of the Sibyl, the majestic priestess of Apollo and Hecate Trivia, custodian of the divine oracles and the Gates of Hades. Aeneas landed on the shores of Cumae and climbed to her antrum, where he was shown the future as well as the Tartaro chasms.

It is likely that Virgil, as a poet, only intended to create an ideal situation rather than a factual description. It was only with the so-called pseudo-Giustino (IV century A.D.), Procopius and Agathias (VI century A.D.) in later centuries that a detailed description of the antrum was made, yet their testimony, late and influenced by local traditions, is felt by many experts to be unreliable. Two sources deserve closer attention that even seem to exclude the existence of an oracle of the Cumaean Sibyl, at least in the Late Age. In short, Pausanias in II century A.D. maintains that the people of Cumae had no oracle of the Sibyl to show but only an urn with ashes held in the Temple of Apollo. This claim seems to confirm indirectly the information handed down in the Life (IV century A.D.) of Emperor Clodius Albinus (196-197 A.D.), in accordance with which he travelled to consult the oracle in the Temple of Apollo in Cumae.

Interest in the figure of the Sibyl survived the disappearance of the ancient world, so the even in the Middle Ages efforts were made to identify, on the basis of Virgil's poetry, the site of the Sibylline Oracle. The emphasis given to the episode of Aeneas' descent into the underworld, guided by the prophetess, however, meant that the antrum was sought on the shores of Lake Averno, locating it in the setting today known as the "Grotto of the Sibyl". This identification was accepted throughout the Renaissance and repeated, among others, by Petrarch and Boccaccio.

A visit to the antrum of Averno remained almost until the last century one of the most evocative stop-offs of the Grand Tour. In the 1700s, Goethe and Mozart were both told that Lake Averno was the home of the Sibyl, while the ruins of the Acropolis of Cumae, by now buried, had been abandoned for centuries.

It was only as of the mid-1800s that the interest of archaeologists moved to Cumae, leading them – but only in 1932 – to the discovery of the antrum of the Sibyl. Maiuri inasmuch could claim: "*The long trapezoidal corridor as high and solemn as the nave of a church, and the vaulted grotto and the large niches made up a unique combination. It was the Grotto of the Sibyl, the Antrum of the prophecy appearing to us in the poetic vision of Virgil and the prosaic yet no less moving description of the anonymous Christian author of IV century*".

This hypothesis was recently brought into doubt again, since it is now believed that the tunnel, that can be dated IV-V century B.C., had a military function. The antrum should therefore be sought near the Temple of Apollo, itself near the peribolus, where there is a almost completely underground setting – the "Greek cistern".

We do not know exactly how consultation of the oracle took place. Virgil narrates that the Sibyl guided the Trojan hero Aeneas from the hill of Cumae to the shores of Lake Averno to interrogate the shade of his father, who prophesised the imperial destinies of Rome.

The prophecies of the Sibyl came about in a rather ambiguous manner. There is the famous sentence: "*ibis redibis non perieris in bello*", where the destiny of the questioner depends on the negative – that is, whether it is linked with "*redibis*" ("*you will not return, you will die*") or "*perieris*" ("*you will not die, so you will return*"). On other occasions, the prophecies were written on leaves, with one word on each leaf; the leaves were then thrown into the wind.

Other oracular sanctuaries, such as the one in Delphi, provide us more information. Here, in the Temple of Apollo, the Pizian Sibyl sitting on a tripod set over a hole exhaling underground fumes, breathed these vapours and pronounced unrelated sentences, that were then recomposed by the priests into prophecies.

Another Greek oracular sanctuary, the Nekromanteion in Epirus, near the Acheron, the river of the dead, has provided a great deal of interesting information about the way the oracles were interrogated. The questioners were guests of the sanctuary for several days during which they followed a very strict diet. In the courtyard, archaeologists discovered the skins of beans and lupins which, when eaten in large quantities and on an empty stomach, cause hallucinations (this is perhaps the reason why Pythagoras did not allow his followers to eat them).

When the "patients" were considered "ready", they were conducted along a labyrinthine corridor that, twisting and turning, probably caused their heads to spin; they then reached a room known as the Gateway to Hades. Here, a hoist – some pieces of which were found during excavations – was used to suspend from the ceiling the "shades of the dead" who pronounced prophecies through the voices of the priests hidden in a gap.

For poets after Virgil, the greatness of the Cumaean Sibyl gave way to popular elements. Propertius, Ovid and Lucan outline the figure of the long-lived Sibyl enjoying a thousand years of life, while the *Satyricon* by the playful Petronius describes a decrepit Sibyl that Apollo made immortal but not eternally young, reduced to a tiny being closed in a bottle invoking – in Greek – death.

While the Pagans forgot the Sibyl, by II century B.C. this figure had been absorbed into the Hebrew tradition that restored the use of oracles and gave them voice through texts defined as the "Sibylline Oracles" announcing the end of Rome and corrupt Imperial power.

It was precisely thanks to this mediation that the Christians recovered the Cumaean Sibyl from oblivion, spreading in its name an obscure vision of the future that gave life to the Christian Sibylline Oracles. Inasmuch, Christian authors such as Lattanzio, Eusebius of Caesarea and Constantine discovered that the IV Eclogue of Virgil's *Bucolicae* – where the Cumaean Sibyl announced the miraculous birth of a divine child (Octavian) and the onset of a new era (the Augustan age) – could also be interpreted as the announcement of the birth of Jesus and the advent of Christianity.

In the Middle Ages, the Cumaean Sibyl was fully included among the prophets foreseeing the Christian age and the end of pagan times, as sentenced by Thomas from Celano placing her as a witness, next to David, on the day of Universal Judgement: "*Dies irae, dies illa, teste David cum Sibylla*".

PAESTUM

Ground plan of the ancient city of Paestum.

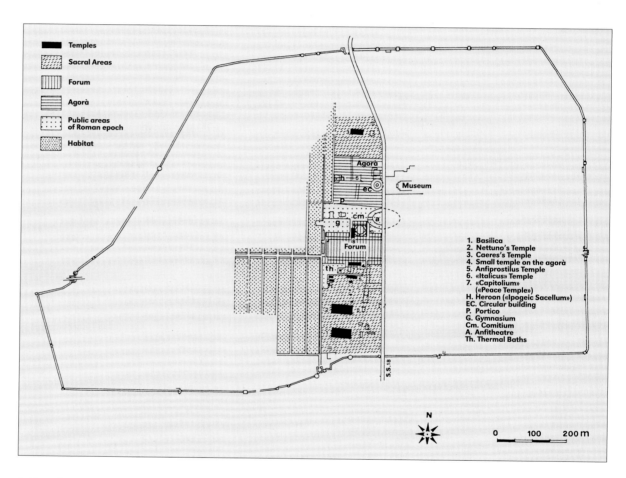

Temples
Sacral Areas
Forum
Agorà
Public areas of Roman epoch
Habitat

Agorà
Museum
Forum

1. Basilica
2. Nettuno's Temple
3. Caeres's Temple
4. Small temple on the agorà
5. Anfiprostilus Temple
6. «Italicus» Temple
7. «Capitolium» («Peace Temple»)
H. Heroon («Ipogeic Sacellum»)
EC. Circular building
P. Portico
G. Gymnasium
Cm. Comitium
A. Anfitheatre
Th. Thermal Baths

N

0 100 200 m

"After Campania and the territory of the Sannites (as far as the Frentaeans) on the Tyrrhenian Sea there live the Piceni peoples, a minor branch of the Picentinian peoples of the Adriatic, transferred by the Romans to the Gulf of Poseidonia, now named Pestano, just as the city of Poseidonia standing in the middle of the Gulf is now known as Paestum".

Strabo, *Geographia* V 4,13

"After the estuary of the River Silaris, one reaches Lucania and the sanctuary of Hera Argiva, founded by Jason. Not far away, at 50 stadiums, there rises Posidonia. The Sibarites had raised fortifications overlooking the sea but the inhabitants moved inland; later, the Lucanians took the city and Romans took it in turn from the Lucanians. The swampy river nearby makes it an unhealthy place".

Strabo, *Geographia* VI 1,1

History

Strabo tells that Jason, leading the Argonauts, stopped at the Sele estuary where he dedicated a sanctuary to *Hera*, the protectress of the Argonauts. As they travelled from the south passing Capo Palinuro and then Punta Licosa, they viewed the extensive and fertile plain of Paestum, appearing as a large cavea delimited in the background by the green Picentini Mountains and the pure white Alburni Mountains. The fertility of the plain and the plentiful water of the Sele made this area, then called Pestana, one of the main stop-offs between the Greek east and the Italic west as early as the II millennium B.C., explaining the foundation and flourishing of a city as rich as Paestum.

Life in this delightful area in truth dates back to the Eneolithic Age (III millennium B.C.). In short, 1500 metres north of the walls, in 1943 – building a temporary runway during the American landings at Salerno – a necropolis came to light that testified to a culture that from that place took the name "Gaudo Culture". The necropolis comprised tombs in small grottos, cut into the limestone embankment, with multiple burials. The burial treasures included pulp vases worked by hand and baked directly in fires, arrow tips and chert dag-

The remains of the
"ekklesiasterion" of Paestum,
a building with a circular
ground plan intended for
public meetings.

gers, as well as several copper daggers. These people had Aegean-Anatolian origins; they reached the plain directly from the sea or from the Adriatic, crossing the peninsula. It is inasmuch possible that later visits by Greeks colonists may have echoed these routes travelled since pre-history which had never been forgotten.

The city of Paestum, then called *Poseidonia*, was founded by Sibarian colonists around 600 B.C. Strabo (I century A.D.) suggests that foundation was preceded by the creation of a fortified outpost, perhaps standing on the Agropoli promontory. Solinus, a grammarian of III century A.D., mentions the foundation of *Poseidonia* by the Dorians, so that it is supposed that the city was founded by the Dorian minority ousted from Sibari by the Achaean majority. During the VII century, Sibari, set to become one of the main economic centres in Magna Graecia, founded several trading stations on the Tyrrhenian. *Poseidonia* was the most northern of these subcolonies, standing at the node for trade towards the interior, the Ionian, Latium and Etruria.

In the VI century, *Poseidonia* became one of the most important landmarks in the Tyrrhenian, as shown by the mediation with the native Enotrian people, that helped the Phocaean exiles to found Elea (*Velia*) around 540 B.C., and the aid given to the Sibarites in the reconstruction of their city, razed by Crotone in 510 B.C.

At the end of V century B.C., as seen in the documentation of the necropolis with a funeral ritual, the Lucanians took control of the city, without however disrupting the use and function of public and religious places. It was then that the city was renamed *Paistom*.

During the IV century, the colony experienced a period of demographic expansion; between 335 and 331, it was occupied by Greek Alexander Molossus, but soon returned to the Lucanians.

In 273 B.C., the Latin colony gave it the name Paestum. During the war with Hannibal, it aided Rome as a federated city. It was a time of major changes in the town: the *Forum* was reduced in size compared to the Greek agorà but spread into the area of the northern sanctuary.

Paestum was inhabited until the High Middle Ages and was abandoned in VIII century A.D. because of Saracen raids and the extension of the swamplands.

The city

Standing in the centre of the fertile plain on the left bank of the River Sele, the city developed on a slightly raised limestone shelf compared to the surrounding land. The town occupied an area of about 120 hectares, surrounded by an imposing system of fortifications made up of twin masonry walls with connection dykes and in-fills of earth and rubble. The perimeter of the wall had twenty-eight towers with square and circular bases and four main gates, of which only three remain today: Porta Sirena to the east, Porta Giustizia to the south, Porta Marina to the west and Porta Aurea to the north.

From its very foundation, the urban plan of the city remained inside this perimeter. The residential and public areas were distinctly separated. The latter, extending about 1 km north-south and 300 metres east-west, in turn had three sections: a central area for the agorà with political functions and two lateral areas, to the south and north, for the great sanctuaries of the town.

The northern area had the Temple of Athena (the so-called Temple of Ceres), while the southern portion had the Temple of Hera (the so-called Basilica) and the Temple of Neptune (perhaps dedicated to Apollo). The disposition of the sanctuaries, with a common orientation that differed from the layout of the streets and buildings, highlights the desire for a clear distinction between spaces for the gods and spaces for people.

The street plan dates back to the period of the foundation of the city but was effectively only finalised in the last twenty-five years of VI century B.C. It focused on two large arteries (*plateiai*) departing from the main gates and meeting at a right angle; one, 10 metres wide (north-south from Porta Aurea to Porta Giustizia), and the other, 20 metres wide (east-west from Porta Sirena to Porta Marina). Two other parallel arteries departed north and south of the latter. The three *plateiai* east-west were intersected by smaller streets (*stenopoi*) marking off long, narrow blocks.

The agorà

An enormous square, delimited by the east-west median artery and the parallel one to the north, was home to the Greek agorà. It was only from the second half of IV century B.C. that two areas were distinguished, one to the south for commercial activity, where the Roman colony later set up its Forum,

and one to the north with political and holy functions. Two important monuments stood here: the *ekklesiasterion*, the building for meetings, and the so-called "Sacello ipogeico" for hero worship.

The *ekklesiasterion*, built around 480-470 B.C., was circular with concentric steps with access through two entrances. A stele was found inside the building, datable IV-III century B.C., with a dedication in Oscan to Jupiter, the patron divinity of politics housed here.

The "Sacello Ipogeico", in reality a cenotaph, was built around 520 B.C. It was designed as a chamber tomb with stone walls and a double-sloping roof in slabs of stone and tiles, probably covered by a tumulus of earth. A table in the interior had five iron spits, while eight very large bronze vases were aligned along the walls containing clots of honey and an Attic amphora with black figures and a depiction of the ascent of Hercules to Olympus. It was a *heroon* for worship of the hero who founded the colony placed emblematically in the centre of the political area of the city. With the arrival of the Romans, the monument was surrounded by a rectangular compound and covered with earth, while cult worship was interrupted.

The Forum

Following the Romanisation of the city as of III century B.C., the area of the agorà was disrupted by the building of the Forum. The square was surrounded on three sides by *tabernae* with two chambers, while the north side opened on to the *Comitium*, the most important monument of the colony. The meetings of the Curia and the judgements were held here. A rectangular wall in blocks delimited the area. It supported the circular steps of the building but also defined the space so that the Curia was at the north in accordance with the dispositions of the Roman ritual. Meetings, in short, were held in relation to the course of the sun, observed by facing south.

Behind the building, close to the north-east end of the Forum, there stood the amphitheatre, in an unusually central position for ancient urbanistics. The monument was split into two parts by the modern road, built on a Bourbon layout. The building involved two construction stages: the first in I century B.C. with the elliptical analemma of the cavea in blocks of limestone. At the end of I century A.D., in a climate of monumental work in the city and its buildings, the amphitheatre was extended with a

new tribune and relative access staircases. The entrance gates, placed on the north-south axis, were surmounted by brick vaults.

The temples

The imposing temples of Paestum are one of the greatest examples of the Doric order in Magna Graecia. It was only around the mid-1700s, at the same time as the discoveries of Herculaneum and Pompeii, that the city and its temples became one of the stop-offs on the "Grand Tour" and was visited, among others, also by Winckelmann, Piranesi and Goethe. In this way, the temples of Paestum became fundamental in the later fortune of the Doric order in European architecture.

The area of the northern sanctuary has the Temple of Ceres, in reality dedicated to Athena, dating from end VI century B.C. It represents the transition stage from the Archaic epoch to early Classicism and achieves the canonical proportional ratio with 6 columns on the fronts and 13 on the long sides. The *peristasis* encloses a deep cell, open to the east towards a colonnade supported by Ionic columns. This layout evidently indicates a desire to exalt the facade at the entrance to the temple and the cell as a place home to the cult statue.

Two monumental staircases set into the walls between the pronaos and the cell gave access to the roof for maintenance work.

The sophistication of the site was achieved thanks to the use of two different stones. The trabeation above the frieze, comprising triglyphs and metopes, had a decorated band on the exterior with a relief wave-like motif. This was all crowned by a moulding with large ovolos in sandstone. Heads of lions alternating with palmettes were used as rainwater spouts. Traces of colour, in particular red and blue, on the cornices and the tympanum give an idea of the original multi-colour finishing.

In VII-VIII century A.D., the building was converted into a church with the closure of the intercolumns and the demolition of the cell walls, while the southern ambulacrum was used as a burial place. The Temple of Hera, the so-called Basilica, and the Temple of Neptune, in turn, stood in the northern sanctuary.

Building work on the former began around mid-VI century B.C. and was completed in 520-510 B.C., after some changes to the design of the cell. The *peristasis* has 9 columns on the fronts and 18 on the long sides. The cell is divided in two by a central colonnade of six columns and has an eastern chamber open towards the colonnade of the pronaos and a western chamber (*adyton*), closed towards the *peristasis*, where the cult statue was raised. The capitals are covered by very rich floral decorations, while the frieze had triglyphs and metopes carved separately and probably in sandstone. The roof had peaks with lion-head water spouts, carved as a single workpiece with the guttering tiles decorated with multi-colour lotus flowers and small palms.

The so-called Temple of Neptune, dedicated perhaps to Apollo, is a mature interpretation of the Doric order. The crepidoma with three steps supports the colonnade of the *peristasis* with 6 columns on the fronts and 14 on the long sides. The cell, set in perfect symmetry into the *peristasis* but raised above it, had a pronaos, with two columns between the sides, and the opistodomus. The interior of the cell was divided into three naves by two rows of seven columns in two overlapping orders that supported, together with the walls, the lamina of the ceiling and the roof. The frieze had a smooth metope and triglyphs. The tympanum of the frontons, smooth and without traces of sculptural decoration, was framed by a rampant *geison*. It is possible that the roof was in marble and was removed after the building was abandoned. To the east of the two temples there are altars where worship took place.

In conclusion, the southern holy area was home to the worship of the main divinities of the city: Hera, Apollo, as suggested by finds of several headstones linked with his cult similar to those found at Metaponto, and Zeus, mentioned in an inscription with the appellative Xenios, the hospitable.

The homes

The zone to the west of the city was occupied by residential blocks with homes of various dimensions and richness. An exceptional example is the so-called "House of the pool" occupying an area of 2800 square metres. It had a portico courtyard with brick columns; a large pool stood in the middle. This building involved several stages; the pool dates from the first imperial age and was subsequently filled and replaced by an *impluvium* to collect rainwater.

The "House with the marble impluvium" occupies half of the east-west block. The entrance and vestibule, to the south, gave access to the atrium

Opposite: the Basilica of
Paestum or Temple of Hera.

Pages 36-37: the slab enclosing
the "Tomb of the Diver"
(480-470 B.C.). Paestum,
National Archaeological
Museum.

and its marble impluvium below which, during restoration work, a mosaic was found that is now in the Museum. The atrium was the focus for different rooms (cubicula and alae) while the north side had the tablinum that linked with the peristyle.

The Archaeological Museum

Paestum National Archaeological Museum was inaugurated in 1952 as a home to the Archaic metopes of the thesauros of the Sanctuary of Hera Argiva (Heraion) on the estuary of the Sele, previously placed in an Antiquarium. The metopes, placed at the original height, can be dated around 560 B.C. and depict scenes of the myth of Heracles as well as scenes relating to the Trojan cycle. The adjacent hall displays the metopes from the main temple depicting young dancing girls wearing Ionic garments (500 B.C.), architectural elements from the main temple and other metopes from unidentifiable buildings.

The finds of greatest prestige in the Museum include painted Lucanian tombs. These tombs can be dated in 390-370 B.C.; the figurative space is marked by vegetal and geometrical motifs, while the central part has painted vases, vegetal crowns and holy bands. A later stage, that lasted up to about 340 B.C., saw the introduction of a new figurative motif – the "return of the warrior". The deceased is depicted with armour and weapons on horseback with the bodies of enemies defeated in battle; he is awaited by a woman, depicted in the act of libations. The other slabs have depictions of funeral games. It was only as of mid-IV century B.C. that women's tombs saw the introduction of a new theme – women intent in female tasks or portrayed in scenes of funerary mourning.

The "Tomb of the Diver" is also particularly important. The male tomb is a kind of chest made up of four slabs of travertine with a large coverage slab. Decorated internally, along the four slabs depict a funeral banquet, while the coverage slab portrays a male figure in the act of diving into a pool of water from a pillar-like "trampoline" made up of blocks. While the banquet scenes reflect the ideology of the symposium, favoured among the aristocracy, the diving scene is charged with intense symbolic meaning, perhaps that of the passage from life to death. The tomb, on the basis of the style of depictions and the typology of the burial treasure (a lyre with a tortoise shell as sounding box and a lekythos), can be dated around 480-470 B.C.

The mid-IV century B.C. is also the date of a chamber tomb from Agropolis, where two individuals were buried: a man, whose burial gifts comprised an hydria by Assteas with the Myth of Bellerofon, a strigil and weapons, and a woman with clay fruit, cheese and cakes. The rear partition is painted with the image of the lady, accompanied by a maid offering a drink to her husband attended by a servant.

A splendid example of Pestan coroplastics is a seated statue depicting Zeus, with Ionic influences, dated 530 B.C., it was found in the southern urban sanctuary. There is also a rich series of architectural terrecotta dedicated to Hera depicting the goddess in all her manifestations: as a wet-nurse, the goddess of horses, enthroned with pomegranate, etc.

The ceramics and pottery of the IV century B.C. also saw major developments with Pestan production with red figures: the amphora of Python, signed, with the birth of Helen, the oinochoe with the judgement of Paris before Hermes, the painter of Aphrodite, the Attic amphora with red figures by the painter of Nikoxenos with Hercules and Cerberus and the investiture of the Amazons.

Particularly important bronze finds include the vases found in the heroon located in the agorà and a statue of the silen Marsias, dated III century B.C., found in the compitum (crossroads), marked in the Roman age by an altar dedicated to the Lares compitales.

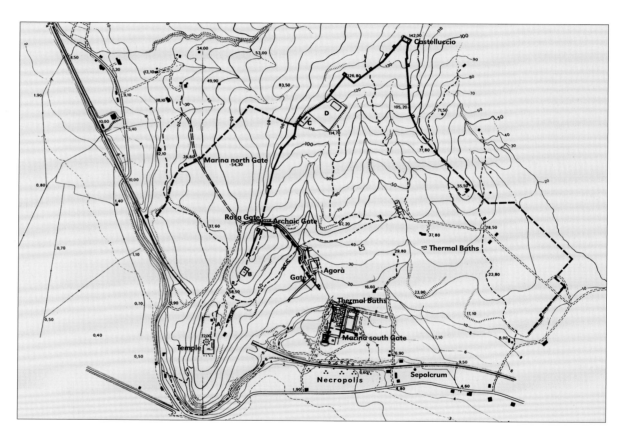

"*Opposite the island (Leucosia), the promontory in front of Sirenusse rises to form the Gulf of Posidonia. On rounding the promontory, another adjacent gulf opens out with the city called Hyele by the Phocaeans who founded it and Ele by others after the name of a fountain. Today, it is known as Elea; Parmenides and Zenon, philosophers of the School of Pythagoras, were born here. Their work, and that of their predecessors, suggests that the city was governed with good laws, even to the extent that the local people withstood and repulsed the Lucans and Posidonians despite being inferior in numbers and territory. Yet the sterility of the soil obliged them to be seafarers, salting fish and the like. Antioch says that after Focea was taken by Arpago, the general of Ciro, many people escaped by ship with their families, sailing first to Corsica and then to Massalia, led by Creontiate; on being repulsed, they travelled onwards to found Elea. (Others say that it took its name from the River Eleeto); the city is about 200 stadiums distant from Poseidonia. After Elea comes the promontory of Palinurus*".

History

Herodotus narrates that Elea – Velia for the Romans – was founded in 540 B.C by the Phocaeans fleeing Asia Minor from the Persians. After a vain attempt to settle in Alalia, Corsica, the exiles found refuge in Rhegion, where they met a Poseidonian who told them of a place on the Cilentum coast where they could establish a new city. This site stood between Punta Licosa and Cape Palinuro – a promontory overlooking the sea with two deep inlets offering safe haven for mooring and repairing ships. The city soon became famous for its prosperous trade and the beauty of its places.

It was also famed for its "good laws" and the "Eleatic School" of pre-Socratean philosophy founded by Parmenides and Zenon. Parmenides was born in Elea (Plato, *Parmenides* 127 B.C.) between 515 and 510 B.C. His thinking was outlined in a didactic poem traditionally known as *On Nature* that could still be read in its entirety in VI century A.D. Here, he defined the essence of being: *"What is engendered is also immortal, alike, unique, immovable and without end. It never was nor will be, because it is at once continuous and indivisible. So, what origin can one seek? How and whence did it grow? I shall not allow being or non-being to be said or thought. What is not can neither be said nor thought".*

From the top of the acropolis, watching the breakers, these verses of Parmenides come to mind: *"The waves that drag me as far as my soul could ever desire took me after the goddesses set me along the lofty way towards that reason that guides every wise man ... The goddess welcomed me benevolently, took me in her right hand and said: oh young man who together with immortal guides comes to our home ... good health to you! ... there is no malign power that has brought you on this way but a divine command and justice ... Yet in any case, this you will also learn: who seeks in all directions must also judge appearances".*

The city, thanks to its strength, withstood the joint attack launched by the Lucans and Poseidonians in the second half of V century B.C. In IV century B.C. – to defend its independence – it had to seek aid from Dionysios I, the tyrant of Syracuse, and joined the Italiot League.

When Taranto fell in 272 B.C., Velia became one of the naval allies of Rome. In the Roman age, the Greek name Hyele was changed to Velia. It became a Roman municipality in 88 B.C., yet Rome allowed

the use of Greek in official ceremonies and permitted the issue of its own coinage.

The city

The archaic city settled by the first generation of colonists (540-480 B.C.), occupied the acropolis and the hillsides behind it, dominating the two large inlets to the north and south – today silted up but at that time still safe ports. There are no surviving traces of port structures.

From its foundation, the city was protected by defences embracing the town and its three suburbs: the acropolis itself and two quarters of the lower city. These walls were remodelled several times: the most ancient walls were built with simple bricks laid on a polygonal base; they became more monumental in the first half of V century B.C. with the addition of towers; around the end of IV century B.C., lastly, they were rebuilt using a chequered technique ("velina") characterised by regular sandstone blocks alternating with small, unhewn blocks of stone rather than head blocks. The southern "Porta Marina" was built later and was the starting point for the street linking the southern and northern quarters.

The "Porta Rosa", built in the closing decades of IV century B.C., stood at the end of this road. The name "Porta" (gate) is incorrect, since it was actually a tunnel about 6 metres long and 3 metres wide which linked to the two quarters. Similarly, the name "Rosa" (pink) does not refer to the colour of

View of the Mediaeval tower overlooking the Acropolis and the southern quarter of Velia.

Opposite page: marble portrait of Parmenides (I century A.D.). Velia, Archaeological excavations.

the stone but the dedication made by the excavator – Mario Napoli – in honour of his wife. "Porta Rosa" had a round arch entirely in sandstone, with ashlars installed without using mortar; it was surmounted by a small, load-bearing arch. The "gate" required cutting into the hill as the narrowest point of the gully and supporting the flanks with sturdy retaining walls.

The acropolis

The hill of Velia – where the tower of the Norman-Anjou tower stands today – was home to the acropolis in the Greek age. The installation of the castle keep utterly compromised ancient topography. The first town developed here, yet little remains of the original structures, not the least since around 480 B.C. the terrace was used to build a sanctuary, perhaps dedicated to Athena. The residential area expanded along the slopes over three terraces. An unusual technique was used to build the homes: the perimeter walls at the base were polygonal with perfectly matched curves, supporting simple brick structures finished with plasterwork. This particular building technique was perhaps used to overcome the steep gradient, whereby the perimeter walls had to withstand significant stresses. The homes were simple with two or three rooms; most family life took place in the entrance, while the room at the rear held the treasures of the *oikos*. The town can be dated – on the basis of building typology and technique – to the closing decades of the VI century B.C. and inasmuch emerged alongside the foundation of the colony. The site was soon abandoned – as early as 480-470 B.C. – when it was obliterated by a terracing wall with four-sided blocks. The acropolis was then reorganised and became the centre for the public, civil and religious life of the community. The temple was built on the summit and probably dedicated to Athena Polias – the goddess also favoured in the Phocaeans homeland and found in Elea on coins and mentioned in various votary inscriptions. Today, only the base and one corner of the cell of the building are visible. The castle was built on top in XI-XII century A.D.

The north-east corner of the terrace saw the construction of the theatre, built as part of the monumental projects for the acropolis. The current building reveals the renovations implemented during the Imperial age (II-III century A.D.) of a previous building of the Hellenistic Age (IV-III centu-

ry B.C.). The cavea, supported in part by the slope of the hill and in part by an artificial landfill, had 20-22 rows of seats. Few traces of the stage remain, while one can still see the remains of the *parodoi*. The theatre was used until V century A.D. and was then cut by the Mediaeval moat.

Other terraces were built on the ridge of the acropolis, towards the north-east, and also included fortifications. The first, closest to the acropolis, was home to the sanctuary of Poseidon, worshipped with the appellative of *Asphaleios* – the protector of ships and sailors. Zeus was worshipped on the second terrace, beyond Porta Rosa. Inside a *temenos*, a paved square with an altar (V century B.C.) made up the place of worship. Zeus was worshipped as *Orios*, the protector of the winds and summer, *Pompaios*, the guide and *Olympios Kairos*, the propitiator of happiness.

The Pantheon of Elea probably also included another divinity: Asclepius, son of Apollo and a healing god. It is likely that the building in the central area of the city, along the street leading to Porta Rosa and so far identified as the Greek *agorà*, may actually on the other hand be an *Asklepieion*. In short, it is a large, rectangular square surrounded on three sides by columns and closed at one end by a monumental fountain. Channels and small basins were arranged around the perimeter to collect and regulate the water from a spring above. Water seems to be the central element of the complex and this suggests that some form of medical treatment took place here.

The southern quarter

The southern part of the city outlines the evolution of the town from the foundation of the colony through to the Roman age. The oldest homes (V century B.C.) overlooked the marina, since the ancient coastline was further inland than today. A flood around mid-V century B.C. buried the old quarter. The blocks built in the next period had a narrow, elongated design and probably focused on the crossroads of the three main streets (*plateiai*) running east-west intersecting with smaller streets (*stenopoi*) running north-south. Homes were built within this grid with peristyles and often with splendid mosaic floors.

The entrance to the city was through Porta Marina to the south. A large paved road with spacious pavements separated the homes of Insula I from a building dating from the Augustan age that was re-worked in II century A.D. This complex comprised a courtyard with a colonnade on three sides and a central altar. The rear part of the complex was on two levels; the upper level formed a garden, while the lower level – with a crypto-portico with barrel vaults – extended around an open area. The discovery inside this complex of statues and portraits of doctors – including Parmenides – suggests that it was the home of the famous Eleatic School of Medicine. On the other hand, some experts suggest that it was a college of the Augustals – a sanctuary where the Emperor was worshipped – given the discovery here of nine portraits of the imperial family.

At the end of the street, there was a holy well (*bothros*) of the Hellenistic Age, surrounded by a perimeter fence and covered by a circular roof 1.70 metres in diameter and 7.50 metres wide. Small terracotta statues, coins and fragments of vases were found inside. The fact that some terracottas and the compound were marked with the Greek EP (epsylon-rho) suggests that the sanctuary was dedicated to "Eros".

The same quarter also had the baths built in II century A.D. They had a *laconicum*, with terracotta piping on the walls and under the flooring used to heat the area. The *frigidarium* was paved with a mosaic with white and black *tesserae* depicting a marine environment. At the rear, there was the basin for cold baths; the walls were decorated by a series of niches that originally held statues.

Another bath complex was located near a spring above the *Asklepieion*. Built in III century B.C., it was one of the best-known ancient baths in Magna Graecia. The flooring in the changing room had hexagonal tiles in terracotta, while the flooring in the hot bath area was in potsherd decorated with mosaics. The baths also had a room with oval basins for individual bathing.

The city was famed since the Hellenistic Age for its production of hollow bricks, known as "Velina bricks". A small Roman mausoleum (I century A.D.) – the funerary building no. 7 in the southern necropolis of Porta Marina – had cladding made with fragments of *Velina* bricks that even imitate the reticulated masonry technique.

Marble statuette – Asclepius. Velia, Archaeological excavations.

THE ROMANS AND CAMPANIA FELIX

"Let us first speak of Campania. The coastline extends from Sinuessa as far as Misenum to form a broad gulf and then another, much larger gulf, known as Crater, opening out between the two capes (Misenum and Athenaion). Campania occupies the entire coastal hinterland and its well-blessed plain, surrounded by fertile hills and the mountains of the Samnites and the Oscans. Antiochos says that this region was inhabited by Opicians, also known as the Ausonians. Polibius, on the other hand, identifies two peoples when he states that the Opicians and the Ausonians lived in the land around Crater. Others claim that Campania was initially inhabited by the Opicians and the Ausonians, and then by Sidicean Oscan peoples, the Cumaeans and the Tyrrheneans – conquerors all attracted by the fertility of its soils. The Tyrrhenaeans founded twelve cities hereabouts, giving the name Capua to the capital city. Their prosperity made them weak and feeble; and just as they were forced to abandon the Po Plains, so in Campania they were supplanted by the Samnites, who in turn were unable to prevent the supremacy of the Romans.

The fertile soil produces a fine cereal – the wheat used to make a superb flour surpassing rice and every other food product based on cereals. It is also said that certain plains in Campania produce two harvests of spelt, a third harvest of millet and that, at times, even produce a fourth harvest of vegetables. The Romans also enjoyed the best local wines, such as Falernum, Statanum and Calenum; yet by now even Surrentinum today bears comparison with these following recent experiments proving its affinity for ageing. Production of olive oil is also impressive throughout the Venafro region bordering on these plains".

Strabo, *Geographia* V 4, 3

Territorial assumptions

The splendid Campania region was defined by Pliny (Como 23-Stabia 79 A.D.) "*Campania Felix*" in his *Geographia*: "*This was the onset for the fame of Campania … It was subsequently dominated by the Oscans, the Greeks, the Umbrans, the Etruscans and the Campanians. This "riviera" also boasts Naples, itself founded by the Chalcidaeans, and named Partenope after the tomb of a siren; Herculaneum, Pompeii, close to Vesuvius and the River Sarno; the territory of Nuceria and Nuceria itself, only nine miles from the sea; Sorrento and the Minerva promontory, once home to the Sirens*" (*Naturalis Historia* III 60, 1-4).

This region – despite the high risks – was always densely inhabited. During the Roman imperial age, Pompeii had a population of at least 20,000 inhabitants, Herculaneum at least 10,000 and without doubt the population of *Neapolis* and *Puteoli* was ten-times higher, Rome in these times already boasted one million inhabitants.

With Vesuvius on one border and the sea on the other, the ancients were well aware that they lived in one of the most evocative scenarios of the entire Mediterranean; this is demonstrated not only by literary testimony but also by the very numerous Roman villas built from Miseno as far as Capo di Sorrento.

Obviously, the beauty of the landscapes and the richness of resources would not alone have sufficed to encourage tourism and resorts – political stability was also essential, and this was ensured by the Roman conquest over a period lasting almost two centuries.

The Roman conquest

The Roman republic expanded its dominion over southern Italy in order to counter the Italic peo-

ples allied with Hannibal during the expedition against Rome in III century B.C. The expansion process was slow and complex, since these were effectively guerrilla wars.

It was on this occasion – during the Second Punic War – that Taranto, in the face of Roman encirclement, turned to Pyrrhus, King of Epirus, who fought against both Romans and Carthaginians. He was defeated by the former at Benevento in 275 B.C., with the result that in 273 B.C. a Latin colony in *Poseidonia* was established. *Neapolis* on the other hand, an "ally city" of the Romans since 327 B.C., continued to witness absolute Greek pre-eminence.

While Hannibal was present in Magna Graecia, the Italics made alliances with several Italiot cities. Since the territory had become ungovernable, the Romans decided to enact further colonial expansion, as in Salernum in 194 B.C. The purpose of colonisation was to set up a military presence and provide colonists with agricultural land.

The creation of these colonies coincided with sys-tematic depredations, such as the capture of Taranto in 209, the sack of the treasury of Proserpina in Locri in 205 and the ruin of the sanctuary of Hera Lacinia in Crotone, which was deprived of its tiles in Greek marble. Part of this booty was possibly re-used to build the walls of *Nuceria*.

Subordination to Rome is demonstrated by the copies of the laws promulgated in the *Urbs*, such as the *senatus consultum de Bachanalibus* dated 184 B.C. and the spread of the Latin language. For example, Cumae asked Rome in 180 B.C. to have access to official documents alongside Greek and Oscan records. Inasmuch, official documents for municipal laws were issued in Latin as of the second half of II century B.C., Oscan was still approved, while Greek continued to be used in *Neapolis* in private spheres.

By now, the close link between ancient Magna Graecia and Rome is demonstrated by the opening of the road from Reggio to Capua. It was essentially built for military purposes and was completed in the second half of II century B.C. The headstone

tionships between Naples and Velia with the sanctuary of Cos.

Further influx of colonisation occurred in 122 B.C., following the agrarian laws of Gaius Graccus, which assigned agricultural land to the poorest Roman citizens. One of these colonies was set up in Capua. In view of such widespread well-being, the risings against Rome by the Italic cities in II and I century B.C. should not be viewed as "wars of independence" but as the attempt by the Italic peoples to be granted the same rights as the Romans. The outcome was the extension of Roman citizenship to all the inhabitants of the peninsula, from the Po to the Strait, following the social war that took place in 90-88 B.C. The situation in the Italiot cities was different; some of these cities preferred to remain "federated" with Rome, since the pacts or *foedera* were at times more advantageous than full citizenship.

In 82 B.C., during the Social War, Sulla conquered *Neapolis*. Thereafter, the Campania coastline became increasingly peaceful and was popular with nobles and senators. All the great figures, and subsequently even the Emperors, had properties in the area. The coastal area became a favourite resort where Roman aristocrats built their luxurious villas. The Romans were the forerunners of modern economic exploitation of the natural spas in these volcanic areas. A certain *Caius Sergius Orata* invented the hanging pools of the hot springs at Baia; he is attributed with the invention of the "Roman spas". Moreover, *Marcus Crassus Frugi*, set up thermal-mineral spas at Torre Annunziata for paying guests – still functional today – while in Pozzuoli he built an artificial island to exploit the hot water spring bubbling from the sea.

Caesar, Augustus and Nero set up other colonial settlements for the veterans of their armies. The Augustan age, with the conquest of Egypt in 30 B.C. and the instauration of the *pax romana*, itself saw widespread wealth that found expression in public and private architecture as well as the monumental rebuilding of public areas intended to exalt the ideological values of the Empire. The Age of Nero also saw widespread well-being, testified by the splendid decorations that once embellished the last decades of the cities buried by Vesuvius in 79 A.D. Subsequent austerity policies paradoxically mean that if this eruption had taken place a few centuries later we would not have found such rich sites.

found at Polla, halfway along this road, mentions this purpose, its length (475 km), the bridges, the milestones and the cities crossed: Capua, Nuceria, Muranum, Cosenza, Vibo Valentia and Reggio. Nevertheless, most connections were still by sea, as witnessed by poet Lucilio's description of his trip from Rome to Sicily.

In 146 B.C., Rome conquered Corinth and Greece – as well as Carthage and northern Africa. This new supremacy and the sudden wealth it brought about were the basis for the major urban and monumental changes that took place during II century B.C. in all the cities of Italy, including those in Campania. This process of enrichment was completed by the donation of the Kingdom of Pergamon by Attalos III in 133 B.C. and the conquests made during the Asian wars. The economic situation of these cities benefited from the expansion of the Mediterranean market as far as the coasts of Asia Minor. This is evidenced by the oriental ships serving the ports of Dicearchia and Pozzuoli in II century, by the presence of Italic merchants at Delos, Rhodes and the Black Sea and the close rela-

Territorial and social aspects

The Roman conquest therefore modified the appearance of the cities, urban layouts and territorial outlines defined by Greek colonisation in VIII-VII century B.C.

The colonies saw the construction of buildings typical of the Roman lifestyle: the *agorai* were converted into *fora* and huge public spas were built alongside amphitheatres for entertainment. This utterly modified the appearance of these cities, formerly dominated by their huge temples.

The status quo was troubled by occasional revolts sent in motion by the many slaves bought on the eastern markets to work in the great agricultural estates. Wealthy Romans purchased these slaves and managed the estates.

Such estates became the characteristic feature of the southern landscape throughout the Roman age and especially in the Imperial period. The writers of the late Republic – Cato, Varro and Columella – provide us with information about the organisation of farms and the produce. In short, archaeology still reveals numerous "rustic villas". These villas, over and above their dimensions, adopted a standard model: a part for production activity with millstones, presses, oven, store rooms and slave quarters, etc., and a residential area, with baths and sumptuous mosaic and fresco decorations. On the other hand, the main activities in cities focused on administrative management and commercialisation local produce.

Oriental cults

One of the innovations that came with Romanisation concerned the influx and consolidation of oriental cults. To all intents and purposes, relationships between Campania and Egypt had been very intense since the Archaic Age yet became even closer in the Imperial Age, as clearly shown in *Puteoli*, Pompeii and *Beneventum*.

The cult of Isis in the Roman world, in its search for individual spirituality, appealed to the lower social strata – such as women and slaves – since it professed defence of the humble by the goddess. A remedy for existential unrest and fear of impending destiny could not be assured by official and social religion but only by a direct relationship with the "divine", that Isis – as the synthesis of all goddesses and the perfect "Mother-figure" – could ensure. Inasmuch, the cult soon spread to the middle classes (landlords, merchants and freemen) straying from traditional social values in their search for more individual eschatological approaches.

Magna Graecia and Mezzogiorno

"*L'Europe finit à Naples et même elle y finit assez mal. La Calabre, la Sicile et tout le reste c'est de l'Afrique*". So wrote a French traveller from Sicily towards the end of XIX century (Creuze de Lesser, *Voyage en Italie et en Sicile fait en 1801 et 1802*, Paris, P. Didot l'Aîné, 1806). Yet regions such as Campania or Calabria in the Greek age were among the richest in the entire Mediterranean; mention need only be made of the Sibari's proverbial examples of luxury or the "indolence of Capua" that sapped the strength of Hannibal's troops, as described by Livius (XXIII 18) and Strabo (V 250).

Still today, "Magna Graecia" is synonymous with wealth, sophistication in life and culture – as clearly demonstrated by architecture, art and literature – while the term "Mezzogiorno" on the other hand implies under-development and ignorance. When did such deterioration take place? Many experts of the "southern question" are utterly convinced that it began with Roman domination and became worse in the Middle Ages.

With the loss of its autonomy, Magna Graecia declined and became dependent on the Roman world, and was inevitably involved in its vicissitudes. In short, the ceaseless warfare in II and I century B.C. – the Sannite wars, the Pyrrhic wars, the Second Punic War and the Social War, the revolt led by Spartacus, and the Civil Wars – caused widespread devastation. The consequences were also often hugely important – including the annihilation of entire ethnic groups, such as the Sannites. For example, *Apulia*, once prosperous but devastated during the war against Hannibal, became an area of transhumance economy on a huge scale and – together with Samnium – had few cities but many villages, as Strabo reported in the Augustan age.

Moreover, while the land in the Magna Graecia age was gradually and progressively exploited by local peoples, in the Imperial Roman Age the great landowners were mostly Roman senators, who resided elsewhere, or unscrupulous freemen who only sought economic advantage.

Lastly, the barbarian invasions in V century A.D. and natural calamities, such as the plague in 543, meant that, by the end of VI century, there were very few traces of these ancient peoples.

Opposite page: view of Via Spaccanapoli (built over the Decumanus Maximus).

NAPLES

"After Dicearchia there is Neapolis, a city of Cumaeans; later on, it also welcomed a colony of Chalcidaeans and some colonists from Pithecusa and Athens, which is why it was called Neapolis. The place was apparently home to the tomb of a Siren, Partenope, and was home to a gymnastic contest, in accordance with an ancient oracle … Here, there are still numerous traces of the Greek lifestyle, such as the grammar schools, the ephebes, the fratries and Greeks names, despite the Roman population. This city, in our times, is home every five years to holy games with competitions of music and gymnastics lasting several days that even rival the most celebrated festivals in Greece itself.

There is also an underground gallery, excavated into the mountain between Dicearchia and Neapolis, just like the one in Cumae, which even has a road long and wide enough to allow simultaneous passage by two waggons travelling in opposite directions; moreover, thanks to the apertures made in several points, daylight reaches the very depths of the mountain. Neapolis also boasts springs of spa water and resorts by no means inferior to those of Baia …

In any case, the Greek lifestyle was upheld in Neapolis by people retiring from Rome in search of peace and quiet after teaching or working in Rome because of old age or illness. Even those Romans who love this kind of lifestyle – seeing so many people residing here, attracted by the way of life – are happily setting up their homes".

Strabo, *Geographia* V 4, 7

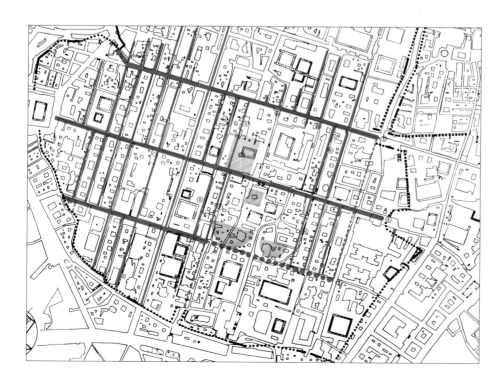

History

Ancient literary tradition suggests that (end IX-early VIII century B.C.) sailors from Rhodes founded a trading colony on the hill of Pizzofalcone and the small island of Megaris – present-day Castel dell'Ovo.

By the mid-VII century B.C., the initial bridgehead was transformed by the Greeks of Cumae, during their expansion in Campania, into a full-scale town known as Partenope. The Neapolitan tradition concerning the existence and origin of Partenope was confirmed by the necropolis found in Via Nicotera, whereby this first settlement can be dated around 650-550 B.C., the period of Cumaean expansion towards the Gulf of Naples, that for many years was known as the "Gulf of Cumae".

The Cumaeans probably lost this stronghold during the war against the Etruscans (524 B.C.). They rebuilt the city around 470 B.C., when, having defeated the Etruscans with the aid of the Syracusans, they founded *Neapolis* to the east of the first site of Partenope (that then came to be known as Palepolis, the "old city").

The relationships between the different peoples in Campania encouraged the Romans to take an interest in Naples in IV century B.C., initially offering their protection and subsequently beginning a conflict that came to an end in 327 B.C. with an agreement that established *Neapolis* as an "allied city". The pact, that for many years spared Naples from the risk of warfare, envisaged absolute pre-eminence of the Greeks in the city over the Samnites, a people against whom Rome was engaged in a bitter war.

In 90 B.C., following the Social War (90-88 B.C. fought by the *socii*, that is to say the Italic allies, against Rome in order to win Roman citizenship and related privileges), *Neapolis* achieved Roman citizenship. The old Greek magistracy formally retained its status but its substance changed, since the city was forced to take part in the political conflicts and civil wars that broke out in Rome immediately after the end of the social war.

In 88 B.C., war broke out between Marius and Sulla, when the merchant classes of *Neapolis* took the side of Consul Caius Marius, the leader of the popular party opposing the Sulla's aristocratic faction,

which on the other hand was supported by the great landowners. Following the defeat of Marius, Sulla in 82 B.C. also conquered *Neapolis*, and his supported murdered almost all its citizens and confiscated the city's triremes. *Pithecusa*, the present-day island of Ischia, was taken from the Neapolitans. This also interrupted production of the so-called 'Campana A' pottery, manufactured as of III century B.C. in Naples and its surroundings, as well as in *Pithecusa* itself (the clay came from *Pithecusa*), formerly exported by sea throughout the western Mediterranean together with wine jars.

Inasmuch, the old ruling class was not only physically eliminated but also lost the very basis of its power: the merchant class involved in maritime trade was replaced by a residential class based on income from rents and land estates. It was at this

time that Naples began to emerge as a peaceful city ideal for *otium* inhabited by nobles and senators. At this time, Roman senator Lucullus (who died in 57 B.C.) decided to retire – at the end of his political and military career – to the Pizzofalcone area and the island of Megaris, where he built a splendid villa famed for its fish pools and flowering gardens. Still today, "Lucullian meals" is a common expression making perhaps unaware reference to his sophisticated life style.

The Empire period deliberately exalted and flaunted the traditional Hellenic character of the city, that wilfully continued to use the Greek language, spoken by Nero during his visit to Naples in 64 A.D. yet equally witnessed in burial inscriptions in the Sanità Quarter, at least until II century A.D.

Civic institutions and associations (*fratriae*) re-

View of the western side of Castel dell'Ovo where the last Roman Emperor, Romulus Augustulus, was imprisoned.

building sumptuous and pleasurable villas often visited by Emperors and their courts. All the great figures – such as Marius, Sulla, Crassus, Caesar, Pompey, Ortensius, Lucullus and Cicero – owned properties in the area.

Roman culture in Naples came to its peak in the Augustan age through the presence of poets and writers such Virgil, Catullus, Horace, Lucretius and Papinius Statius. The Roman aristocrats built their finest residences between Posillipo, Chiaia and present-day Castel dell'Ovo. They were full of books, statues, marbles, rare and highly-prized objects sought on the markets of Greece and the Orient. The most famous is the villa of Vedius Pollio, a friend of Augustus, later inherited by the Emperor himself. The Greek name itself – *Pausilypon* – alludes to its function as a place of rest, the "end of troubles". Emperor Marcus Aurelius, in II century A.D., perhaps made Naples a colony, as testified by an inscription.

Christianity spread rapidly throughout the region as early as I century A.D., since the port of Pozzuoli was a gateway to all the religious currents in the Mediterranean. Between end-II and early-III century A.D., Aspreno was the first Bishop of *Neapolis*. The significant development of the Neapolitan Church is witnessed by the benefits granted by Constantine, where Naples enjoyed a privilege shared by few other cities in Italy of a Basilica (Santa Restituta), today a chapel incorporated into the Cathedral.

The most significant examples of paleo-Christian culture in Naples are the catacombs of Capodimonte hill – the underground cemeteries that began to develop as of II century A.D., remaining in use until X century.

There is little news about *Neapolis* from III century A.D. Signs of decadence came to the fore in IV-V century: famines, depression and abandoned fields. In 440 B.C., in the period of the barbarian invasions, Emperor Valentinian III built new city walls and towers as a counter-measure against attacks from sea and land, as witnessed by an inscription and the discovery of such a towerin the area around Piazza Nicola Amore.

The Roman Empire came to an end in Naples. The splendid villa once owned by Lucullus, and later transformed into Castel dell'Ovo, was where Odoacres, King of the Erulians, exiled Romolus Augustulus, the last Emperor of Rome, who died here in 476 A.D.

tained Greek as their official language; the five-yearly games held in the city on the model of the Olympic Games (*Italikà Romaia Sebastà Isolympia*) were also Greek and alternated musical contests with gymnastics and horse riding.

At this time, Naples was a kind of "Florence of Antiquity", popular with literary figures and aristocrats for its peace and quiet, beautiful landscapes, mild climate and ancient culture.

Moreover, the city – as witnessed by geographer Strabo, who lived during the Augustan age – boasted many hot spas and baths which were extremely popular with the Romans. The town of sailors and merchants gave way to a resort city for rest and entertainment.

The coastal area of Naples and the Phlegrean Fields became favoured by the Roman ruling class,

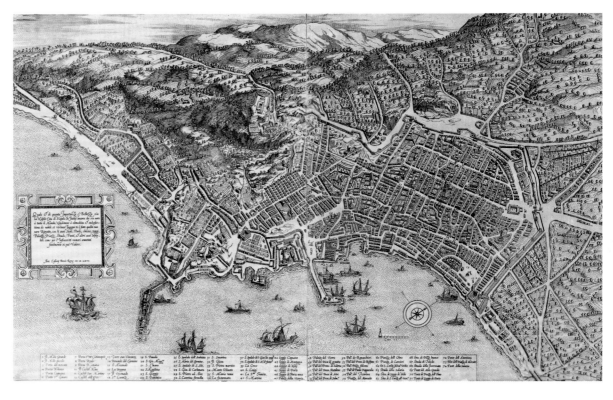

The urban layout

The first settlement at *Partenope*, later known as *Palepolis*, stood in the present-day area of Pizzofalcone, a promontory surrounded on three sides by the sea and separated from the hinterland by the deep Chiaia Gorge; its necropolis developed in the area today crossed by Via Nicotera.

The new city of *Neapolis* was founded around 470 B.C. The "new city" stood on a stretch of land descending to the sea from the high ground of Sant'Aniello at Caponapoli (about m 70 above sea level), marked off by a series of natural gorges carved by streams that are still today easily recognised: Via Salvator Rosa and Via Foria on the north and northwest sides and, to the south, Via Toledo, Via Sant'Anna dei Lombardi and Via Mezzocannone.

Historiographic tradition has long debated the ancient port of *Neapolis*, in particular its location and the outline of the coast. It probably stood on the eastern rim of Mount Echia-Pizzofalcone, where the "Plebiscito" and "Municipio" stand today. In short, the coastline has seen significant changes since Antiquity to our own times, with various landfills of alluvial origin that have extended it. Another landing place, as seen in Mediaeval documents, was without doubt the beach at the end of Via Mezzocannone. Recently – during work on the Subway in the Town Hall Square and Piazza Bovio – core sam-

pling and stratigraphic excavations were performed that enabled a reasonably close reconstruction of the 1500s Lafréry ground plan: the coast, at least during I century A.D., probably extended as far as present-day Via Medina, in front of the modern Town Hall, where recent investigations have brought to light the wooden poles of a pier and three perfectly preserved Roman ships.

The Graeco-Roman city corresponded with the current ancient city centre. This is demonstrated by the surrounding fortifications and the ancient urban ground plan, still today recognisable in the grid pattern of the blocks in this zone. The continuity of the urban ground plan is a characteristic element of Naples and something that few other modern cities can boast.

The layout of the walls was reconstructed thanks to finds involving many sections. The walls ran from the hill of Sant'Aniello at Caponapoli, along Via Settembrini, as far as Castel Capuano and Forcella, and then follows Corso Umberto I as far as Piazza Bovio, climbing on the western side towards Piazza Bellini and Via Costantinopoli, closing the loop in Piazza Cavour. The new city inside the walls had a regular ground plan, made up of rectangular blocks with three main roads running east-west (*platéiai*), about 15 metres wide (Via Sapienza-Via Anticaglia-Via Pisanelli, Via Tribunali and Via San Biagio ai Li-

brai); these are intersected at right angles by a series of minor roads (*stenopoi*), 3 to 3.50 metres wide. The upper part of the city – the acropolis – was used as a city sanctuary, as witnessed by a votary offering to Demetra found in the former San Gaudioso monastery.

The central part, on the other hand, was home to the monumental and civil area, standing on two terraces because of the gradient of the hill. Both squares were intended for public use even in the original town plan, that is the *agorà* in the Greek city, where most administrative, political, economic and judiciary functions took place. In the Roman age, the civic centre of the Greek city retained its functions on becoming the Forum. The upper terrace (marked off by Via Anticaglia) had an essentially political function, as shown by the Temple of the Dioscuri (Castor and Pollux) and the theatres. The lower terrace (marked off by Via San Biagio ai Librai), on the other hand, had a commercial function, given the remains found of the market in the San Lorenzo Maggiore complex. It is likely that these dual functions reflected a similar organisation of the square (*agorà*) in Greek times. On the other hand, there is little archaeological testimony of residential buildings from the Classic Age.

The necropolis were located outside the city gates. Over and above the necropolis of *Palepoli*, in Via Nicotera, mention can be made of the necropolis in Via San Tommaso d'Aquino and the necropolis that came to light beneath Castel Capuano, the site of the present-day Courts.

The years between the end of the Republic and the onset of the Empire also saw the construction of a great many leisure villas all along the coast. They were so numerous and adjacent that, as suggested by geographer Strabo, the landscape viewed from the sea resembled a single city. The most important was the Villa of Lucullus, later known as the *castrum* or *castellum lucullanum*, where Odoacre, King of the Erulians, exiled the last Roman Emperor, Romolus Augustulus. The villa occupied an immense area, from the present-day Corso Vittorio Emanuele (Largo delle Quattro Stagioni, now a station on the Cuma Railway) as far as the island of Megaride (Castel dell'Ovo); other famous villas included *Pausilypon* (hence the name of the entire hill of Posillipo), once owned by Vedius Pollio and afterwards inherited by Augustus, and the Villa of Pollio Felix on the coast now corresponding to Riviera di Chiaia.

Communication routes and fortifications

There is no certain information about communication routes in the Greek age, although it is possible to reconstruct the Roman roads. Two main roads ensured connections with Pozzuoli (*Puteoli*) and the Phlegrean area, one passing through a tunnel (*crypta*) and the other known as the "hill street" (*via per colles*). The street passing through the tunnel departed from the gate in Piazza San Domenico Maggiore, followed the present-day Via Chiaia to Riviera di Chiaia and, at Mergellina, entered the *Crypta Neapolitana,* the tunnel through the hill of Posillipo, thereby connecting Mergellina with Via Terracina and hence the territory of Pozzuoli. The *Crypta* was probably the work of the famous architect of Augustus, Cocceius, who also supervised the development of the major project for the strategic improvement of the Phlegrean ports, including the gallery tunnel (named "Grotta di Cocceio") that linked Cumae and Lake Averno, home to the new port (*portus Iulius*). The hillside road, known in the Middle Ages as *Via Antiniana*, departed from the gate close to San Pietro a Maiella, climbed Salita Tarsia, Via Conte della Cerra, Via Annella di Massimo, Via Belvedere and Corso Europa, and then descended on the opposite side towards Loggetta as far as Via Terracina, where it joined the road from the *Crypta*. A coastal road, on the other hand, linked Pompeii and Nocera (*Nuceria*), where there was also an inland road – the Via Popilia – that linked Capua and Reggio Calabria.

The Serino aqueduct was built in the Augustan age, remains of which can be seen at Capodichino in a series of brick arches known as the "Ponti Rossi". The Serino springs (in the province of Avellino) supplied one branch serving Benevento, while the other arrived as far as Casoria and Capodichino and hence to Naples, then continuing as far as the Phlegrean Fields where it terminated in a huge cistern – the *Piscina Mirabilis* – at Miseno (Bacoli), where it supplied the imperial fleet.

The city was surrounded from its foundation by an imposing system of fortifications, still preserved and visible in important sections. These fortifications were in all about 3.7 kilometres long and enclosed an area of about 72 hectares. The walls and the town ground plan are effectively the only remaining architectural structures of the Greek city. The masonry walls followed the irregular terrain of the plateau, sloping down from north to south and cut by deep gorges.

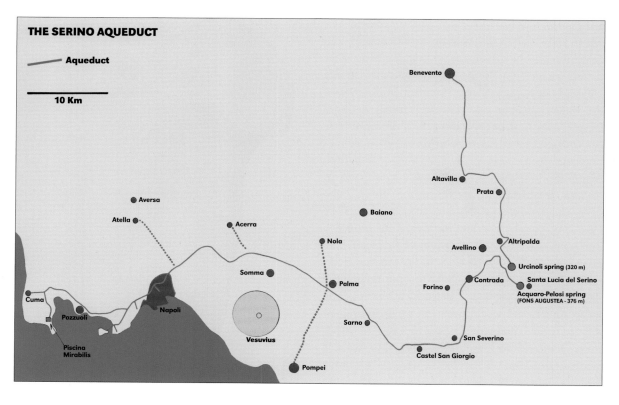

THE SERINO AQUEDUCT

Aqueduct

10 Km

Benevento
Altavilla
Prata
Aversa
Baiano
Atella
Acerra
Nola
Altripalda
Avellino
Urcinoli spring (320 m)
Somma
Contrada
Santa Lucia del Serino
Palma
Forino
Acquaro-Pelosi spring (FONS AUGUSTEA - 376 m)
Cuma
Pozzuoli
Napoli
Sarno
Piscina Mirabilis
Vesuvius
San Severino
Castel San Giorgio
Pompei

Above: female head in terracotta, from Sant'Aniello a Caponapoli.
Right: ground plan of the Serino aqueduct.

Page 54: statue of Nike, a Flavian copy of a Greek original – end V century B.C.
Page 55: torso of an athlete. Naples, National Archaeological Museum.

Despite the destruction following urban rebuilding in the late 1800s, the large sections still extant have made it possible to define these walls. Numerous discoveries were made at the end of XIX century during major urban reclamation work following the Unification of Italy.

Two main chronological phases for these fortifications have been identified: the first can be dated to the early V century B.C., contemporary with the foundation of the city, while the second can be dated as of the second half of IV century B.C. and was built during the Samnitic wars. In 440 B.C., under Valentinian III, an inscription found between Piazza Bovio and the Town Hall Square testifies to the expansion of the fortifications in the port area.

The two stages are distinguished by the materials used and construction techniques. The most ancient stage (V century B.C.) involved large, cut to square blocks known as "ortóstati". The more recent stage (IV century B.C.) saw a construction technique based on horizontal squared blocks. A well-preserved portion of these walls can be seen in Piazza Bellini, that came to light in 1954; it can be dated at the second half of IV century B.C. on the basis of ceramic materials found in the *émplekton*. A gate came to light at Forcella during reclamation work (the so-called *Porta Furcillensis*,

named after the fork-like road junction). On the other hand, there are no remaining traces of the towers. The ancient city also had road tunnels under the surrounding hills.

The *Crypta Neapolitana* was cut into the side of the Vomero hill in the Augustan age to improve communications between Pozzuoli and Naples. Strabo wrote that it was the work of Cocceio and wide enough to allow two waggons to pass in opposite directions. The tunnel is 705 m long, 4.50 m wide and 4.50 to 18.50 m high. The entrances for this magnificent work of engineering were near the Church of Piedigrotta and at Fuorigrotta, not far from the exit of the modern tunnel. In the 1400s, Alfonso of Aragon commissioned renovation and extension work which involved lowering the pavement.

The "Grotta di Seiano", also known as the "Grotta di Posillipo", passed under the hill of Posillipo between Coroglio and Gaiola to provide monumental access to the Imperial Villa of Posillipo. It came to light in 1840; it was re-opened on the orders of King Ferdinand II Bourbon but later abandoned. Excavated entirely into the tuff – 780 m long, 4-7 m wide and 4-9 metres high – it is still today an impressive undertaking. Ventilation was provided by three side tunnels open on to the Bay of Trentaremi.

The sanctuaries

The main cults in Naples during the Greek and Roman ages can be deduced from a wealth of epigraphic and literary documentation. The Neapolitan poet Statius, who lived I century A.D., considered Apollo, Demeter and the Dioscuri as the gods of the city. Geographer Strabo in I century A.D. mentioned that the tomb of the siren Partenope was still venerated in his own times.

The Sanctuary of Demeter probably stood on the acropolis – the hill of Sant'Aniello at Caponapoli, where – in the area today occupied by the Clinic of Medical Semiotics – a votary offering was found. These offerings – about 700 objects found in a trench 7 metres deep – are largely female figures, especially with high, truncated conical caps (*pólos*) typical of the cult of Demeter. The sanctuaries of Demeter found in Sicily (Agrigento, Syracuse and Morgantina) have revealed objects very similar to those found around Naples, thereby confirming the close relationships between *Neapolis* and Sicily in IV century B.C.

The Sanctuary of the siren Partenope, on the other hand, probably stood on the coast, perhaps near the port. Literary tradition claims that Ulysses provoked the suicide of the Sirens and that the body of one of them, Partenope, was swept up on to the beach near Naples, where it was honoured every year with libations and sacrifices of oxen.

The cult of the Dioscuri, of Greek origin, was handed down to Roman religion. This cult was particularly popular in the Augustan age, when it was linked with the heirs of the imperial house. In short, the two divine brothers resembled the two adopted sons of Augustus, Lucius and Caius Caesar, and – after their death – Tiberius and Drusus. The cult was celebrated in a temple in the Forum area. The remains are now part of the facade of the Church of San Paolo Maggiore in Piazza San Gaetano. The Roman temple, built I century A.D., remained intact for many centuries until, in VIII-IX century, a Christian church dedicated to St. Paul was built on top of it.

Francisco de Hollanda, a Portuguese artist of the school of Michelangelo, in 1540 made a drawing of the facade that is still the most accurate testimony of the Roman temple, especially as regards the reproduction of the sculptures of the fronton and the transcription of the dedication on the architrave. Andrea Palladio in 1570 also included the Neapolitan temple in Book IV of his treatise *Architecture*, although he arbitrarily included a sacrificial scene in the fronton.

Today, the remains of the Roman temple only comprise two columns with bases, still *in situ*, and a fragment of the dedication, re-used in 1637 as a tombstone on the Charterhouse of San Martino. The relics incorporated into the facade of the Church can be dated to the Tiberian age. The dedication on the architrave indicates that the building was erected in honour of the Dioscuri and the city by Tiberius Julius Tarsus and Pelagon, freemen of Emperor Tiberius. This chronology is confirmed by the style of the architectural decorations as well the reticulated masonry technique used in the podium, that can be seen in the Chapel of the Holy Crucifix. The decoration of the fronton perhaps depicted the Dioscuri between Diana and Apollo and two other figures, identified as the personifications of the earth (*Tellus*) and of sea (*Oceanus*) flanked by two Tritons. The Dioscuri were represented as the

The Greek walls in Piazza Bellini, city centre.

Above: the "Crypta Neapolitana", the ancient tunnel between Piedigrotta and Fuorigrotta, in a 1700s print by F. Piranesi.

Opposite page: facade of the Church of San Paolo Maggiore.

area paved with a white mosaic. The centre of the area had a circular structure (*thólos*). The building, very similar to the *Macellum* in Pompeii, was accessed from the *platéia*, corresponding to the present-day Via Tribunali.

The slope of the site meant that the building extended over a terrace with a series of rooms, found at a depth of about 7 metres. Excavations underneath the transept of the church highlighted about 60 metres of road running in a north-south direction. The road was 3 m wide, paved and dated around V century A.D.

In I century A.D., several workshops (*tabernae*) were built on the western side, while a crypto-portico was built on the southern side. The *tabernae*, entered from the street, had two chambers in accordance with a standard module. The northern limit of the street revealed the city's treasury building. This building had two narrow, communicating chambers, with an external facade in brick. It was identified on the basis of the sturdy door closure system and the massive metal grille on the window. The Forum, dating from the closing years of the reign of Nero and the early years of the Flavian period, was significantly renovated after the earthquake in 62 A.D. that damaged several sites in Campania, including Pompeii itself.

The buildings and the road were used until V century A.D., when the mud left after floods caused the area to be abandoned. In VI century A.D., the paleo-Christian Basilica was built on top of this stratum of mud.

The High Middle Ages saw the construction, over the in-filled ancient road, of the "Seggio" – the administrative head offices of the city. The name derives from the colonnade building where elected nobles and representatives of the people met. The "Seggio" and the paleo-Christian Basilica remained in use until the building of the Anjou church by the Franciscan Friars in XIII century.

The theatres

The ancient city boasted an intense theatrical life. Two theatres were built in the Roman age to the north of the *Forum*, near the present-day Piazza San Gaetano. We do not know whether they were built on top of similar buildings of the Greek age but it is likely – by analogy with other Greek cities – that the Roman theatres occupied the sites of former buildings for public meetings and performances (*ekklesiastérion* and *bouleutérion*).

guardians of universal harmony, ensuring plentiful fruit and water for the city, as well as the endless sequence of day and night, through the figures of Apollo (the Sun) and Diana (the Moon). The original religious message of the Greek age was joined in Roman times by political values, since the Dioscuri – the twins who decided in fraternal love to live and die in alternation one day each – became the guardians of the continued social peace (*concordia*) established by Emperor Augustus. The reworking of the temple in I century A.D. expressed the attention paid by Augustus and his successors to the modernisation of *Neapolis*.

The site underneath the Basilica and Convent of San Lorenzo Maggiore, in Piazza San Gaetano, has revealed remains of the ancient city, with Greek, Roman and Mediaeval stratifications. The archaeological excavations, begun in 1954 during restoration work on the church, uncovered the Roman market of *Neapolis* (*Macellum*). The remains came to light about two metres below the paving of the 1700s cloister of the Convent of San Lorenzo. The building comprised a series of workshops (*tabernae*) arranged beneath a marble portico, that in turn marked off an outside rectangular

The imposing dimensions of the theatres, embracing the Temple of the Dioscuri, scenically dominated the upper terrace. Poet Statius (I century A.D.), born in Naples and proud of the beauties of his city, described the theatres as a *gemina moles*, that is as an apparently single complex that in reality had two purposes.

The outdoor theatre, used for theatrical performances, was already known in XVII century. It stood in the area between Via San Paolo, Via Anticaglia, Vico Giganti and the cloisters of the Convent of the Teatin Fathers. It was probably flanked by the indoor theatre (*Odeion*), where musical contests were held.

The very large remains of the outside theatre are now housed inside the modern buildings. It was possible to reconstruct the ground plan thanks to excavations undertaken last century: the maximum diameter was 102 m, while the orchestra had a diameter of about 20 m. The two large brick arches that can be seen along Via Anticaglia, that takes its name precisely from these structures, probably acted as external buttresses ("barbicans") for the cavea. Part of the terraced seats of the cavea is still visible inside the cellars and the courtyards of the homes, while the wall in the cloister of the Teatin Fathers was once the base wall of the stage. The first stage of the theatre dates back to the Augustan age (end I century B.C.- early I century A.D.). After the earthquakes in 62 and 64 A.D. and the eruption in 79 A.D., that destroyed Pompeii and Herculaneum, damage in Naples also had to be repaired.

These buildings were recognised in 1400s low relief in the Maschio Angioino – today lost – depicting the procession of Alfonso of Aragon beside a temple with six columns at the front, identified as the Temple of the Dioscuri.

On the basis of the description by poet Statius and the curved outline of Via San Paolo-Via Pisanelli, it is assumed that the *Odeion* stood inside the block defined by these streets. The only remains are perhaps the six reticulated rooms that came to light along Via San Paolo. Moreover, finds in Via San Paolo included two columns in "cipollino" marble and a base dedicated to flautist P. Aelius Antigenides, who won several contests in Rome, Naples and Pozzuoli.

The institution of the five-year games modelled on the great games of Olympia (*Italikà Romàia Sebastà Isolympia*) dates to 2 A.D. Events included horse races and gymnastics, musical contests and plays held in the two theatres. The importance of these

The "Macellum" (covered market) of Neapolis, in two models of the complex of San Lorenzo Maggiore (Studio Romatre, Architect M. Travaglini, Rome).

Opposite page: statue from the Temple of the Dioscuri. Naples, National Archaeological Museum.

games is witnessed by the fact that Augustus himself attended them in 14 A.D., that is to say immediately prior to his death. Emperor Claudius in 42 A.D. won the first prize, staging a Greek comedy he wrote in honour of his brother, Germanicus.

The Neapolitan people were held in high regard by Emperor Nero, who honoured them with a premiere of his musical show before performing it on stages in Greece. Historian Svetonius mentions an episode in 64 A.D. during one of these performances: a violent earthquake shook the theatre but Nero phlegmatically continued to sing and perform. The exact date is provided by historian Tacitus who, without actually mentioning an earthquake, tells that the theatre collapsed after the performance without harming the audience. Between 138 and 161 A.D., Marcus Aurelius attended performances in Naples, ironically recalling the excessive adulation of the writers of the eulogies he was obliged to listen to. As of II century A.D. the importance of the Neapolitan contests was overshadowed by the games held in nearby Pozzuoli.

The baths

The most complete example of documented baths in *Neapolis* is found in the Convent of Santa Chiara. The building, dating from second half I century A.D., was accessed from the ancient street

now marked by Via Benedetto Croce. The baths, fed by the Serino aqueduct, comprised an area for steam baths (*laconicum*), in turn linked with rooms for lukewarm baths (*tepidaria*). Along the wall of the *tepidarium*, there are terracotta pipes for the passage of hot air (*tubuli*). A large rectangular hall in brick may be identified as the site for cold water baths (*frigidarium*) or as a nymphaeum. The hot bath area (*calidarium*) probably stood in the portion as yet unexplored. These settings revealed a great deal of pottery dating from 1300s-1700s (now on show in the Museum dell'Opera), probably associated with life in the convent, when the bath area became a tip.

View of the Baths of Santa Chiara.

Opposite page. Top: buttresses in Via Anticaglia. Bottom: view of the excavations of the Baths of Carminiello ai Mannesi.

Another Roman thermal building came to light following bombing during the last World War, that destroyed the Church of Santa Maria del Carmine ai Mannesi. It stood to the east of present-day Via Duomo and south of the *plateia* in Via Tribunali. The complex, in use from the end of I century A.D. to IV century A.D., has two levels. This area revealed marble sculptures, including a head of Mercury from the age of Tiberius and a torso of a satyr. During the Imperial age, the lower floor saw the installation of a Mithraeum, that is a place for the cult of Mithra, the eastern god of the sun. A stucco relief depicts the god about to sacrifice a bull. The cult, which promised resurrection and eternity, was held in grottos and underground places; it spread throughout Campania, especially among soldiers and slaves.

Other Roman baths were found at Fuorigrotta, along Via Terracina. They stood along the Naples-Pozzuoli road and belonged to a place of rest (*statio*); in short, the area also revealed remains of homes, a mausoleum, sections of the Roman road and parts of the Roman Serino aqueduct. The building, dating around II century A.D., has changing rooms (*apodyterium*), a room for cold baths (*frigidarium*), another for hot baths (*calidarium*) and various other areas for warm baths (*tepidaria*). The route was circular to allow gradual progression from cold to hot areas. The rooms were heated through a double flooring. The lower flooring, made up of tiles, supported small columns in terracotta (*suspensurae*) that sustained the upper flooring decorated with marble mosaics. An oven (*praefurnium*) heated the water for the hot baths and generated hot air that flowed under the floors, all intercommunicating, rising from the floors along the walls through a gap made with tiles and pins (*tegulae mammatae*) or terracotta pipes (*tubuli*). The changing rooms are still today decorated with a floor mosaic with a Sea Nymph seated on the spiral tail of a Triton. The flooring of the *frigidarium* was decorated with a mosaic depicting a procession of marine monsters: a sea horse, a panther, a dragon and a bull. Near the entrance there is a marble latrine, with a mosaic depicting two dolphins with twisted tails.

A particularly evocative example of thermal architecture stands in front of the present-day New Spas in Agnano, on the slopes of Mount Spina. It is amazing to think the site has been in use since Antiquity through to our own days. The imposing complex, now only massive ruins, was characteristic of the Phlegrean area, since it exploited the natural underground heat to warm certain rooms, as at the Baia baths. The Agnano baths, like those in Via Terracina, date from II century A.D. and were used until the high Middle Ages.

The building, supplied by the Serino aqueduct, had several levels. The cold baths (*frigidarium*) revealed several sculptures, currently on show in the modern spa: a group with Hermes and Dionysus, a marine Venus and two other statues identified as Ganymede and Venus wearing the weapons of Mars. A circular route was taken from the *frigidarium* to the heated rooms. Some of these were heated by the natural underground heat and others, such as the hot baths (*calidarium*), artificially with an oven (*praefurnium*). The room heating system involved a double flooring: warm air circulated between the two floors, separated by small terracotta columns (*suspensurae*).

The villas

Between the end of the Republican age and the early years of the Imperial age, the entire coastline of Naples and the Phlegrean Fields became a residential area with many villas. The beauty of the places, the mild climate, the presence of spa waters and the fascination exerted by Greek traditions encouraged the Roman ruling class to build luxurious homes. This development was also encouraged by the completion of new roads in the Naples-Phlegrean Fields area, including the so-called *Crypta Neapolitana* tunnel between Piedigrotta and Fuorigrotta. Moreover, the presence of the Emperors staying in these villas with their courts also made the Gulf of Naples famous all over the Roman world.

Pietra Salata, off Cape Posillipo, has numerous submerged remains of a seaside villa standing on artificial foundations and complete with porticos. At Marechiaro, the remains of a *domus* barely emerge from the sea, that – since the early years of last century – presented a circular building, in part reticulated and in part cut into the tuff. Numerous materials from the Roman age were re-used to build the Church of S. Maria del Faro, where the use of this place name in documents dating from the Anjou period suggest that there was a lighthouse even in Roman times.

Near Gaiola, there is the best-preserved and most evocative Roman building in the area, the so-called "House of the Spirits". It is a three-storey reticulated building of the Augustan age. The first floor is partially submerged, yet traces of marine erosion can also be seen on the walls.

The most famous villa built along the coast was *Pausilypon*, whose Greek name (meaning "untroubled place") was later used for the entire hill. The Villa covered a truly huge area, from the slopes of the hill as far as the Gaiola Islands. This is one of the first examples of villas built by adapting architecture to the nature of the site. Other examples are the Villa of Emperor Hadrian at Tivoli, the Villa of Tiberius at Capri and the Villa of Pollio Felix at Sorrento. The complex had a monumental access in the so-called "Grotto of Seiano" (today "Grotto of Posillipo"), that tunnelled by about 800 metres into the hill of Posillipo, linking Coroglio and Gaiola.

The first owner was the rich Roman noble Publius Vedius Pollio, an important political figure at the court of Augustus. On his death in 15 B.C., he left his properties as a bequest to Augustus and his successors. They extended and adapted it to the needs of an Imperial residence.

The villa in short comprised various buildings arranged scenically on terraces that exploited the landscape potential of the slope. Buildings, gardens, avenues, spas and baths and servant quarters were arranged on the slopes of the hill, while grottos, tri-

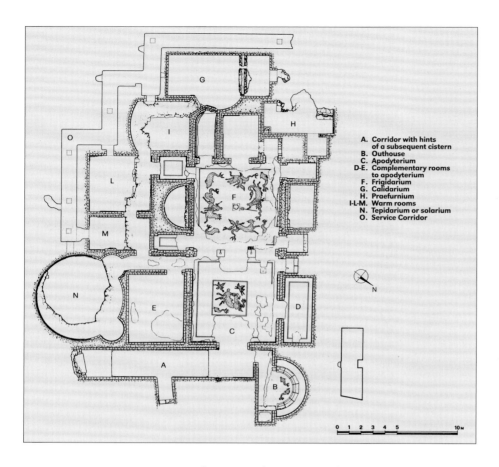

A. Corridor with hints
   of a subsequent cistern
B. Outhouse
C. Apodyterium
D-E. Complementary rooms
     to apodyterium
F. Frigidarium
G. Calidarium
H. Praefurnium
I-L-M. Warm rooms
N. Tepidarium or solarium
O. Service Corridor

0 1 2 3 4 5   10 M

*Above: ground plan
of the Baths in Via Terracina.
Right: the Baths of Agnano.*

*Opposite page: sea nymph,
from the Imperial Villa at
Posillipo. Naples, National
Archaeological Museum.*

cliniums and porticos made up the sea-side quarter. The ruins known as "Virgil's School" were in fact a nymphaeum overlooking the sea. The name derives from the Mediaeval legend whereby the poet taught his magical arts here. The villa also had landings, with piers and quays today submerged by the effect of Bradyseism. The Gaiola Islands, then linked with firm land, had fish breeding pools.

The highest terrace was home to the most representative settings, with two buildings for performances, a theatre and an *odéon*. These buildings indicate that the complex was designed to host a small Imperial court. The reticulated theatre was capable of holding about two thousand spectators and was clad with slabs of marble. There was a very large pool in the middle for aquatic performances (*kolymbetra*). The villa also had spas with a circular hall for hot baths (*calidarium*).

The necropolis

The city of the living, initially animated by Greek culture and later by Roman luxury, was counterpoised by the city of the dead.

The archaic necropolis was identified in Via Nicotera, near Monte di Dio. In the Classic Age, the main necropolis was almost certainly the one identified outside the gate located at Forcella in the area beneath Castel Capuano, today home to the Courts.

The Hellenistic Age was characterised by funeral monuments cut into the sides of the hills in the north-east area immediately outside the fortifications, that is in the area outside Porta San Gennaro, towards Via dei Vergini e Cristallini, in the current Sanità Quarter. Since they were subsequently buried – today several are even more than eleven metres below the present-day road level – they were for some considerable time erroneously interpreted as "ipogei", that is underground cemeteries.

The models of these monumental tombs, dating from end-IV to mid-III century B.C., were inspired by Macedonia. The burial chamber is usually rectangular, surmounted by a barrel vault or a double span with a caisson ceiling; access was through a stepped corridor (*dromos*). The sarcophagi for the deposition of the dead, carved and decorated to represent funeral beds, were placed around the walls of the chamber. Pictorial decorations in red, yellow, black and sky blue often embellish the inside walls of the burial rooms: crowns of ivy hanging from nails, festoons and garlands, bunches of grapes, pomegranates, pines and eggs – as well as painted objects depicting silver candelabra, skylights and vases. Funerary offerings, found in the sarcophagi or placed on the protruding cornices, included mirrors and bronze broaches, iron strigils, balm jars, oil jars, small amphora and clay jugs, and in some cases terracotta statuettes.

Subsequent inscriptions show that the tombs were re-used for some considerable time, until the early years of the Empire, even by people not belonging to the family groups for which they were built. This is also the reference period for the cinerary urns placed in a series of niches and the reliefs on slabs of terracotta and marble with scenes of farewell of the deceased.

The complex in Via Cristallini, given its exceptional conservation status, is the most significant example. Excavated between 1889 and 1896, it is made up of four adjacent but independent rooms completely cut into the tuff. Every tomb has a vestibule and a chamber underneath it housing the sarcophagi resembling funeral beds with mattresses, pillows and decorated feet. The entrance to one of the tombs is flanked by two columns carved into the tuff, that perhaps once belonged to a monumental facade. Pictorial decorations are very varied, with small pillars and capitals with two scrolls with a head of Medusa or leaves in the centre. The head of Medusa in relief on the back wall painted inside a "tondo" decorated with leaves and snakes is of exceptional quality.

The most significant tomb of the Roman epoch is the so-called "Tomb of Virgil" standing at the entrance to the *Crypta Neapolitana*. This monument, dating from the early Imperial age and comprising a cube-like base with a cylindrical drum, is in the so-called "colombarium" style with niches in the walls of the chamber where the cinerary urns were placed. Inside the base, there is the burial chamber, covered by a barrel vault and illuminated by three slits. The tomb today seems to stand unusually high, since the work commissioned by Alfonso of Aragon in the adjacent *Crypta* lowered the flooring of the gallery and the surrounding area compared to the original Roman floor. In reality, this is one of the many funeral monuments of the Augustan age that flanked the ancient road, yet the humanist tradition arbitrarily identified it as the tomb of the great poet. In short, after his death in Brindisi, his remains were apparently taken to Naples and placed near the second military milestone on the road from Naples to *Puteoli*. Inasmuch, the true tomb – no longer extant – should be approximately located inside the present-day Villa Comunale. In any case, in 1930, during celebrations of Virgil's second millennium, it was decided to restore and renovate his presumed tomb and give some kind of official recognition to the attribution. It is an evoca-

tive coincidence that the nearby Church of Piedigrotta has the tomb of another great Italian poet, Giacomo Leopardi.

We know that already in Antiquity the true tomb of Virgil was visited by literary figures and poets, such as Statius and Silio Italico, but also later by Petrarch and Boccaccio. We know that his true tomb had an engraving of the last verses composed by the poet on his death bed: "*Mantua gave me birth, Puglia enthralled me; now I belong to Partenope. I sang of pastures, fields and warriors*".

The paleo-Christian city

The catacombs are the most significant testimony of paleo-Christian culture. The term "catacombs", subsequently used to define all underground cemeteries, originates from the name given to the place where the mortal remains of St. Peter and St. Paul were placed underneath the Basilica of San Sebastiano in Rome, that is "in a hollow" (*ad catacumbas*). In short, the catacombs, standing outside the city walls, were used by the first Christians to celebrate religious functions and to bury the first martyrs. The most important Neapolitan catacombs are those

of San Gennaro a Capodimonte, San Gaudioso in the Church of Santa Maria della Sanità and San Severo alla Sanità. They began to develop in Naples as of II century A.D. through to X century. Christianity spread rapidly all over the region as early as I century A.D. through the port of Pozzuoli.

The Catacomb of San Gennaro was so-named by *Ianuarius*, Bishop of Benevento, after the reliquaries of the Saint were transferred here in V century A.D. The mortal remains of the Saint were then transferred in 831 by the Prince of Benevento to Naples Cathedral, where they are still housed. Following the transfer of the reliquaries of San Gennaro, the desire of the faithful to be buried near the Saint – by then the Patron Saint of city – encouraged the expansion of the catacomb.

The catacomb is the most important in view of its size and its paleo-Christian paintings and decorations. Access is from the Church of Madre del Buon Consiglio, in Via Capodimonte. The cemetery has two storeys. The lower floor is the most ancient core. Originally, it was an underground site built in II century A.D. for a noble pagan family. This initial core was later extended to become the cemetery and religious centre of the Christian community, after the burial here of Agrippino, one of the first bishops of the city. In VIII century, Bishop Paul II built a baptistery here.

The centre of the upper catacomb comprises the "Bishops' Crypt" where the bishops of Naples were buried in V century. There are also the remains of mosaics depicting the busts of the bishops, such as the one portraying the Bishop of Carthage *Quod vult deus* who, fleeing from the persecutions of the Vandals, died in Naples in 454 A.D. The upper catacomb has the most interesting testimony of V-IX century paleo-Christian art in Naples.

The most ancient portrait of San Gennaro (V century) has a dedication and monogram of Christ with the typical letters "alpha" and "omega". The Saint also appears in a painting of the early VI century with two mountains in the background, identified as Vesuvius and Monte Somma.

Great Christian buildings in Naples owe their origins to Emperor Constantine, who is attributed with the foundation of the most ancient church in the city. The Constantine Basilica, founded in IV century A.D. on a temple dedicated to Apollo, came to be known in IX century as the Basilica of Santa Restituta, after the reliquaries of the African martyr were brought here.

Statue of Isis, from Regio Nilensis. Naples, National Archaeological Museum.

Opposite page: "Cristallini" undeground tombs, chamber tomb.

The original ground plan with five naves was altered in the Anjou period, when the Basilica was incorporated into the Cathedral. The two external naves were converted into chapels. Remains of the Constantine building include the basilica ground plan and the columns in a large chapel on the left side of the Cathedral.

The right-hand nave of the Basilica of Santa Restituta leads to the Baptistery of San Giovanni in Fonte, founded by Bishop Severus (363-409 A.D.). It is the most ancient baptistery in the western world. It has a square ground plan and a dome with an eight-sided tambour. The mosaics depict evangelical scenes and symbols evoking the ancient baptismal liturgy. Towards the end of V century, a new Basilica was built alongside the first cathedral by Bishop Stefano (499-501), named Stefania after him.

The new Basilica, dedicated to the Saviour, probably stood on the eastern side of the Basilica of Constantine, facing in the same direction yet separated by a road. Excavations have highlighted a road bed, dating IV-V century, and some sections of a V century mosaic floor, perhaps even the flooring of the Stefanía church. The Neapolitan bishopric at the time therefore comprised two Basilicas and a Baptistery. The Neapolitan example is one of numerous examples of "double cathedrals" well-known in Christian architecture.

The two cathedrals were joined by a large atrium. A bronze horse stood in the centre, that tradition claims was the magical work of Virgil who could heal horses. The horse was destroyed in 1322, when is was re-cast to make the Cathedral bells.

The survival of the ancient

The particular fascination of a city such as *Neapolis*, growing ceaselessly on the same site for more than two thousand years, also lies in the fact that unusual dialogues are created between modern inhabitants and the vestiges of its past.

This is the case of an allegorical statue of the Nile and its minor tributaries, that the Neapolitans identify as Naples and its many sons. The statue today stands in Largo Corpo di Napoli, between Piazza San Domenico Maggiore and Via San Biagio ai Librai. Mentioned as early as XIV century in "*Chronicles of Partenope*", it was incorporated into the Donnaregina monastery. In the 1500s, it was several times restored and then placed on its present base in 1734. The river god is depicted as an old, bearded man lain on a rock from which water bubbles. The right hand holds a cornucopia, symbol of plenty. The head of a crocodile emerges from the feet of the statue, while several putti symbolise the branches of the river. A sphinx makes an allusion to Egypt. The statue, dated around I century A.D., perhaps belonged to a sanctuary dedicated to the Egyptian goddess Isis; the area was possibly home to Egyptian merchants from Alexandria (*Regio Nilensis* or Vico degli Alessandrini).

Another example is the Graeco-Roman tuff quarries that were converted in later epochs into cemeteries. The most evocative is the Fontanelle Cemetery, cut into the hill of Materdei. Access is from the Church of Maria Santissima del Carmine. It comprises numerous rooms used as a city ossarium, especially after the plagues. In the late-1800s, certain devoted parishioners gave some order to the thousands of skeletons found here. Since then, popular devotion has grown for these deceased, identified as the souls of Purgatory in need of care. The faithful chose certain skeletons, calling them by name and offering their devotion in order to obtain favours and miracles.

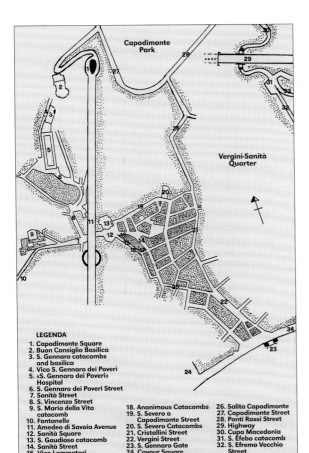

Capodimonte Park

Capodimonte Square

Vergini-Sanità Quarter

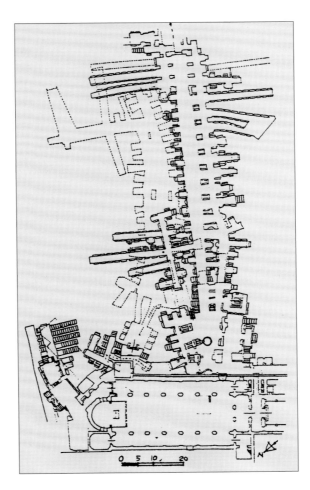

0 5 10. 20

Left: general ground plan of the catacombs of Naples. Right: ground plan of the catacombs of San Gennaro. Below: catacombs of San Gennaro, view of the upper area.

Virgil the Seer

In *Itinerarium Syriacum*, Petrarch mentions that King Robert d'Anjou, having heard in Naples that the *Crypta Neapolitana* may have been built by Virgil, asked him for more information; on which, Petrarch shrewdly replied *"I've never read that Virgil was also a miner"*.

Yet, in accordance with popular tradition, the Latin poet not only built the tunnel between Naples and Bagnoli, and in a single night to boot, but even the *cloache*, the aqueducts and the spa baths of the Phlegrean Fields, while – through his pupil Merlin – even paved with malign spirits the road between Rome and Naples, creating the Appian Way! He, who created the city with its walls, was also attributed with the building of Castel dell'Ovo; the castle stood not on a foundation stone but on an egg ensuring magical solidity – but, if found and broken, like "Achilles' heel", the castle and the city itself would have collapsed.

Evidently, in the late-ancient period and the Middles Ages, as the town shrank and population decreased – but also with the loss of the previous technological knowledge, the people faced by such gigantic monuments they were no longer themselves been able to realise – like the baths, walls, theatres, etc. – thought they were the work of a Roman magician and, since it was still claimed that Virgil had lived in Posillipo, they attributed to him all these impressive works as if built by magic.

These legends must have been taken very seriously, since Konrad of Querfurt, Bishop of Hildesheim, travelling in Italy with Arrigo VI, wrote a letter in 1196 describing that the conquest of Naples was made possible since the "palladium" built by Virgil protecting it – comprising a crystal bottle containing a small model of the city – had cracked.

The flourishing activities of the seer are listed in *Cronica di Partenope*, a XIV century text with as many as seventeen chapters dedicated to the description of the artifices and prodigies performed to protect the Neapolitans against a variety of calamities. Whereas for us *Publius Virgilius Maro* is quite simply the national Roman poet, on the other hand, for the country folk of Lucrino and Lake Averno, Virgil is he who through Aeneas descended to the underworld, was the lover of the Cumaean Sibyl, saved the city of Naples on several occasions and, if their forebears were still alive, so many other stories could still be told … As when, following the example of Moses who created a bronze serpent to ward off calamities, he created a gold fly to avert an enormous swarm of flies infesting the Neapolitans. Or when, following an epidemic causing widespread deaths of horses, he cast a bronze head of a horse and prescribed that every sick horse should walk three times around its metal companion to be miraculously cured. The gigantic horse, perhaps part of a Roman equestrian statue, stood in Piazza del Duomo and later ended up in the courtyard of Palazzo Carafa.

The so-called "School of Virgil" at Marechiaro, in an 1800s gouache, unknown artist. Naples, private collection.

Virgil lived on the hill of Posillipo, yet wandered every day around the smoking volcanic countryside between Averno and Cumae – not to seek inspiration, as historians of literature claim – but to perfect his magical arts. In his own garden, he cultivated extraordinary plants and medicinal herbs that grew lushly even without rain, while in the partly submerged ruins of a nymphaeum, known as the "School of Virgil", he brought together his disciples to teach them his magic.

The "seer" was also obliged to take Vesuvius into hand. He made a metal archer whose arrows were aimed at the demon of the volcano, which therefore kept quiet. Unfortunately, a stupid man released the arrow: Vesuvius was wounded and roared with pain.

The plague in 1497 saw San Gennaro regain possession of the city, usurping the "magician" Virgil who throughout the Middle Ages and the Renaissance, had charmed the souls of the Neapolitans, and through endless miracles – combating the plague, earthquakes and especially eruptions – clearly showed his powers and became the patron saint of the city.

The memory of Virgil in Naples must have remained particularly vivid even after his death. For example, poet Silius Italicus (I century A.D.) purchased his home where he celebrated his birthday every year.

In late Antiquity, the figure of the poet began to take on esoteric valences, made possible by the prophetic interpretation of the fourth eclogue of the *Bucolics* that narrated the birth of prodigious child who initiated a golden age, that the Christians interpreted as Jesus Christ.

This was how Bernard of Chartres commented in the XII century the first six books of the Aeneid, interpreting them allegorically as the Biblical Genesis. Virgil's poetry was viewed as a source forerunning Christian doctrine and clerics took the poet as their guide in their approach to knowledge and awareness leading to the truth, to God. This is the background that precisely induced Dante to choose, a century later, the great Latin poet as his "Duke and Maestro" in his travel to the underworld – the "Divine Comedy".

THE NATIONAL ARCHAEOLOGICAL MUSEUM OF NAPLES

*Opposite page: view of
the National Archaeological
Museum.*

The building and history of the collection

The National Archaeological Museum of Naples is the largest in the world as regards the number of objects. The Museum was founded in the 1700s when Naples, thanks to excavations in Pompeii and Herculaneum, also saw the birth of scientific archaeology.

As of 1816, with the restoration of the Bourbon kingdom under Ferdinando, it became the Royal Bourbon Museum; the new name glorified the dynasty that saw Ferdinando IV become Ferdinando I, King of the Two Sicilies. The king celebrated his patronage of the arts by engaging Antonio Canova to sculpt a marble statue of Ferdinando I wearing a Greek helmet, resembling Athena as the patron of the arts, to be placed in the large niche in the middle of the back wall of the staircase.

The Museum essentially comprises the *Farnese Collection*, the *Pompeian Collection* and the various finds made since the 1700s in various excavations all over southern Italy. The Farnese Collection was brought to Naples by Bourbon King Carlo, who inherited the finest collection of Roman Antiquities from his mother, Elisabetta Farnese.

The great figures who directed the Royal Museum (today the National Archaeological Museum) include Alexandre Dumas, Giuseppe Fiorelli, Ettore Pais, Amedeo Maiuri, Alfonso de Franciscis and Stefano De Caro.

THE FARNESE COLLECTION

Farnese Hercules

One of the most impressive works, if only for its dimensions, is the so-called "Farnese Hercules", found in 1545 in the central hall of the Baths of Caracalla. It was moved from this site, as part of project designed by Michelangelo, to the courtyard of the Palazzo Farnese in Rome, where it was shown together with another major work – the Farnese Bull. The similar, so-called Latin Hercules was sent in 1788 to the Royal Court of Caserta. The splendid marble sculpture – a copy of an original in bronze by Lisippus – was immediately recognised as a major work – not the least for its colossal dimensions and the signature in Greek by the copy-artist engraved into the rock underneath the club "*Glycon Athenaios epoiei*" ("carved by Glykon of Athens"). The enlargement of the Lisippus' original work is explained by the fact that the sculpture was displayed in Caracalla's Baths, itself a building of colossal dimensions.

The hero, apparently tired and exhausted after completing one of his feats, leans fully on his right leg, resting his huge body on the club in turn placed on a rock and set into his left armpit. The right arm, behind his back, seems to hide something and it is only by walking around the statue that one sees he is holding the cause of his fatigue: the golden apples of the Garden of the Esperides. In short, Euristeus had ordered Hercules, as his last feat, to bring him the golden apples from the garden of the Esperides. This feat obliged him to steal from the Esperides the golden apples that Gea had given to Juno as a wedding present and kept at the western borders of the earth. Stealing the golden apples was the feat that demanded Hercules' greatest strength and shrewdness. The garden was guarded by a dragon, Ladon, who the hero killed with a single arrow. Atlas, who helped him, asked Hercules to support the sky while he

The Farnese Hercules, a gigantic statue found in 1545 in the Baths of Caracalla, Rome.

went to steal the apples. Yet, when Atlas returned with the apples, he was unwilling to resume bearing the sky on his shoulders. In short, he wanted to take the apples to Argus, while Hercules continued to take his place. The hero then asked Atlas to hold up the sky for a moment so that he could rearrange his lion skin and, with this excuse, replaced the sky on the shoulders of Atlas and fled with the apples.

The Tyrannicides

At the end of VI century B.C., the young Armodius and Aristogeiton became the symbol of Athenian democracy after killing Ipparcus, the younger son of the tyrant Pisistratus. They were condemned to death for this deed, yet Athens dedicated two bronze statues to their memory – the work of Antenor – displayed in the agorà of Athens. The original bronze group was then taken by the Persians when they occupied Athens in 480 B.C. and transferred to Susa. It was only a century and a half later that Alexander the Great took the work back to Athens. In 477 B.C., after victory over the Persians in the battles of Salamina and Marathon, a new bronze statuary group was commissioned of Kritios and Nesiotes. Their work was extremely popular, given the number of reproductions made even in antiquity itself.

The two marble statues, from the Farnese Collection, were found at Hadrian's Villa in Tivoli, and are copies made in II century A.D. of the second group. The head of Aristogeiton is a chalk model of a head in the Vatican. Probably, the group, today comprising two single statues, represented Armodius, the boldest, who marches forwards in attack with his sword, while the older Aristogeiton stood back slightly to protect, with his left arm outstretched, the exposed left flank of the younger man.

The Farnese Bull

Another impressively monumental work is the "Farnese Bull", nicknamed the "marble mountain". The gigantic sculpture was found in the 1500s, together with "Hercules resting", in the Gymnasium of the Baths of Caracalla in Rome. It was studied by Michelangelo, who transformed it into a fountain so that it could be placed in the centre of a garden standing between Palazzo Farnese and Palazzo Farnesina. It was moved in the 1700s to Naples, with the Farnese Collection, and

exhibited until 1826 in the Royal Avenue at Chiaia, the present-day City Hall.

The torment of Dirces was a theme dear to the ancients and found its greatest expression in the "Farnese Bull", the prototype of which was a masterpiece carved in II century B.C. by the sculptors from Rhodes Apollonius and Tauriscus. The sculpture depicts Queen Dirces as she is bound by her stepsons Anfion and Zetos to a bull ready to drag her to the top of Mount Citeron, in Beotia, as punishment for mistreating them and their legitimate mother, Antiope. Dirces was tied under the rampant bull, begging for mercy holding the right leg of stepson Anfion, identified by his lyre. Antiope watches from behind, holding the spear of her son Zetos, as the vendetta unfolds.

The event took place in the mountains in the presence of a young shepherd, perhaps the personification of Mount Citeron or even Dionysus, standing between the symbols of the Dionysian ritual that Dirces, a Bacchante, was about to undertake.

The Farnese Cup

Archaeology has many examples of highly-prized works that ended up underground since, over the centuries, they were always handed down between powerful families. This is the case of the "Farnese Cup", a splendid cup in sardonyx agate from the Hellenistic age, perhaps made in II-I century B.C. In short, we know that it first belonged to the Ptolemy kings of Egypt, then to Augustus and then to Frederick II of Svevia; it subsequently disappeared for a long period in Persia, only to reappear in the collection of Lorenzo il Magnifico de Medici who took it to Rome in 1471. The work involved the cameo technique using a single stone comprising strata of different colours. The cup, with a relief *gorgoneion* on the exterior, has a scene on the interior comprising eight allegorical figures set in Egypt, as symbolised by a Sphinx standing at the base. The Nile is represented on the left, sitting enthroned and supporting a rich cornucopia together with the young Triptolemy, educated by Demetra in the art of crop-growing. Isis sits majestically at their feet. They are followed by the *Horai* and the *Etesii* winds, in flight at top-right. Although there have been many interpretations of this allegory in Hellenist-Alexandrian subjects, the entire scene in any case seems to exalt the fertility of Egypt.

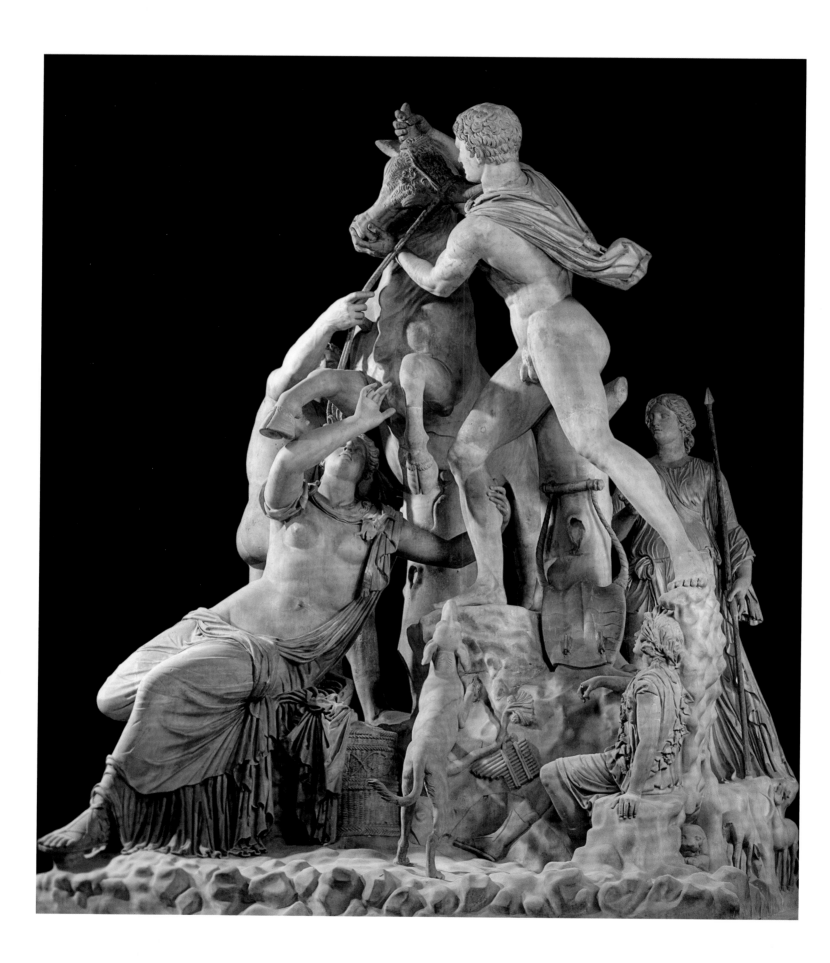

FINDS IN THE CITIES BURIED BY VESUVIUS

The Mosaic of Alexander

The "Mosaic of Alexander" is the most famous in the world both for its monumental dimensions (5.82 × 3.13 metres) and its historic meaning. Found in the "House of the Faun" at Pompeii on 24 October 1831, it was set into the flooring of the large exedra north of the central peristyle. The work is dated II century B.C. It is a work of supreme quality: in short, it was laid using the so-called *opus vermiculatum* technique involving about one million tesserae measuring three millimetres per side; the gaps were caused, on the other hand, following transport on waggons from Pompeii to Naples in the 1800s.

The mosaic represents the decisive battle between Alexander the Great and Darius III of Persia at Gaugamela (331 B.C.), although it is also traditionally identified with the battle of Issos (333 B.C.). The identification with Gaugamela, in arid Assyria, better explains the barren tree standing to the left of the field. Alexander is shown on the left, on horseback, attacking the chariot of the Persian king. The Persian army is by now surrounded, as witnessed by the long "sarissa" spears of the Macedons. Realising that the life of the king is endangered, the Persian charioteer pulls the horses to the right to avoid the attack, while an official – a member of the famous "Immortal" bodyguards –

shields the king and is struck by Alexander's spear. The face of the young Macedon prince is god-like and proud, while the Persian king seems shocked and surprised. The theme of the battle between the two kings was inspired by a painting by a great Hellenistic "maestro", a certain Philoxenos of Eretria mentioned by Pliny (*Naturalis Historia* 35, 110) and known for his depiction of a battle between Alexander and Darius. The access threshold to the exedra, also on display in the hall, has a river landscape with ducks, an *ichneumon* attacking a cobra, a hippopotamus, a crocodile and two ibis; the evident reference to the Nile may suggest that the Mosaic of Alexander should be interpreted in the artistic language of Egypt under the Ptolemy kings: Alexander defeated Darius thanks to the intervention of the goddess Isis, the patron of the Nile but also the goddess of fortune responsible for human destiny.

Johann Wolfgang Goethe, on hearing of the huge mosaic, wrote in 1832, a few days before his death: *"The present and the future will never do justice to such a wonder of art and we shall always have to return, after explanations and study, to pure and simple marvel"*.

The Spear Bearer of Policletos

The statue, in pure white Luni marble, was found in 1797 in the Samnitic Gymnasium of Pompeii. Since then, it has been known as the best Roman copy of the "Spear Bearer", a famous bronze work by Policletos of Argos cast around 440 B.C. that

perhaps depicted the hero Achilles. The "Spear Bearer" was defined by Pliny as the finest example of the "*Canon*", that is the model for excellence of proper artistic equilibrium in representing the human body. Recently, however, the statue has been identified not with the "Spear Bearer" but with another work by Policletus, the "*nudus telo incessens*", that is the sword bearer.

Inasmuch, we should imagine this statue as having a sword in the right hand and a spear and shield in the left, like the young Cheredemos depicted in the stele of the same name on show in the National Archaeological Museum of Athens. In this case,

the "Spear Bearer" mentioned by Pliny should be identified as another statue, the "Westmacott Ephebus" now in Great Britain. This new interpretation, in any case, detracts nothing from the perfection and equilibrium reflected in the Pompeii copy – qualities that characterise all Policletos' work.

Portrait of Paquius Proculus

The painting "Paquius Proculus and his wife" was found in House VII 2, 6 at Pompeii. This house had a bakery annex (*pistrinum*), so that it is assumed that the portrait depicts the owner of the house and the *pistrinum* annex. It was initially thought to portray *Paquius Proculus*, a name that appeared in the electoral inscriptions painted outside. It was only later realised – after interpreting an inscription on the right of the entrance, that the true name of the owner was *Terentius Neo*.

The man is portrayed wearing a toga and a *volumen* to the right; his wife has a diptych and a stylus charmingly held to her lips in accordance with an iconography invented by the Greeks for poetesses and the muses, yet … were they truly literate?

The realism of the two portraits, expressed through the pose of the wife and the country hardness of her husband, contrasts with aristocratic character of the overall pose. Evidently, the provincial middle classes imitated aristocratic models, as clearly shown by the lady's delight in her fashionable hair-do of the Neronian age and pearl ear-rings.

The so-called Sappho portrait

Like the portrait of Paquius Proculus, a famous "tondo" from Pompeii depicts a lovely young girl with a triptych and a stylus charmingly held to her lips, as if inspired by poetry. The precious gold hair-net, letting slip a frivolous lock of curls, and the gold ear-rings are a symbol of the well-being of her family. It was assumed in the past that it was a portrait of Greek poetess Sappho, yet it is certain that the painting was a *pendant* with another of a young boy on a roll of papyrus, so that we can be sure that the portrait of the young girl does not depict a famous figure of the past but is a common example of provincial "intellectual" couples in Pompeii.

The Mosaic of Alexander. Opposite page: detail with the figure of Alexander the Great.

Side: portrait of Paquius Procolus and his wife. Right: the so-called Sappho portrait.

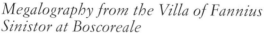

Megalography from the Villa of Fannius Sinistor at Boscoreale

The monumental painting ("megalography") was hung in the main hall of the Villa of Fannius Sinistor in Boscoreale, a town near Pompeii. The owner of the house, in I century B.C., commissioned copies on the walls of the famous originals depicting Hellenistic kings living 300 years earlier, that he and his guests could admire while lying on their tricliniums.

It is an allegorical work. A cynical philosopher, perhaps Menedemus of Eretria, wearing a heavy cloak and huge Peripatetic shoes, gazes beyond a column as if admiring a vision: the victory of Macedonia over Persia. Macedonia, seated on mountains, is characterised by the Macedon shield with an eight-pointed star and the Macedon headgear, the *kausia*, in turn with the tubular gold diadem of the kings. On the right – in a subordinate and thus subjected position – there is Asia, characterised by Persian felt caps, the *tiara*.

In order to understand the entire cycle, these paintings must be integrated with others, today in the Metropolitan Museum, New York, which, in accordance with a recent interpretation, depict the father of Alexander the Great, Philip II (whose tomb was discovered at Vergina, in Greece) together with his mother Eurydices. There follows Olympia, the mother of Alexander and accomplice in the assassination of her husband Philip II, represented while playing a lyre. A priestess performs *katoptromantìa*, that is foresees the future through mirrors; the honed surface of the shield, in short, is a prediction of the birth of the new king, Alexander.

In 40 B.C. in short, roughly when these paintings were made on the walls of Boscoreale, Caesar was preparing his expedition against the Parthians, the descendants of the ancient Persians. This historic theme was therefore very "up to date".

The silverware of Pompeii

Special mention must also be made of the silverware from Pompeii held in the National Museum of Naples, where they are one of the largest and most important existing collections. Mention need only be made that of the 500 hundred silver vases of the Roman age now found all over the world, almost half are housed in Naples.

The various services especially include the one found in 1930 by Amedeo Maiuri in the "House of Menander" in Pompeii (I 10, 4), a treasure comprising as many as 118 items with an overall weight of 84 kg.

Roman silverware can be divided into cups (*argentum potorium*), including *scyphi, canthari* and *calathi*, etc.; bowls (*argentum escarium*), including trays, *phialai,* pateras, plates, etc. and bathroom items (*argentum balneare*), including presentation boxes, scoops, mirrors and broaches, etc.

Silver table ware is the most common. Table services included goblets, sold in pairs, and plates sold by fours or multiples of four. These are genuine "*sets*" that reflect the customs in the Graeco-Roman world; in the Gallic-Roman world, for example, such services were sold in threes and multiples of three. The most common silverware includes: the high oval or semi-spherical chalice (*cantharus*), the low cylindrical bowl (*scyphus*) and a truncated conical beaker (*calathus*). These items were ideal for decorations on the main body.

An embossing technique was used. This involved cold beating metal sheet with a hammer to emboss the figure on the other side; details were then finished by chasing or engraving. The decorated metal sheet was then attached to the smooth sides of the vase and welded top and bottom. These vases therefore had double walls: the smooth inside wall, with edging and foot worked separately, and an external wall, decorated with embossed and chased reliefs. Subsequently, the silversmith added generally cast and solid handles. The reliefs were often copied from mould dies in turn inspired by Hellenistic originals.

The vases embellished tables, so they were decorated with topics that exalted the virtues of wine and love, such as the loves of Mars and Venus. Numerous Dionysian themes are explained by their associations with wine. Mythological stories are more rarely narrated.

Sir William Hamilton: the birth of volcanology and archaeology

Admiral Nelson and Lady Hamilton in an 1800s painting by Ettore Cercone. Naples, San Martino National Museum.

One of the most fascinating figures in Neapolitan's archaeology and volcanology was Sir William Hamilton, the British Ambassador to the Kingdom of the Two Sicilies. He arrived in Naples in 1764 and remained in residence for thirty-five years – half his lifetime (1729-1803) – and only left the city in 1798, on the eve of the French occupation.

Hamilton was one of the leading figures in 1700s European culture and, in view of his eclectic interests, may be considered as a representative figure of the century of the *Encyclopédie*. Many of the personalities who arrived in Italy considered him an essential landmark and, inasmuch, the British Embassy in Naples, then in Palazzo Sessa, became a crossroads of culture and society life, where visitors could meet nobles, politicians, scientists, painters and musicians.

He is popularly more famous as the husband of the frivolous Lady Emma Hamilton, who was later the lover of Admiral Horatio Nelson; Hamilton, in reality, was a true authority in the field of Vesuvian studies, as well as a great collector and admirer of classical antiquities: his first collection included 730 vases, 165 terracottas, 300 items of glassware, 600 bronzes, 150 ivories, 150 engraved gemstones, 100 gold-ware objects and 6000 coins. It may well be said that the British Museum only became a true museum after acquiring this collection in 1772.

He personally published a book dealing with his first collection of vases from Campania in four splendid volumes complete with drawings. The book was titled "*Antiquités Etrusques, Grecques et Romaines tirées du Cabinet de M. Hamilton*". The Readers' Notes suggest that the splendid water-colour plates should not necessarily be kept in the library but were also ideal "*for furnishing an apartment or embellishing a collection of prints*". Moreover, this work included "*a delightful surprise for pottery workers and makers of vases in silver, copper, glass and marble, etc.*". Craftsmen, facing a shortage of models, could find here more than 200 new items to copy. In short, the Ambassador consulted in England with the famous Wedgwood chinaware producers, providing instructions and suggestions for the production of wares in the Etruscan style.

Hamilton's interests were wide-ranging and by no means limited to volcanology and archaeology. He was also a fine violinist and a painting today in London portrays him during a concert in Palazzo Sessa with Leopold and Wolfgang Amadeus Mozart, then 14 years old. An enthusiast of botany, he convinced Queen Maria Carolina to engage a gardener-botanist from London to create an English garden in the park of the Royal Palace of Caserta, the first example of landscape architecture ever implemented in Italy.

GUGLIELMUS HAMILTON

He purchased from the famous English explorer James Cook an excellent Polynesian ethnographic collection – with garments, statues of gods, weapons, musical instruments, etc. – as a gift for the King of Naples, who included it in the Farnesiano di Capodimonte Museum. Today, this collection is one of the most important sections in the "Luigi Pigorini" National Museum of Pre-History and Ethnography in Rome.

In his first year of residence in Naples, Hamilton became extremely popular – so much so that even the austere Prime Minister Bernardo Tanucci commented to the King that "*the new English envoy, Hamilton, has earned deserved and universal esteem in Naples*". The palace in Naples, in Via Cappella Vecchia, was rented from Marquis Sessa, and included not only embassy offices but also Hamilton's his own apartments – and unlike today – was not crowded by other buildings but had a clear view over the Gulf and splendid gardens. Goethe described it in 1787, after a visit: "*Hamilton has made himself a fine nest here … His apartment, in the English style, is extremely delightful and the view from the corner room is perhaps unique. The sea is close by, with Capri opposite and Posillipo to the right; the promenade of the Royal Villa runs on one side, with an old Jesuit building to the left, then the coastal road to Sorrento as far as Cape Minerva. It is very difficult, at least in Europe, to find such a place, especially in the centre of a such a large and populous city*".

Hamilton was immediately able to devote himself to everything that interested him, at least until the French Revolution overturned the balance of power in Europe and completely absorbed him in his true tasks of diplomacy. He soon began to collection antiquities. In 1765, he presented a request to be able to export them, with the motivation "*of having received an engagement from England to procure several medals*" and "*since a ship will sail tomorrow for London, I beg Your Excellency to grant me a permit to load them*". Prime Minister Tanucci withheld permission since "*... the laws of the Kingdom forbid the removal of monuments*". This means in general that works of art could be exported but not those taken from excavations. Later, the Ambassador learnt how to get round these laws and exported his entire collection to England. This not only included antiquities but also an art gallery with works by Veronese, Tintoretto, Titian, Rubens, Velasquez, the Carracci and Luca Giordano, etc., following the suggestions of Joshua Reynolds.

Over above art and archaeology, his other great passion became Vesuvius, as he wrote in person: "*I have observed with particular attention the behaviour of Vesuvius ... from the day of my arrival in this capital*". He also made frequent visits to Vesuvius. In 1765, on reaching the peak, he noticed about 50 metres from the crater a dark cone emitting blue flames. "*I was examining the phenomenon when I heard a strong explosion. All of a sudden, a column of black smoke followed by a reddish flare gushed from the mouth of the volcano and a few minutes later I was caught in a shower of stones, one of which almost struck me. I hurried away and determined to be more careful in the future ...*". He continued to observe the re-awakenings of the volcano ... but from his home with a telescope ...

Towards the end of March 1766, he realised that an eruption was about to take place: "*the smoke increased, carrying ash with it*". "*On Good Friday, 28 March, at seven in the evening, the lava bubbled out of the crater and, after splitting into two streams, moved towards Portici ... On seeing the lava, I immediately left Naples, together with a group of countrymen keen to observe this phenomenon at close hand ... The lava flowed like a river of molten metal, resembling liquid glass; huge, semi-combusted cylindrical stones floated on top of it, rolling over each other as they fell down the sides of the mountain and forming a singular and astonishing waterfall of fire*".

The last major eruption after the one in 79 A.D. and before the arrival of Hamilton occurred in 1631. Obviously, there were many other eruptions between the two (at least eleven are calculated today). There was already a huge bibliography dealing with the eruption in 1631 – at least 232 titles – but "*all silly, credulous and superstitious*". Hamilton was the first to examine and describe Vesuvius in scientific terms. He even realised two centuries in advance the importance of paleo-soils; for him, the only method to reveal the secrets of Vesuvius was meticulous study of geology and stratigraphy.

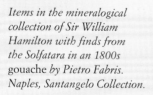

Items in the mineralogical collection of Sir William Hamilton with finds from the Solfatara in an 1800s gouache by Pietro Fabris. Naples, Santangelo Collection.

Hamilton had sent to the British Museum "*a complete collection with all the matter expelled by Mount Vesuvius*"; moreover, he also sent the Royal Society a number of reports about the eruptive activity of Vesuvius, later collected in a book that became famous – the *Phlegrean Fields*. These letters are considered as the starting point for modern volcanology. He also commissioned painter Pietro Fabris to illustrate the work. He produced 40 *gouaches*, the originals of which are now in the British Library, London. His views of various parts of the Gulf made it possible to document different stages in its evolution; this is why other documentation also deals with Agnano, Averno and Astroni, as well as Etna and the Aeolian Islands. These illustrations, although intended to ensure rigorous scientific documentation, also helped promote the beauties of the Neapolitan landscape all over Europe. Observing these volcanic landscapes, Hamilton realised that "*these terrifying works of Nature should be viewed in a creative rather than a destructive context*"; in short "*could not the underground fire be considered as the great plough that Nature uses to overturn the bowels the earth, so that fresh land to be worked replaces that we have exploited with too many harvests?*". Moreover "*would not so many precious minerals remain at unreachable depths unless carried to the surface by such work of Nature?*". The *gouaches napolitaines* are today highly sought after by antiquarians. The technique is similar but not identical to that of "tempera". The fashion was initially spread in the Kingdom of Naples by Pietro Fabris and subsequently by German artist Philipp Hackert. Their success was also due to the fact that, at the time of the Grand Tour, they provided documentation of sites visited that could easily be packed in personal baggage. When, however, the first "organised trip" left London in 1841 guided by Thomas Cook, the period of the Grand Tour as a means of "personal education" was already over. Since then, "travellers" have become merely "tourists" and the *gouaches* have become merely standardised souvenirs.

Although he completed his work on the *Phlegrean Fields* in 1779, Hamilton continued to devote himself to volcanology, this time aided by Father Antonio Piaggio (who himself invented the machine for unwinding the Herculaneum papyri). The aged Piaggio prepared for him – simply by observing the volcano from his balcony in Herculaneum, a "Vesuvian Diary" where every day he made notes and drawings of activities between the eruption in 1779 and the next in 1794. The diary of Father Piaggio, today in the Library of the Royal Society in London, has as many as three thousand three hundred pages.

In the meantime, Hamilton also continued expanding his new art collection. Having sold the first collection to the British Museum, he immediately began a second, even more appealing and extensive collection. Not the least because his young wife was a spendthrift, Hamilton later also decided to sell this collection. In 1798, French threats became pressing and the English sent Admiral Nelson, the victor at Abukir, and his fleet to Naples. The Hamiltons moved with the royal family to Palermo, sending to England eight large crates containing the second collection on "HMS Colossus".

The ship was wrecked in 1798 during a storm off the Scilly Islands in the English Channel. In 1974, an English underwater researcher, Roland Morris, recovered as many as 42,000 sherds from the sea-bed. Later, restoration experts at the British Museum managed to re-compose about a dozen vases, including an Attic basin with red figures by the Painter of Peleus with a Dionysian procession.

In 1786, Hamilton, then 53, called Emma Hart to Naples, an attractive 19 year-old girl he had met three years earlier as the betrothed of his nephew. Emma became Hamilton's lover and they married in 1791. Emma's splendid figure brightened up his life by recalling the classic beauty of ancient sculptures. He even set up in his home a kind of black-lined cabin with a gold frame where Emma, during receptions, performed in the poses of the ancient women of Herculaneum, the famous "*attitudes de Madame Hamilton*". These performances delighted J.W. Goethe but outraged Vicar Herder, who wrote from Rome on 21 February 1789 to his wife Karoline: "*the entertainment involves Hamilton's mistress, Madam Harte, performing in a thousand poses wearing Greek garments ... it is evident that this ingenuous monkey is far from the true sentiment of that noble art ...*".

In 1798, Emma became the lover of Admiral Nelson and Hamilton wrote "*I see that my wife devotes all her attentions to Lord Nelson, but I can't complain*" and then "*I appreciate the purity of the friendship that Lord Nelson feels for Emma ...*". Emma nevertheless gave birth in the early 1800s to Nelson's daughter, Orazia. In 1802, Hamilton had to return to England, where he died on 6 April 1803 in his Piccadilly home in the presence of Emma and Nelson. Nelson died at Trafalgar in 1805, while Emma died on 15 January 1815 alone, old and forgotten by one and all in Calais, France, aged 51.

THE PHLEGREAN FIELDS

Map of the Phlegrean Fields.

Opposite page.
Top: model of the Phlegrean
Fields (Studio Romatre,
Arch. M. Travaglini, Rome).
Bottom: view of the Phlegrean
Fields from Ischia in a gouache
by Pietro Fabris.

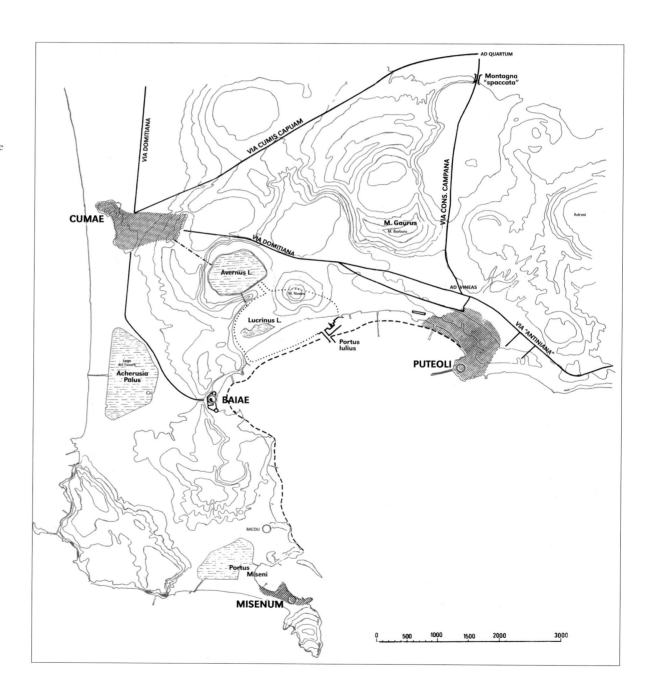

BACOLI

Bacoli, on the hill overlooking the ancient port, has an enormous rectangular cistern (70 × 25 metres), with a volume of about 12,600 cubic metres, known as the *Piscina Mirabilis*, cut into the tuff for 15 metres in height, one of the largest of the Roman age. The complex, of rare beauty, resembles an enormous underground Basilica and is also depicted in the evocative engravings of Francesco Piranesi. This cistern was the arrival point for the Serino aqueduct, built in the Augustan age to supply the Roman fleet anchored in the Bay of Miseno. The interior, with barrel vaults, is scanned by forty-eight cross-shaped pillars arranged in four roles forming five long naves and thirteen short naves; the external roof terrace, paved with pottery sherds, communicates with the interior through a series of aeration and lighting pits.

The reticulated masonry structures in brick for the side walls and tuff blocks for the pillars dating from the Augustan age have impermeable pottery sherd cladding. The floor of the short central nave has a basin 1.10 metres deep with the outlet mouth at one end, that was used as a decantation tank (*piscina limaria*). The inlet duct is near the western entrance; the lack of outlet openings suggests that

the water was taken from the top, by means of hydraulic machines, and channelled and distributed. The exterior of the north-west side has twelve small rooms, built in mixed and striped materials with barrel vault roofs, that was a later extension of the cistern. The complex was built end I-early II century A.D.

MISENO

Miseno is today a suburb of Bacoli, standing between the Miliscola beach and the "dead" sea closing the Gulf of Pozzuoli to the west. The name derives from the trumpeter of Aeneas, who drowned in these waters. In short, Virgil (*Aeneid* VI, verses 156-235) tells that Miseno, after the death of his companion Hector and the fall of Troy, departed with Aeneas. On reaching the Phlegrean coast, proud of his trumpet-playing talent, he dared to challenge the gods in a musical contest, but was drowned by Triton.

Miseno was an excellent natural harbour and stood between the ports used by Cumae in the Gulf of Naples, so much so that Dionysios of Alicarnassus considered its role fundamental within the scope of the defensive strategy of the Cumaeans against the Etruscans in 524 B.C. Its coasts, from end II century and throughout I century B.C., were home to sumptuous villas: the villa of Cornelia, mother of the Gracchi, was perhaps one of the first to be built in the Phlegrean area and was probably acquired by Marius before being for bought by Lucullus.

The area soon regained its ancient vocation as a port when Agrippa favoured it over *Portus Iulius* and moved the Roman Tyrrhenian fleet to the double basin of Miseno. The fleet was stationed here between 31 (battle of Azium) and 12 B.C. (death of Agrippa). In these years, the military colony was established that gave the town of *Misenum* its urban compactness and administrative autonomy, removing it from the typical residential character of the "regio baiana".

The semi-submerged remains of the "Sacellum of the Augustali" at Miseno are evocatively beautiful. The building, found in 1967, has a central room and two side rooms opening on to a courtyard with a portico. Used for worship of the emperors elevated to divinity, it was home to priests belonging to a college known as *Collegium Augustalium*. Inasmuch, it was mentioned in local inscriptions as *"Templum Augusti quod est Augustalium"* ("Tem-

The tomb of Agrippina, mother of Nero, at Bacoli, in an etching (1800s). Naples, National Library.

Page 88, top: view of Lake Avernus. Bottom: Cape Miseno, the "Sacellum" of the Augustals.

Page 89: equestrian statue in bronze of Emperor Nerva, from the "Sacellum" of the Augustals. Baia, Castle.

BAIA

"... Baia, in the wake of a wealth of residential buildings built close to each other, has seen the emergence of another city by no means smaller than Dicearchia".
Strabo, *Geographia* V 4, 7

History

The history of Baia goes back to times prior to Greek colonisation, as witnessed by finds of stone anchors dated between the end of the Bronze Age and the start of the Iron Age. With the foundation of Cumae, Baia joined this territory.

The term *Baiae* was mentioned for the first time in III century B.C. by Licophron, who located here the tomb of the hero named *Baios*, a companion of Ulysses. Such was the success of tourism here in Antiquity, that the word "baia" (bay) became current usage to designate any attractive coastal inlet. In short, as early as the late Republican age exponents of Roman aristocracy built sumptuous homes here, attracted by the mild climate, the fascinating landscape and, above all, its thermal waters. Sources confirm the presence of influential public figures whose homes characterised the urban system lacking in apparent regularity defined by Pliny as "*more baiano*", where, in the natural basin formed by a semi-submerged volcanic caldera, the villas of the aristocrats and public buildings extended on overlapping levels sloping down the hillside to the sea.

In the Republican period these villas still had a function of *fructus*, yet with the advent of the Empire they took on an exclusively residential function. Augustus was not particularly fond of these places and his successor Tiberius preferred the more secluded Capri, but other emperors and eminent figures of the imperial families visited the *regio baiana*.

Marcellus vainly sought here the remedy for his illnesses. Caligula celebrated his elevation to divinity by building a pontoon crossing the area, which he then rode over wearing the armour of Alexander. Emperor Claudius often visited Baia. Nero was very fond of these places, so much so that he conceived grandiose projects, such as that conveying all spa water into a large basin intended to link Miseno with the Averno, yet he also enacted here tragic iniquities, such as the murder of his mother Agrippina, who he saw as an obstacle to his politi-

ple of Augustus, that is of the Augustals"). The complex has revealed statues of Emperors Vespasian, Titus and Nerva, as well as various divinities, such as Asclepius, Apollo and Venus, the protectress goddess of the *gens Iulia*. Built in honour of Augustus, the temple was enlarged and embellished during the reigns of the Antonin Emperors (mid-II century A.D.). Renovation work was commissioned by *Cassia Victoria* in honour of her husband, *Laecanius Primitivus*, the Augustal priest at the time of Marcus Aurelius. The building was destroyed towards end II century A.D., probably following earthquakes linked with Bradyseism events causing the collapse of the tuff hillside above.

The decline of Miseno began in IV century A.D., when a policy of expansion and de-centralisation of naval units was implemented. In VI century A.D., there was even no memory of the military port of *Misenum*.

cal decisions. With the advent of the Flavii, Baia become more austere once again but this brief pause was interrupted by Domitian, who restored all its debauchery. The *regio baiana* was then at the peak of its fame.

During II century, *Baiae* saw no decrease in the presence of imperial families. Hadrian sought remedies for his illness in the spa cures and died here in 138 A.D. Antoninus Pius and Commodus were also frequent visitors to the area; yet it was with Alexander Severus, in III century A.D., that all its splendours were regained. He built in Baia, in honour of his mother Julia Mamaea, a *palatium cum stagno* that is a luxurious imperial residence. The fortunes of Baia were in any case linked with those of the empire, and the Phlegrean regions were equally affected by its decline: in short, the Goth wars initially and Bradyseism later saw the area definitely abandoned. Between VII and VIII century, much of the city was submerged under several metres of water.

Interest in the area came to the fore again during the Middle Ages. The fascination of its ruins struck Petrarch and Boccaccio, frequent visitors to the seaside around *Baiae*; the former relived the glories of the past, the latter exalted the life of parties and debauchery. In the wake of these great writers, the Neapolitan humanists, as equally the Aragon court, resumed the fashion of Baia. The society life of the place was described by Pontano, inspired by the love poems of Catullus and the satires of Martial.

The warfare between the Aragons and French (1493-1503) and then the disastrous volcanic event that saw the birth of Monte Nuovo in 1538, soon saw Baia and the Phlegrean Fields forgotten.

Today, Baia is far from its ancient splendour. Man has spoiled the landscape, while building and quarry work have destroyed its ancient vestiges. Only the Archaeological Park and the underwater ruins have been saved. The recent creation of the underwater Archaeological Park – the first in Italy – means that the evocative port is no longer a "cemetery" of laid up ships, while the consequent ban on navigation avoids ships carrying heavy loads of pozzolana cement damaging underwater structures with their keels.

The port

The Baia area in Antiquity had a different configuration to that seen today. Seneca, Tacitus and Mar-

Baia, Temple of Venus, painting by F. Vervloet (1795-1878), private collection.

tial defined it as *lacus baianus*, highlighting with this term its distinct separation from the sea. The ancient name betrays its volcanic nature; in short, it comprises the semi-submerged cone of an ancient volcano separated from the sea by a strip of sand into which a channel was cut to link the lake with the open sea. Underwater prospecting has confirmed the presence of an access channel of the Augustan age, 33 metres wide, that linked the *lacus* with the sea – channel with two large, parallel embankments more than 200 metres long.

Despite the evidence of semi-submerged Roman buildings, the illusion of industrial progress brought about in XX century massive excavations in the area, with the consequent pouring of cement foundations on which the modern shipyards were then installed. Dredging work recovered several sculptures and architectural elements from the palace of Severus.

The "Temple of Diana"

The fame of Baia in Antiquity was connected with its spas, of which several imposing buildings still exist on firm land. The north-east part of the archaeological area has a domed building known as the "Temple of Diana". The attribution to the goddess was made following the find of marble low reliefs depicting animals and a fragment of a frieze on which the name of Diana was carved.

The entrance to the complex was on the southern side. The hall was built using various materials, with

Sculptures from Baia.
Side: Apollo of Omphalos.
Right: Aphrodite Sosandra.
Opposite page: Dioscuro.
Naples, National
Archaeological Museum.

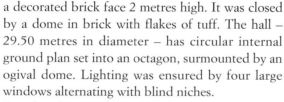

a decorated brick face 2 metres high. It was closed by a dome in brick with flakes of tuff. The hall – 29.50 metres in diameter – has circular internal ground plan set into an octagon, surmounted by an ogival dome. Lighting was ensured by four large windows alternating with blind niches.

Dated in the age of Severus (III century A.D.), the building still today arouses great interest since, although literally split by the earthquake that occurred at the same time as the "birth" of Monte Nuovo, it is still standing, demonstrating the construction skills of Roman engineers.

The "Temple of Mercury"

The so-called Temple of Mercury has been known since the Middle Ages. Whatever its true function – *frigidarium* (for cold baths) or *natatio* (indoor pool) – the building has been a major tourist attraction since the 1700s and has never ceased to arouse admiration for the unreal appearance of the interior, where water reaches the base of the vault, and the imposing architecture of the roof.

It is a spa area adjacent to the so-called Sector of Mercury. Built at the end of I century B.C., it remained in use until the age of Severus (III century A.D.). The circular internal ground plan, 21.46 metres in diameter, is set into a square. In this way, the

external form was rather austere, with a view only of the emerging volume of the dome. The dome, built with brick and wedge-shaped flakes of tuff, is the most ancient example in Roman architecture of a large, spherical roof. The central *lumen*, together with four large windows in the vault, provided lighting. The walls had a series of niches, four of which with a semi-circular design that are no longer visible, and two larger ones currently protruding from the water. The main entrance was probably near the eastern niche, while the western niche perhaps had a natural spring. The interior was almost certainly richly decorated.

The effects of Bradyseism are also visible in this monument, that at the time of maximum immersion saw the sea rise as high as the vault, as witnessed by traces of erosion on the base of the dome.

The Nymphaeum at Punta Epitaffio

In 1969, a heavy sea revealed at Punta Epitaffio a nymphaeum with statues of Ulysses and his companion *Baios*. Excavation operations began in 1981. Underwater surveys revealed, at a distance of 130 metres by the shore, the *palatium* built under Hadrian above the Pisoni Villa, attributed on the basis of the find of a lead *fistula* bearing the inscription "*L. Piso*".

Models of the Baia Archaeological Park (Studio Romatre, Arch. M. Travaglini, Rome).

The structure, found at a depth of 7 metres opposite Punta Epitaffio, has a rectangular shape with a semi-circular apse on the base side and four rectangular niches on each of the long sides; two secondary entrances are aligned with the niches, while the main entrance, surmounted by an arch, opened on to the sea. It was defined as a nymphaeum since the decoration of certain walls imitates natural rock. In reality, it was used as a triclinium – a banquet hall. Its sumptuousness suggests that it was owned by a very high-ranking person.

The U-shaped triclinium table has a continual masonry structure. The triclinium beds were placed on top of it: two on the short base side and at least four on each of the long sides. The table was separated from the walls to leave space for a marble channel, where water flowed. The central part of the hall was also submerged, so that diners could imagine being suspended between the waves as they were served with meals on floating plates.

The interior of the nymphaeum has superb sculptural decorations: the apse, resembling a grotto, had a depiction of the blinding of Poliphemus, captured at the moment when Ulysses offered the giant a goblet of wine; on the other side, his companion Baio appears with a wineskin, while the figure of Poliphemus has not survived. The niches on the sides have statues of the parents of Emperor Claudius and his sons; the cycle was completed by two statues of Dionysus. The west wall had a statue-portrait of Antonia Minor, the mother of Emperor Claudius, depicted as the Venus Mother-Figure, the mythical mother of the *gens Iulia*. Antonia's rank as empress is witnessed by her precious tracery diadem with small palms alternating with pomegranate flowers. The woman is joined by a small boy on the left who leans towards her shoulder. The figure has been interpreted as Eros in the womb of Venus as well as *Thanatos*, "death", in view of the detail of crossed feet alluding to Antonia's suicide. The head of the young boy is severely damaged but it is likely that his hair was worked separately, perhaps with gold leaf. Holes suggest that wings were fitted to his shoulders. A statue-portrait of a young girl was found on the opposite side, wearing a chiton and cloak but with a bare bust. Her noble origins seem to be suggested by the precious comb set in her hair, comprising two rows of pearls joined by four gold clasps. It is suggested that the young girl is Octavia Claudia, daughter of Claudius and Messalina and grand-daughter of Antonia Minor.

The east side also had two rather similar statues depicting Dionysus. One, of which only fragments remain, showed the god crowned with ivy and corymbs, with his left leg on a trunk with a large bunch of grapes; the right arm held separate of the body suggests the statue held a *kantharos*. A *kantharos* was also probably held in the right hand of the other figure of Dionysus who, leaning on a pillar over which drapery was thrown, looks at the panther at his feet, ready to sip the wine spilt from the goblet.

PORTUS JULIUS

Between 38 and 36 B.C., during the war against Sextus Pompeius, Octavian's admiral, Agrippa, built with architect *Lucius Cocceius Auctus* a new military base, the *Portus Julius*, in the lake complex of Averno-Lucrino.

The new port was built by cutting through the strip of sand that separated Lucrino from the sea and excavating a navigable channel between the two lakes. Lucrino was probably the port as such where ships could be moored, while Averno was probably the yard where ships could be repaired. The immense port complex, named *Portus Iulius* in honour of Caesar, was reinforced by quays that protected the basins from heavy seas and underground tunnels that improved connections with Cumae and *Puteoli*. It is possible, however, that Bradyseism silted up the site which was no longer considered reliable, since only seven years later, in 31 B.C., it was replaced by the military port at Misero, and continued to perform only commercial functions at least until the late empire (IV century A.D.).

LAKE AVERNO

The harsh nature of the volcanic crater that forms the Averno basin, surrounded by dense woods and sacred to the infernal divinities for very ancient religious beliefs, kept the lake free of residential settlements until the end of I century B.C. In short, Greek geographer Strabo wrote as follows in the age of Augustus: *"Averno is surrounded by steep cliffs dominating it on every side, except for the mouth, where crops are now grown but initially wild and inaccessible with tall trees shading the gulf and inspiring superstition. The inhabitants of the place also claimed that birds, flying over the area, fell into the water struck by its exhalations"*.

This geographical description is matched by the poetics of Virgil in Book VI of the Aeneid (verses 237-242) describing the terrifying lake as follows: *"There was a deep grotto, a vast and horrid chasm, / defended by the black lake and the shaded woods. / No bird could safely fly / over this place: such was the exhalation / from the black chasm rising to the sky"*.

The lake was formed almost 4000 years ago following an eruption and had always been considered as a sacred area: the wooded slopes shading the deep waters, the sulphurous exhalations and the thermal springs encouraged the appearance of fantastic tales. In accordance with popular etymology, reported by Servius, the commentator of the Aeneid, *"Avernus a non aves"*, that is *"named Averno because there are no birds"*. We must assume that even in the Greek age there was a widespread conviction that the lake gave direct access to Hades and the underworld. This belief was so strongly rooted that Hannibal in 209 B.C. travelled here to make a sacrifice to the gods of the underworld.

Reasons of state, however, prevailed over religious beliefs since, in 37 B.C., admiral Marcus Vipsanius Agrippa transformed the lake, that mythology claimed was fed by the Styx, into a large shipyard. Averno was almost entirely deforested and adaptation work completely disrupted the ancient status of the area.

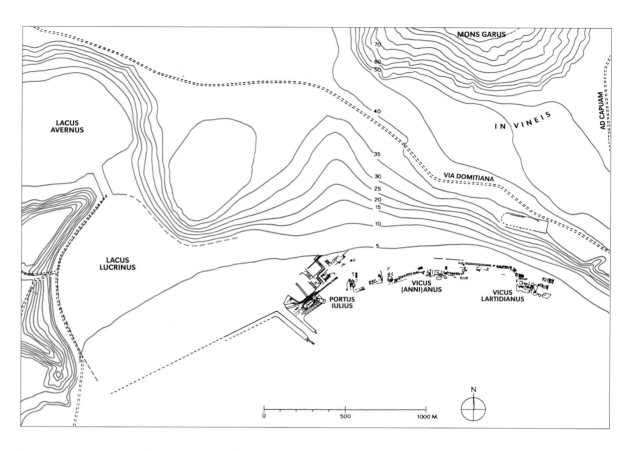

Improvements to land connections also saw the creation of two underground tunnels towards Lucrino and Cumae. The first, traditionally known as the "Antrum of the Sibyl", was entirely cut into the tuff bed, is about four metres wide and has a round vault. Its rooms, installed when the area no longer had military functions, were home to baths exploiting the natural thermal springs. Yet travellers in the 1300s (such as Petrarch and Boccaccio) as well as in the 1700s and 1800s (such as Mozart, Goethe, etc.) were shown it as the antrum of the Sibyl. The grotto can still be visited today, by torchlight as in Antiquity.

The other road (*crypta*), one kilometre long, ensured communications between Averno and the Cumaean territory through Monte Grillo. Strabo suggests that it was designed by architect Lucius Cocceius Auctus, known for also having built the Neapolitan Crypta that linked *Neapolis* and *Puteoli*, and the temple on the acropolis of *Puteoli*. This tunnel, also entirely cut into the tuff, was illuminated by six light wells and was wide enough to allow two waggons to pass simultaneously. Unfortunately, it was severely damaged after the last war since, having been used as an arsenal by the Germans during the Second World War, it was blown up.

Remains of underground rooms known as the "Font of the Sibyl" stand on the west side of the lake. They stand on different levels and communicate through staircases. The ceilings are barrel vaults, while the walls are finished with plaster. They perhaps belonged to a villa and were used as baths.

The large spa hall visible on the shore of the lake is known as the "Temple of Apollo". The remains of the monumental building, that exploited natural hydro-mineral springs, have sunk somewhat as a result of Bradyseism.

POZZUOLI (PUTEOLI)

"There follows the shore of Dicearchia and the city itself, that was originally a port built by the Cumaeans on the edge of the rock; the Romans then settled here, after the war against Hannibal and changed its name to Puteoli (Pozzuoli) after the many wells. Some suggest that the name derived from the bad odour of the water, since the entire region as far as Baia and Cumae is replete with sulphur, fire and hot springs. It is also thought that this is why Cumae was called Flegra and that the emissions of fire and water caused the injuries to the Gi-

Averno, gouache
by Pietro Fabris (1776).
Naples, Santangelo Collection.

ants who fell here through shocks. The city was a huge emporium, and artificial anchorages were installed thanks to the favourable nature of the land, that in short produces lime that is easily set and consolidated. Gravel, stones and lime were mixed to build sea dams and the large inlets where the great merchant ships could tie up safely."

Strabo, *Geographia* V 4, 6

History

The pre-Roman history of *Puteoli* (Pozzuoli) is based more on literary sources that on archaeological data (more or less lacking). The Greek geographer Strabo handed down news that *Puteoli* in the Archaic age was a stopping point for the Euboean colonists of Cumae. A different tradition, handed down by Polybios and Lucilius, suggests the arrival here of a small group of Samians, fleeing in 528 B.C. from the tyranny of Policrates. They gave the city the name *Dicearchia* (city of fair government) in contrast to the unjust government of their homeland. The arrival of the Samians was probably warmly welcomed by the Cumaeans who, in those years, were embattled against the Etruscans and Italics. Some objects of oriental origin, probably Samian, such as a marble sarcophagus found in the necropo-lis of Cumae and a stele with palmettes in the Ionic-Oriental style from Francolise but carved in local stone, can be considered as testimony of the relationships between Campania and the Orient. In any case, the only archaeological evidence bearing witness to effective pre-Roman settlement of the site of *Puteoli* is limited to a sub-geometrical fragment of an *oinochoe* (wine jar) dating from the end of VII century B.C., manufactured in *Pithecusa*, and the handle of an Ionic goblet dated around the second half of VI century B.C. perhaps of Samian origin.

The lack of archaeological data may be explained by the imposing renovation work on the site at the time of the foundation of the Roman colony. The first testimony of the name *Dicearchia* in literary tradition dates to II century B.C. and appears among pro-Hellenist writers such as Polybios and Lucilius, who promoted the Hellenic origin of other sites in Campania such as *Liternum* and *Volturnum*. It may therefore be assumed that the tradition of *Dicearchia* can be ascribed to a literary phenomenon generated by the intellectuals who, in II century, attended the circle of the Scipioni and who, among other things, were among the first to build their villas in the Phlegrean Fields.

FORUM

Archaeological chart of
Puteoli – ancient Pozzuoli.

comprising 300 families. *Puteoli* in just a few years became the main port of Rome, a trading place for goods from Greece, the Anatolian coast, Egypt and Syria.

"Today all of a sudden Alexandrian ships appeared on the horizon that usually precede and announce the arrival of the fleet; they are called tabellarie. They are always welcome in Campania. All Pozzuoli crowded the quays". This was how, in 64 A.D., Seneca (*Epistulae*, 17) described the triumphal entrance into Pozzuoli of the convoy of about 400 ships after a trip lasting ten days; the convoy was escorted by a special fleet, the *Classis Augusta Alexandrina*, to defend these ships loaded with cereals for Rome: every year, twenty million *modii* of wheat (about 1,396,000 tonnes) and sufficient to feed the city for four months, reached Rome through this port. Wheat was imported alongside all the other traditional products of Egypt: stones from the quarries at Siene (syenite), Memphis, the *Mons Claudianus* (pink granite), basalt, porphyry and serpentine for the needs of luxury of the Capital of the Emprire; gems such as emeralds, topaz, amethyst, onyx; typical produce such as papyrus, formerly the monopoly of the Ptolemy kings and now of the Emperor; even the sand of the Nile was used in Rome in the wrestling schools. Alexandria equally gathered, for export to *Puteoli*, products from the farthest lands, the incense and aromatics of Arabia, the cotton and ivory of India and silk from China.

The Phlegrean city soon saw numerous manufacturing activities develop, such as iron and glass processing, perfumes, ointments, fine table ceramics, dyes and pigments. These products were exported not only to Roman markets but throughout the Mediterranean. Local merchants even travelled to much more distant places. There is documentation of their presence in Petra, the Capital of the Nabataeans, today in Jordan.

Numerous oriental communities – Nabataeans, Egyptians, Cappadocians, Phoenicians, Syrians, Bitinians, Cilicians – lived here permanently; for example, an inscription testifies to the cult of Dusaris, the Jupiter of the Nabataeans. The arrival of so many foreigners saw the city expand, from the coast below as far as Lake Lucrino, with the construction of the *emporium* and other commercial buildings on the so-called *ripa*. Residential and monumental constructions, on the other hand, occupied the terrace overlooking the *ripa*, along the road between Capua and *Neapolis*.

There is little information about the city after the advent of the Samnites in Campania but, probably following the conquest of Cumae, it came to be definitively separated from *Neapolis*, the last bulwark of Greek culture in Campania. It was precisely during this stage that the city, by now freed of any dominion, could begin considerable growth and achieve greater liberty. Some experts attribute to this stage a coinage series with the legend *Phistuluis* derived from the name of the Samnitic city Fistelia.

The city was conquered by the Romans in 338 B.C. and re-named *Puteoli*. Its promontory, in the heart of the Phlegrean Fields, was an excellent natural haven and became strategically important in the war against Hannibal, after the defection of Capua and its ally cities. In 215 B.C., 6000 Roman soldiers were stationed here with the task of defending the port and the Rione Terra that was strengthened with fortification works.

With the end of the Punic wars, Scipio the African transferred his own interests to the Phlegrean area, installing at *Puteoli* a *Portorium* in 199 and setting up in 194 B.C. a *civium romanorum* colony

Models of the Serapeum
or "Macellum", the Roman
food market in Puteoli
(Studio Romatre,
Arch. M. Travaglini, Rome).

In 31 B.C., when Augustus created the Roman province of Egypt, there settled in *Puteoli* an Augustean colony. Having created the colony, the Emperor expanded its territory, dividing it into *regiones*, without however modifying the delicate power equilibriums of the Puteolan oligarchy. The ruling families who controlled all enterprise built at their own expense a new Forum in honour of Augustus, standing in a scenic position on the upper terrace. The *Annii* built the Basilica, the *Sextii* financed the building of a portico, while the *Calpurnii* commissioned a new temple on the acropolis.

The archives of the *Sulpicii* merchant-bankers, found in 1959 at Murecine near Pompeii, are important testimony of society in *Puteoli* in the period 30-50 I century A.D. The wax tablets testify to the presence of numerous oriental merchants, but also the great activity of freemen and slaves who played an important role in the economy of *Puteoli*, admittedly with insignificant political weight because of the *lex Visellia* dated 24 A.D. that denied them access to the city magistracy and the *ordo decurionum*.

The only means for social promotion among rich freemen was the *ordo Augustalium*, the priestly college responsible for the imperial cult, that allowed them to have some privileges. The complex equilibriums of *Puteoli* society collapsed under Nero who was called upon to restore the *concordia ordinum* in 58, as ironically recalled by Tacitus. With the ascent of Nero, the attitude of central power to the Puteoli oligarchy changed distinctly, so much so that the *ordo decurionum* began to welcome new men, descendants of freemen, such as the *Bovii* and the *Pollii*. The most evident example was *L. Cassius Cerealis*, who was entrusted with Nero's grandiose building plans as *curator operum publicorum*. An idea of what *Puteoli* society was like is provided by Petronius in the *Satyricon*, through the portrait of the vulgar libertine Trimalchion, made rich through trade and usury. Nero's urban works began with the building of the main amphitheatre, which was intended to be followed by the monumentalisation of the entire up-

per terrace of the city as a theatrical setting greeting people arriving from the port; here, Nero himself commissioned the monumental quay, one of the most imposing architectural works of Antiquity. The main amphitheatre in *Puteoli* was inaugurated by Nero in 66 A.D. with superb games offered to the King of Armenia, Tiridates, travelling to Rome to be crowned by the Emperor. The building of the amphitheatre was erroneously attributed to the Flavians in the lack of testimony referring to Nero, condemned after death to *damnatio memoriae*.

In 61-62 A.D., the apostle Paul began the evangelisation of Italy starting from *Puteoli*, his first landing place on his travels to Rome. Paul arrived here after crossing the Mediterranean on an Alexandrian merchant ship and surviving a shipwreck.

With the advent of the Flavians, *Puteoli* – having supported Vespasian – saw its territory expanded to the detriment of Capua, that on the other hand had sustained Vitellius. Moreover, Capua was cut out of trade routes with the building in 95 A.D. of the *Domitian Way*, commissioned by the Emperor in person, that directly linked Rome and *Puteoli*. In II century, new monuments were built such as the Stadium, the Hadrian's grandiose bath complex (known as the "Temple of Neptune") and the *Macellum* or Serapeum, a vital building in the economy of *Puteoli*. With the transfer of the Annonarian fleet to Ostia, *Puteoli* showed no signs of decline and continued to be, even III-IV century, one of the most important cities in Italy, although the interest of the powerful families had shifted from commerce to purchasing landed estates. It was only in IV century that stagnation began to appear.

As of V century A.D., accentuated Bradyseism caused the lower part of the city to sink bringing about, among other things, the definitive economic crisis. The swamping of the low area almost certainly caused epidemics, that encouraged the Puteolans to seek refuge on the acropolis, if not even in Naples. It decline is indirectly confirmed by the fact the city was no longer mentioned among the fortified centres of Campania that a century later tenaciously resisted the Byzantine troops led by Belisarius. Pozzuoli experienced in VIII-X century A.D. the most critical stages in its sinking. The Rione Terra, constrained in the castle built on the ancient walls, began to resemble a Mediaeval village with a drawbridge. It is indicative that in XI century the Arab geographer Idrisi, listing the centres of Campania in his *Opus Geographicum*, defined Pozzuoli as *cashtili*, a castle.

The Rione Terra

The tuff spur at the centre of the gulf, between Miseno and Posillipo, was the acropolis of the ancient city. The archaic settlements perhaps stood here, of which no trace remains, and it was here that the Roman colony was founded in 194 B.C. The first settlement probably had walls, perhaps recognisable in the blocks of tuff re-used on the north side of the hill. With the Roman colony, the acropolis was completely remodelled. The city took on an orthogonal ground plan adapted to the terrain. The

Opposite page: view of the "Macellum" in Puteoli.

Below: statue of Serapide, from Puteoli. Naples, National Archaeological Museum.

Ampurias

Populonia

Odemira

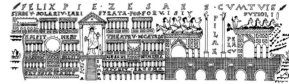

Prague

Pilkington

Rome - Warsaw

ancient road plan can still be recognised in the two decumanums, the *maximus* running about 3 metres underneath the present-day Via del Duomo, and another under the modern Vie Ripa and Crocevia. The section of the decumanum in Via del Duomo, today still in use, was flanked by a series of *tabernae* for catering: a kitchen, a fireplace, some benches and various furniture.

The main north-south road led to the main temple standing on the summit and scenically facing the sea. Roman structures reappeared under the Baroque decorations in 1964, following a fire in the Cathedral. The monument, traditionally identified as the Temple of Augustus, was actually the *Capitolium* for the cult of the Holy Triad comprising Jupiter, Juno and Minerva. There is also a possible connection with a cult of Apollo, that Statius named as the patron of the city, whose simulacrum is represented on the Puteolan flasks inside a temple dominating the city. The building, erected at the time of the institution of the colony, underwent radical conversion work in the Augustan age, under architect Lucius Cocceius Auctus, also known for the construction of the *Crypta Neapolitana* and the tunnels between Lake Averno and Cumae. The temple is a pseudo-peripteral exastyle, having a pronaos with six Corinthian columns on the front and two at the sides; the *intercolumni* were very deep and the cell had walls scanned by dummy square semi-columns. The reticulated building had side bodies set in brick. The cornices were in marble, as also the elevation. The podium was preceded by a broader

platform, accessed through two stairways on the sides of the pronaos. Inside the podium, certain rooms were used as *favissae* or place for votary gifts. The wainscot was decorated by moulding with an Attic base and crowned above by a protruding cornice. The building was already converted into a Christian Basilica V century A.D. and in 1643 was incorporated into the Cathedral.

Recent excavation work has highlighted the outlines of two *insulae* and, underneath the Bishop's Palace, a north-south complex of crypto-porticoes with frescoed walls. This complex – built on a polygonal site later rebuilt with small blocks of tuff and mortar and other additions – stood on the south side of the "decumanus medianus", where numerous fragments of architectural decorations have been found belonging to the temple, as well as statues of various dimensions.

Other buildings that have come to light include the *horrea*, large storerooms with barrel vaults, the *pistrinum* (bakery) in *opus reticulatum*, with a mill and lava stone grindwheels, a large lararium for worship of household and family gods with walls decorated with images of the gods of Olympus and, lastly, another lararium embellished with marble snakes.

Excavations underneath Palazzo Migliaresi have revealed a complex of small rooms fitted only with a stone bed and a rudimentary closet carved into a corner, lacking sources of lighting but with a very simple aeration system; this is an enormous "brothel", the largest ever discovered to date, with an amazing number of rooms.

The quay

The port of *Puteoli*, formerly a Cumaean port, as of the II century B.C. became the *emporium* of Rome. It handled goods from all over the Mediterranean that were then delivered to the Capital by road: wine, wheat, spices, ceramics, building materials, slaves and precious artefacts.

The ancient quay was one of the most impressive architectural applications in Antiquity but is no longer visible today, since its structures were incorporated in the early XX century into the modern docks. However, it is still possible to reconstruct their appearance thanks to the ancient depictions on the glass flasks manufactured in Pozzuoli, the 1700s drawings of Giovan Pietro Bellori and numerous 1700s-1800s designs and engravings.

The wharf was 372 m long and 15-16 m wide; it was supported by arches in turn sustained by 15 rectangular pillars (*pilae*) of about 5-6 m in thickness. It faced east-west and was built in brick, as described by Vitruvius. The Roman engineers conceived this system of arches to offset the undertow and thereby avoid problems of silting; they also avoided arranging the *pilae* along the same outline – developing a slightly arched design – to ensure better resistance to tides. Two triumphal arches opened and closed the quay. The first rose from the ground and was surmounted by a group of Tritons, while the one set into the sea represented Neptune riding his chariot drawn by sea-horses. The arch certainly also had depictions of the "Dioscuri", the "patron-saints" of sailors.

The quay was part of an impressive series of maritime installations (the *ripa puteolana*) that extended from the system of wharfs and piers of the *emporium* (the commercial centre of the port) as far as *Portus Iulius*. Damaged by storms, it was restored under Hadrian and later by Antoninus Pius; it was still in use in the IV century, as shown by an epigraph commemorating its renovation.

Serapeum or Macellum

The Serapeum or *Macellum* is not only a monument of archaeology but also of the history of science; studies of the holes bored by stone-mussels into the columns have ensured a correct definition of Bradyseism. The building – one of the most monumental markets handed down from Antiquity – was partially excavated under Carlo Bourbon at the same time as similar projects involving Herculaneum and Pompeii.

Wrongly named "Serapeum", it was actually a *Macel-*

The Flavian Amphitheatre in ancient Puteoli. It could hold about 20,000 spectators.

lum, that is a Roman food market I-III century A.D., that perhaps even remained in use until IV century A.D. The erroneous attribution was made following the discovery in the rear apse of a statue of Serapis, the divinity worshiped by Alexandrian residents. The statue in white marble is a Roman copy (II century A.D.) of an original work by Bryaxis. It depicts the Egyptian goddess enthroned, as the judge of the deceased, wearing a *modius* headdress, the cylindrical recipient used to store cereals. The existence, in any case, of a temple dedicated to the Egyptian goddess is witnessed by an epigraph – *Lex parieti faciundo* dated 105 A.D. – referring to work on tender in front of a Temple of Serapis in the Republican Age, perhaps installed in the emporium area.

In view of its sources of spring mineral water, in the XIX century the complex was partially used as a spa – as evidenced by traces on the walls of the external *tabernae*. It was only in 1907 that Charles Dubois defined its effective function as a *macellum*, that is to say a food market. The building has a square ground plan (75 × 58 metres); the main entrance leads to a porticoed courtyard with 34 columns in Siene granite. The lateral columns had Attic bases and Corinthian capitals embellished with shells and dolphins, while the colonnade to the rear had

The Temple of Neptune
– in reality, a majestic thermal
complex at Puteoli.

ed by sixteen columns in African marble – that the Bourbons "re-used" in the Royal Palace of Caserta – with bases decorated with Tritons, sea horses and sea-nymphs. The *intercolumni* housed the bases of marble statues and putti, while the centre of the upper platform had an octagonal fountain basin with a perforated slab and a floral pattern.

Meat and fish were sold in the rooms at the sides of the *tholos*; at the far north side, hidden from the view of market passers-by, there were two latrines that, with those in Pergamon, are the most sumptuous known of Antiquity. Lit by three trussed windows supporting columns with statues in niches, they comprised marble mullions and guttering.

The Temple of Neptune

The so-called "Temple of Neptune" is actually a majestic bath complex, standing on the slope of the hill overlooking the port, creating a theatrical setting for sailors. The site dates back to the first half of II century A.D., as confirmed by documents of the age of Hadrian found on site; however, various restoration work was carried out, as documented up to IV century A.D.

The spa complex had an axial ground plan, as follows: rooms for hot baths (*calidarium*), lukewarm baths (*tepidarium*), cold baths (*frigidarium*) and a swimming pool (*natatio*). The ruins, today standing as much as 13 metres above ground level, belong to the upper levels and the rear of the *frigidarium* building. The sides of the apse open on to a series of rooms decorated with mosaics, barrel and cross vaults. The ovens used to heat the water (*praefurnia*) are still in good conservation status. The difference in height between these ruins and those of the *frigidarium* clearly suggest the majestic character of the complex and the various levels of the terraces.

The glass flasks

There is some iconographic testimony that makes it possible to reconstruct the appearance and topography of *Puteoli* between III and IV century A.D.; eight flasks in blown, translucent glass found in different sites throughout Europe and northern Africa. In short, the body of the vase was decorated with views of *Puteoli* and the *Regio Baiana*, with the monuments accompanied by a legend. The flasks are named after the places where they were found or the cities where they are held: Prague, Pilkington, Odemira, Populonia, Ampurias, Rome, Ostia and Cologne.

columns in antique yellow stone. Access to the portico was also gained through four secondary gates facing each other. The portico was surrounded by eighteen workshops (*tabernae*) with marble cladding. These workshops overlooked both the central courtyard and a rear corridor running around the entire building. There was probably also a second floor, since there are also several staircases. The side opposite the main entrance has three columns in "cipollino" marble (11.78 metres high); a fourth column now lies on the ground. They were part of the colonnade portico (*propylon*) in the apse, where the back partition is scanned by three niches. These niches probably housed statues of worship; the central niche probably held the statue of the divinity of the colony (*genius coloniae*), the patron of the market. The apse also revealed two statue bases with inscriptions in honour of Alexander Severus and his wife Barbia Oriana, a statue of Serapis, a group with Orestes and Electra and a group with Dionysus and Faun, all today housed in the National Archaeological Museum in Naples.

The centre of the portico area has a *tholos*, in rockwork clad with slabs of marble. The *tholos*, raised by about 1.79 metres, was accessed by four staircases with parapets in the form of dolphins surround-

As many as six are almost completely integral, with a high, narrow neck and a globular body, on which inscriptions of various types were made – dedications, commemorations, exhortations to drink – probably engraved on the request of the buyer. One may probably assume that they were "souvenirs" purchased by travellers visiting *Puteoli* and the Phlegrean coasts between III and IV century A.D. Other experts, on the other hand, given the prominent position of a large temple at the centre of the figuration, also suggest a religious role concerning the cult of Isis and Serapides. The fact that three vases – Populonia, Ampurias and Rome – were found in burial contexts may support this hypothesis.

The Prague flask – the most complete as regards figuration – has to the left of the main Temple the stadium, the *solarium* and the amphitheatre, all indicated by respective legends: "*stadiu – solariu – ampitheat*". The commercial character of the city is indicated, on the other hand, by the wording "*inpuriu*", *emporium*.

THE SOLFATARA

"*Immediately after* (Puteoli) *one sees the Agorà of Ephestus* (the Solfatara), *a plain surrounded by bold crags, resembling furnaces since many places have blowholes spreading an awful smell all around; the region in short is full of emanations of sulphur*". This was how Strabo, in his *Geographia*, travelling from *Puteoli* to Naples, describes the Solfatara, and it is evocative to think that he saw it exactly as we see it today, with its dreadful exhalations through slits in the ground. Yet, while we moderns seek to arrive at a scientific explanation, the ancients sought for reasons in myth, naming it "the agorà of Hephaestus".

The volcano, in the centre of the Phlegrean Fields, was formed 4000-3000 years ago, so that it is the youngest of the Agnano volcanoes and only slightly before the Astroni formation. It still offers the evocative spectacle of an active volcano: penetrating odours of sulphur, fumarolas, earth tremors and boiling water.

The Solfatara is a recent volcanic episode and no longer fed with magma. In truth, chronicles refer to a later eruption in 1198, but this was probably only a phreatic event. The volcano is formed by pyroclastic rocks generated by the interaction between magma and water, then altered by hydrothermal phenomena that have given rise to multicolour pigmentations.

Volcanic effusions at the Solfatara, gouache *by Pietro Fabris (1776). Naples, Santangelo Collection.*

Bradyseism of the Phlegrean Fields

Map of the craters between
Vesuvius and Cuma,
by G.A. Rizzi Zannoni (1797).
Naples, National Library.

Opposite page.
Top: model explaining the
Bradyseism phenomenon,
by Mastrolorenzo-Dvorčak.
Bottom: view of Monte
Nuovo, gouache by Pietro
Fabris (XVIII century).
Naples, Santangelo Collection.

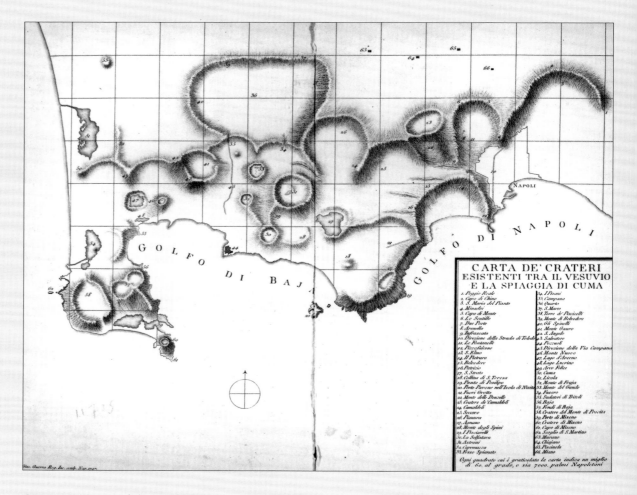

Campania is one of the most important active volcanic areas in the world – with some of the most famous volcanoes, such as Vesuvius, the Phlegrean Fields and the island of Ischia. Despite this, its natural richness – precisely arising from its volcanic nature – has attracted Man to this splendid region since pre-history. It was perhaps because of these resources that a group of Mycenaeans from the Pylos area, around mid-II millennium, settled in Vivara, on the island of Procida, and subsequently – towards end-VIII century – the first Greek colonists from Euboea decided to settle between the island of Ischia and Cumae. These varied resources – fertile land, drinking and spa water as well as plentiful building materials (tuff, lava stone, "pozzolano" cement, etc.) – encouraged men to challenge the risks of dangerous cohabitation with volcanos, that precisely over the last two millennia have unleashed tremendous explosions; mention need only be made of the eruption in 79 A.D. that destroyed Pompeii, yet we know that as early as V-IV century Greek-Syracusan soldiers stationed in Ischia fearfully fled the island after a volcanic explosion.

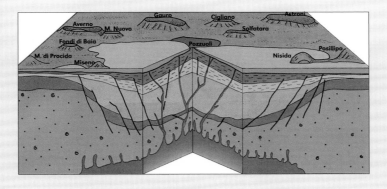

These were not the only hazards – there were also other so-called secondary volcanic phenomena, such as earthquakes and Bradyseisms, frequent in the area to the north of Naples known as the "Phlegrean Fields". The Greek name "Phlegrean Plain" mentioned by Strabo (64 B.C.-21 A.D.) in his *Geographia*, suggests that such "conflagrations" were already well-known. In any case, if – as geologists tell us – the Solfatara volcanic basin ("*the agorà of Hephaistos*" as Strabo named it) was formed 4-3,000 years ago, this means that the first colonists witnessed its formation and in any case breathed – like us – the same acrid sulphurous exhalations and surely wondered where all this awful and lethal material emerging from gaps in the ground came from.

This thought explains why Strabo, in his *Geographia* written in the Augustan age, indicates for the Phlegrean Fields only very arcane myths. The Cimmerians lived here in underground homes, mining metal ores from the bowels of the earth, while the coasts were home to the Lestrigons, the giant monsters who threw huge boulders against the ships of Odysseus. Here, the Giants, defeated and imprisoned underground by the Olympian gods, shook the earth's crust by beating their fists against the walls of their caves (earthquakes?) and threw boulders into the sky (eruptions?) in their efforts to escape. Typhon, who also

rebelled against the gods, was buried beneath the island and that is where his decomposing body issued flames and the sulphurous odours. The hot waters were linked with Periflegetonte and Cocytos, the rivers of the kingdom of the dead, while Hades was identified near Averno and Lucrino was the swamp of Acheron.

The most evident geo-archaeological phenomenon in this area is without doubt "Bradyseism", rising or falling movements of the ground often by several metres. Bradyseism is a phenomenon also found in other parts of the world, yet along the Phlegrean coast it is also well-documented in archaeological terms, especially around Pozzuoli, demonstrating that Man managed to live with the phenomenon from the late-ancient to modern times.

The monument that is by far the best example of this phenomenon – and mentioned in all international manuals – is the so-called "Serapeum" of Pozzuoli. From its initial excavation in the first-half of XVIII century, marks have been seen that show that the sea repeatedly submerged and exposed the building: in fact, the marble columns of the pronaos revealed a broad band perforated by shells (marine lithodomes) between 3.60 and 6.30 metres above the base, which today is more or less at sea level. The Serapeum is therefore a monument of great importance not only for archaeology but also for geology. In XVIII century, the presence of these shells on the columns was ingenuously explained by increases and decreases in sea level. The site even attracted Johann Wolfgang Goethe, an outstanding spirit even in the observation of natural phenomena, who attempted to find an explanation closer to reality. It was only around the mid-1800s that the father of modern geology, Sir Charles Lyell, came up with the correct explanation as the result of lifting and lowering of the earth's crust. The discovery seemed so important to him that he used the view of the columns of the Serapeum as the first plate in his famous book, *Principles of Geology* (London 1847), that marked the onset of modern scientific geology.

The origin of Bradyseism is still today subject to much discussion. The most recent explanatory model, by Neapolitan and American volcanologists, assumes that the lifting of chunks of the earth's crust is caused by the presence below of banks of volcanic materials that swell when impregnated with underground water (rising or negative Bradyseism); if they lose water, their volume is reduced (descending or positive Bradyseism).

Modern geo-archaeology has shown that the phenomenon affects not only the Phlegrean coast but also the Neapolitan coast. In short, Posillipo also has many ruins of Roman villas today below sea level. Marechiaro has the so-called "House of the Spirits" that is almost entirely submerged. This is a reticulated building of the Augustan age that shows, among other things, numerous signs of restoration and renovation dating from the post-Roman period.

The archaeological remains of ancient Baia are in part submerged between Punta Epitaffio and the Castello promontory. Underwater surveys have highlighted that the extreme limit of the Roman buildings is about 400 metres from the present coastline at a depth of about 9 metres. Underwater and aerial surveys have highlighted numerous submerged archaeological remains. Evidence of the submersion of the coast can be found in the ruins of the Temple of Venus that today are about 3 metres below the quay of the port. In particular, at Punta Epitaffio, near the shore, sections of a flagstone street were found 3.75 metres below sea level. Close by, on the other hand, two monumental complexes were also found: a villa belonging to the Pisoni family and a bath complex with a nymphaeum.

Miseno has considerable evidence of coastal submersions. The most important remains are in the port, built by Agrippa after 31 B.C., whose mooring bollards are today sunk by 6-8 metres. The semi-submerged remains of the Augustal Sacellum at Miseno are particularly evocative.

Along the coastline from Pozzuoli to *Portus Iulius* there stretched the famous *ripa puteolana*, that sank in-

Top: *chart of the submerged remains of the Phlegrean Fields.*

Bottom: *miniature from "de Balneis Puteolanis" by Pietro da Eboli (XIII century), illustrating Phlegrean baths in the Middle Ages.*

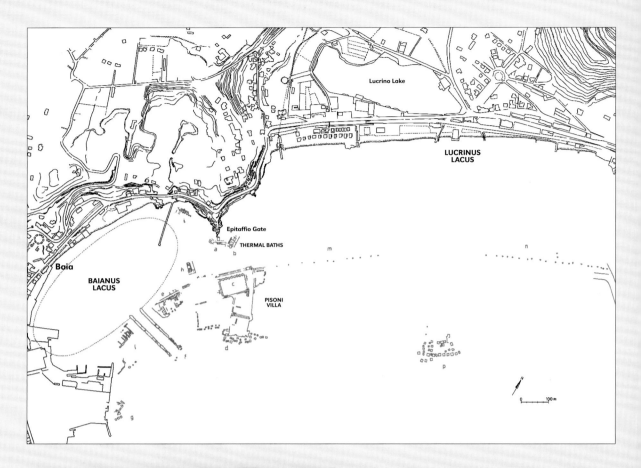

to the sea in the high Middle Ages. *Portus Iulius*, built in 37 B.C. by Agrippa and Octavian, was abandoned in 12 B.C., merely 25 years after its extremely expensive construction, evidently because it had silted up. Its remains can be seen today at up to 7 metres below sea level. The coastline of the Gulf of Pozzuoli in Roman times was in places several hundred metres from the present-day shore-line and has often settled at a depth of 10-11.5 metres below sea level.

In conclusion, geo-archaeological data make it possible to outline a detailed history of Phlegrean Bradyseism over the last 2,000 years, whereby maximum sinking of the Puteolean coast, as of IV century A.D., can be assumed as reaching even 17 metres, although later lifting after a subsequent Phlegrean eruption recovered 6-7 metres in 1538, that also formed Monte Nuovo.

In the Christian age, Bradyseism – that had destroyed flourishing cities such as Baia and Pozzuoli – was interpreted as divine punishment of pagans. In short, an apocryphal document of IX century of the "Acts of the

Apostles" telling the story of the arrival of St Paul in Pozzuoli, mentions the city submerged on the sea-bed at a depth of about 1.85 metres: *"Yet Paul ... told them to 'Follow me' and, leaving Pozzuoli together with those who believed in the Word of God, went to a place called Baia; they saw the city called Pozzuoli with their own eyes, submerged by an arm-length under the sea. And it has remained under the sea, like a monument, until today. ... Yet those who were saved from the city of Pozzuoli submerged by the sea announced to Caesar and Rome that Pozzuoli had sunk with all its inhabitants. And the Emperor ... in a meeting with the Judean leaders, said to them: 'See, because of your prayers I decapitated Paul and this is why the city is sunk below the sea'"*. This sinking may have been checked between mid-VI and VIII century A.D., since Cassiodorus, in a letter in 530 A.D., describes the Gulf of *Puteoli* still in all its splendour.

In the same way, during the Middle Ages, the mythical pagan world of the Phlegrean Fields – known as the descent into the Underworld because of its volcanic exhalations, the pronouncements of the Sibyl and earth movements – was completely absorbed into the *interpretatio christiana*. *"De Balneis Puteolanis"*, verses written at the end of XIII century by Pietro Anzolino da Eboli in honour of Frederick II of Svevia (*Codex Angioinus* 1474, parchment codex of the southern Campania school), includes a list of the spas still active in the Phlegrean area particularly distinguished by the healing properties. One of the miniatures, underneath a view of the Baths at Baia, has a drawing with *"Christ throwing open the doors of Averno or the Inferno"*. By now, the arcane world of the Phlegrean Fields had become part of the Christian imagination.

Even in 1982-1984, the Pozzuoli area was violently struck by Bradyseism phenomena: the land was lifted by up to 2-3 metres and seismic events took place. Quays had to be built everywhere so that boats could moor. Most of the terrified population emigrated elsewhere, yet today, as the memory of such hazards recedes, they are gradually returning. *"There are many admirable things, yet none is greater than Man"* wrote Sophocles in Antigone (lines 332-334): and we must agree with him that Man is truly great if people always take up again the challenges posed by such powerful Nature not to abandon beloved places that, in any case, favour human life through their fertility.

CAPUA

Below: map of Capua.

*Opposite page: view of
the Amphitheatre in Capua.*

"In the hinterland, there is Capua, the main city of Campania. It is truly the "head", as its etymology defines:
in short all the others, in comparison, can be considered as small cities, with the exception of Teanum
Sidicinum, itself important. Teanum also stands on the Appian Way, like the others found between Capua and
Brindisi, that is Calatia, Caudium and Beneventum. Towards Rome, on the other hand, there is Casilinum,
built on the River Volturno, where 540 Prenestines besieged by Hannibal resisted so long that, through
hunger, a mouse weighing just two "mine" was sold for 200 drachmas; the seller died, while those who bought
it survived. Hannibal, seeing them plant turnips near their fortifications, was astonished by their obstinacy,
since they hoped to withstand until the plants bore fruit; it is said that almost all survived, except for a few
men who died of hunger or were killed in battle".

Strabo, *Geographia* V 4, 10

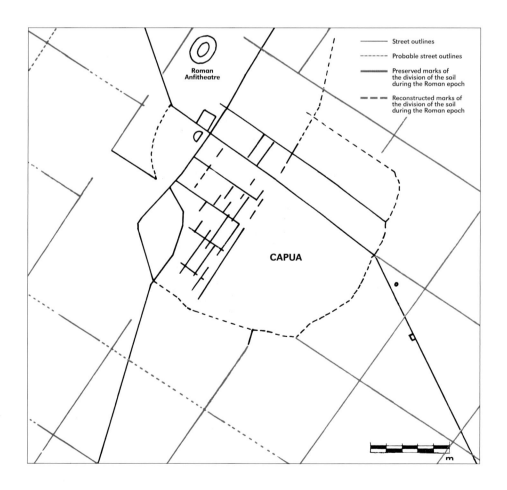

History

Capua was, according to Cicero, a "*modified
Rome*". It was one of the leading centres in ancient Italy as well as the most important city in the
hinterland of Campania. *Capua* today corresponds
with modern Santa Maria Capua Vetere, while the
city currently known as Capua was in reality the ancient *Casilinum*. Velleius Paterculus, who knew local history well as a relative of the Capuan family of
the *Magii*, mentions that the city was founded, together with Nola, in 800 B.C.
The original Oscan settlement was converted by the
Etruscans in the second half of VI century B.C. into
a structured city with a regular plan divided into two
quarters, *Albana* and *Seplasia* for Oscan and Etruscan inhabitants. Etruscan supremacy came to an
end with the unification of the Campanian population in 438 B.C. It was conquered by the Samnites in
424 B.C. (Livius 4, 37.1: "*a Samnitibus captam*"). It
came into the orbit of Rome as of 338 B.C., when it
obtained *civitas sine suffragio*. In 314, a revolt
against Rome was put down and in 312 B.C. the *Appian Way* was built to link Rome and *Capua* directly.
During the Second Punic War, after the Battle of
Canne (216 B.C.) it allied with Hannibal whose
troops lost their resolve while wintering in *Capua*

(Livius 23, 18). It was reconquered by the Romans in 211 B.C., who meted out various punishments: the municipality was dissolved, the *ager campanus* was confiscated and declared *ager publicus*; the senators were condemned to death, the city was subject to a *praefectus* and the population was dispersed in the villages (*pagi*).

Colonised by the Romans in 83 B.C. and regaining citizenship under Caesar in 59-58, Capua re-established its early prosperity thanks to Romanisation. Other colonial settlements took place under Antony in 43 and Octavian in 36 B.C. The building of the *Domitian Way* in 91 A.D. cut if off from major commercial traffic: in short, this new road – branching from the *Appian Way* near Sinuessa – passed directly to Cumae and *Puteoli*, cutting out the city of *Capua*. *Capua* – famed for its important gladiator schools – saw the onset in 73 B.C. of the slave revolt led by Thracian gladiator *Spartacus* who on Vesuvius proclaimed the freedom of all slaves but, faced by Crassus on the Sele in 71 B.C., was defeated and killed together with 50,000 other slaves. 6,000 prisoners were crucified along the Appian Way between *Capua* and Rome. A painting from Pompeii, with a legend in Oscan "*Spartacs*", bears witness to the sympathy of the Samnites for the rebel hero and the sentiments of hostility towards Rome that refused to recognise the rights of Campanian cities.

Christianity soon penetrated into *Capua* with the work of St. Paul. Even in IV century A.D. it was considered the eighth largest city in the Empire. Emperor Constantine made it the head offices of the *Consularis Campaniae* and commissioned a *Basilica Apostolorum*. Razed by the Vandals under Gensericus in 456 A.D., it returned to the fore in VI century A.D. Destroyed yet again by the Saracens in 841, it was rebuilt in 856 by Bishop Landolfo on the site of *Casilinum*, on the River Volturno, present-day Triflisco. By then, the site of the flourishing *Capua*, that Cicero defined in I century B.C. a "*modified Rome*", was reduced to ruins.

The florid economy of the city was the basis for extensive crafts production. It was renowned for its ceramic production, with architectural terrecottas and clay vases as of VII century B.C. (Campanian bucchero) through to the Roman age (black painted ceramics with moulded decorations). Its bronze workshops were already famous in Antiquity and were sacked in the necropolis by the colonists of Caesar (Svetonius, *Caesar* 81). There was a large perfume industry, that made famous the name of the Capuan forum known as "*Seplasia*" (Pliny, *Naturalis historia* 18.111).

Archaeological research

Archaeological research has ascertained that the site of *Capua* was inhabited since IX century B.C., at least in view of the materials found in the necropolis, and that such settlements continued without interruption through to the Roman age and IX century A.D.

There are few traces of the Samnitic period in the town; on the other hand, there are numerous box burials, often painted, of the second half IV-early III century B.C. The Samnitic hegemony saw the construction of the sanctuary outside the town of Fondo Patturelli, to the east of the city. Discovered in 1845 and dated mid-IV century B.C., it revealed numerous Oscan inscriptions, architectural terrecottas and the famous "*Matres Matutae*", known as the "Mothers of Capua" – sculptures in tuff depicting mothers enthroned holding swaddling babies.

The main archaeological evidence in modern Santa Maria Capua Vetere include the amphitheatre, the mithraeum, the cryptoportico, necropolis of every

epoch and Roman funeral mausoleums. The circuit of walls, in part visible and in part hypothesised, seems to have enclosed an area of about two square kilometres. The roads, at right angles, are only matched in part by modern streets. The Appian Way passed along one of the decumanums in crossing the city; there are remains of an honorary arch with three vaults in brick, known as Hadrian's Gate, near the amphitheatre.

The amphitheatre of the II century A.D. was, after the Colosseum, the largest amphitheatre in the Roman world. Rich sculptural decorations included statues such as the Aphrodite of Capua, Eros and Psyche, today in the National Museum, Naples. Remains of a previous amphitheatre of II-I century B.C. have been evocatively linked with the famous school for gladiators. The nearby building, so far thought to be baths, on the other hand is probably the *catabulum* of the paleo-Christian age, that is the place where wild beasts were kept. On the other hand, there are few visible remains of the theatre dating to II century B.C.

Along the Appian Way towards Caserta, there are two funeral monuments of the monumental Roman necropolis, the "Carceri Vecchie" and the "Conocchia", known respectively even in drawings of the Renaissance and the 1700s. The *Capitolium* built under Tiberius (Svetonius, *Tiberius* 40), with the Temple of Jupiter (Tacitus, *Annales* 4, 57), was recently identified between the theatre and the Church of Sant'Erasmo.

In 1922, a painted mithraeum came to light from end II century A.D., one of the most complete buildings of this kind known today. Recent excavations have highlighted structures of Constantine's *Basilica Apostolorum* in the present-day Church of San Pietro.

Hadrian's arch

Also often known as Felice Arch or the Arch of *Capua*, it is an honorary arch or a triumphal gate in brick with 3 arches, of which the southern one has withstood the ravages of time and men; the northern gate, on the other hand, has disappeared, except for the foundations lying in the courtyard of a private home, while only the left pillar remains of the central one. It is thought that it was built in 130 A.D. in honour of Hadrian. A headstone in the centre, dictated by Luigi Settembrini, recalls the Battle of Volturno in 1860.

The amphitheatre

Capua between end II century B.C. and early I century B.C. already had an amphitheatre but also the finest schools for gladiators. The *Capua* Amphitheatre, with a capacity of 40,000 spectators, is second in size only to the Colosseum. The main axis measures about 170 metres and the minor axis about 140 m; it is 40 m high. The building is perhaps linked with the arrival of the Roman colony in 59 B.C. The main entrances opened in a longitudinal direction on the ellipse. The arena was surrounded by three orders of brick bands clad with travertines and marbles; the floor in ancient times comprised wooden planks that could be dismantled. The underground areas, resembling those of the Colosseum and Pozzuoli, are accessed by small stairs. From here, not only fierce an-

Relief with a hunting scene from the Amphitheatre in Capua. Santa Maria Capua a Vetere, Gladiators Museum.

Page 116: statue of Paris, from Capua. Naples, National Archaeological Museum.

Page 117: statue of Apollo, from Capua. Naples, National Archaeological Museum.

imals emerged but also – thanks to hoisting machines – gigantic theatrical scenarios with exotic landscapes and wild beasts, perhaps resembling the landscapes with wild beasts we can admire painted on the walls in Pompeii. The smaller areas were used as changing rooms and stores.

The arches of the ground floor were decorated with gigantic heads on the keystones. In all 19 are known but only two – the busts of Diana and Demetra – are still present on the monument. The arches of the second and third floors were embellished with statues. Some of these can be seen on the facade of the Town Hall and in *Capua* Museum.

Hundreds of statues embellished the exterior arches, on the model of the Colosseum in Rome. The known sculptures all date to the time of Hadrian; these three works are exhibited today in the National Museum, Naples. The first is "Venus"; the goddess is represented in the act of admiring herself using the shield of Ares like a mirror. The second depicts an "Adonis", a statue of a nude young man with floppy and elegant forms, leaning on a trunk, where arrows and a quiver also lie. The third is a female torso identified as "Psyche", excessively honed during restoration work in the 1700s.

When Christianity came to the fore and became, under Constantine, the state religion, the amphitheatres also hosted Christian festivals. Inasmuch an epigraph of *Capua* registers all the Christian festivals, including the rosary for the dead to be recited in the amphitheatre on 13 May.

In keeping with the destiny of the city, the amphitheatre of *Capua* was involved in the sack of Gensericus; yet in the barbarian age it seems not to have lost its function as a field for *venationes*, judging from the new name of "Berolais" or "Virilascio", an ancient-Germanic name, used for the amphitheatres between Latium and Campania, that may mean "arena for bears" from the German "Baer".

The building was expanded and embellished, destroyed and restored many times and became a fortress in the Middle Ages. In the Norman-Svevan age, the radial walls of the *cavea* were cut at the foundations to cause collapse and turn the building into an enormous quarry for building material. In 1736, Carlo III Bourbon ordered the rubble to be removed and Francesco I, with an edict in 1826, halted further looting.

The Gladiator Museum

The Gladiator Museum is a permanent exhibition set up in the *Antiquarium* of the amphitheatre. It is a reconstruction of a sector of the arena where gladiators fought wild beasts. It illustrates the world of gladiators and games through low reliefs in marble with hunting scenes, panels re-enacting the games, friezes and copies of gladiator weapons from the Gladiator Barracks in Pompeii.

The first hall has four keystones from the arches that decorated the first order of the amphitheatre: the heads of Mithra, Juno and Minerva, as well as the copy of the god Vulcan now in the Campano Museum. Underneath, there are two inscriptions dedications to Emperors Hadrian and Antoninus Pius. In the centre, there is a wooden model of the amphitheatre as it appeared in II century A.D.

The first showcase exhibits ceramics from the cisterns and fragments of statues of II century A.D. that once decorated the amphitheatre: the heads of Apollo, Athena and Hercules, fragments of architectural decoration – including two trusses with ox heads – and finds from the necropolis of VII century B.C. pre-dating the amphitheatre.

The second showcase on the other hand exhibits copies of weapons found in the Gladiator Barracks in Pompeii: helmets, pauldrons (shoulder-straps), bronze shields and two decorated greaves. Lastly, copies of clay statues found in Pompeii and votary offerings for *Saturnalia*.

Between the two showcases, a diorama illustrates fighting in the arena. It shows a lion and four gladiators: one with a net and trident, another (*secutor*) (with a helmet and short sword), a Thracian with a sabre and the fourth (*venator*) facing the lion. A commentary recalls the games that Marcus Marcellus organised in *Capua* in honour of Emperor Trajan, when the schools of *Capua* and Rome took to the field, with nineteen pairs of gladiators. The scene depicts the victory of Astiana (with the net) over *secutor* Calenius, "the one from Cales".

The second hall reconstructs the decoration of the balustrade of a vomitorium with fragments found. In the background, there is a relief with a procession of magistrates and lictors entering the amphitheatre; the side balusters on the other hand reproduce animals about to leap into the arena. The fragments depict mythological scenes such as the feats of Hercules, the hunting of the Calidonium-Erymanthian boar, Diana and Acteon, Mars and Rea Silvia, the Torment of Marsias. There are also numerous scenes of sacrifices and others illustrating the building of the amphitheatre. The animals depicted illustrate those used during performances, as demonstrated by analysis of the bones found in the sewers. There are even exotic animals such as elephants, tigers, lionesses, bulls, ibex, dromedaries, African buffalo, bears and elks.

Fragments of pluteus are exhibited on the sides of the room on four panels: the first depicts Hercules sweeping the Augian stables, the two Dioscuri, Hercules and Antheus. The second shows dancing Menades, the god Apollo, Hercules, the torment of Prometheus, whose liver was devoured by the eagle, the torment of Marsias flayed by Apollo, Mars and Rea Silvia, the goddess Diana; the third panel on the other hand has a sacrificial scene with the amphitheatre in the background, personifications of the city with a turreted head, an Amazzonomachia, the building of an amphitheatre, three bearers of *ferculum*; the fourth panel, lastly, has pluteus illustrating the hunt for the Calidonium-Erymanthian boar, Atheon devoured by dogs for having spied Diana and a Centauromachia. The reliefs, in a classical style, seem typical of art in the time of Hadrian.

The Mithraeum

The Mithraeum was discovered in 1922 during excavation work in the courtyard of a private home in Via Morelli.

The cult of Mithra, an ancient Iranian god, was perhaps introduced to *Capua* by the gladiators, in short the god Mithra was a divinity of Indo-Iranian origins. His "mysterious" cult spread throughout Asia Minor, to Alexandria in Egypt, Rome and all the provinces of the Empire.

The building comprises a rectangular underground hall measuring 23 × 3 metres, now 4 m below road level. The vault is decorated with six-pointed green and red stars; the back partition has the altar for sacrifices in front of a large fresco of Mithra, with red garments and hose, killing a gigantic white bull with a tail shaped like an ear of wheat. The side walls have benches for the faithful, above which there are admirable, albeit largely spoilt frescos depicting the various stages of initiation.

Mithra's cloak sparkles with seven stars (a symbol of the planets), while the tip of his Phrygian beret has the shining star of Saturn. On the left there is the sun god with rays and a raven; a ray moves from the sun to Mithra. The moon appears top-right Luna and *Cautes* to the left in Persian garments holding a bow; *Cautopates* is on the right. There are also a scorpion, a snake and a dog. *Oceanus* is depicted bottom left and *Tellus*, the goddess of the earth, on the right. A channel leads from the altar, used to collect the blood of sacrificed animals in a small well. The opposite wall has a painting of the moon and a chariot pulled by two horses.

In short, the god Mithra kills the bull assisted by Sun, Moon, Ocean and Earth. The killing of the bull represents the symbolic sacrifice from which Life originates. The blood of the bull gave birth to wheat, its marrow to harvests and its semen to humans. The raven, snake, dog, scorpion and two children bearing torches indicate different levels of initiation. The Moon on the chariot on the opposite wall indicates the close relationship between animals and the moon, that is between death and resurrection.

The Conocchia

On the Appian Way, on the right of the section between Santa Maria Capua Vetere and Caserta, there is a Roman funerary monument of II century A.D. known as the "Conocchia" after its streamlined shape. The mausoleum has a four-sided main body with concave sides with four cylindrical towers at the corners, on which stands a domed drum embellished by semi-columns and mock arches. It probably belonged to a wealthy local family.

Carceri Vecchie (Old Prisons)

This mausoleum has a large, cylindrical body with a dome, scanned by semi-columns and blind arches supporting the architrave; on top, a second smaller cylindrical body is marked off by pillars. Inside the cell there are traces of frescoes testifying the presence of decorations that have by now disappeared.

Basilica of Santa Maria Maggiore

The Basilica of Santa Maria Maggiore was built in 432 by San Simmaco, Bishop of Capua, who, returning from the Council of Ephesus, decided to dedicate a temple to the Virgin on the model of the one built in Rome by Pope Libero. The Basilica was built on the so-called Grotto of San Prisco, a paleo-Christian crypt of I century A.D. Initially, the building, which had a single nave, was preceded by a tetrastyle portico.

Sanctuary of Diana Tifatina

Three and a half miles north-east of *Capua*, today preserved underneath the Church of Sant'Angelo in

Formis, there stood the famous sanctuary of Diana Tifatina, on the slopes of Monte Tifata. The cult was linked with the Trojan hero *Kapys*, the legendary founder of *Capua*, and especially with the doe hind who suckled him. The animal, sacred to Diana, was apparently sacrificed by Roman Consul Fulvius Flaccus during the siege in 211 B.C. In accordance with periegetes, a goblet belonging to Nestor was displayed, as well as the cranium of an elephant from Hannibal's expedition. Sulla, after the victory over Norbanus in 83, assigned to the sanctuary on the slopes of Tifata the surrounding land rich in healing springs.

The list of the new properties was engraved on a bronze tablet displayed in the cell. The boundaries of the estate must have been extremely extensive, as witnessed by the border-stones with the inscription "*fines agrorum dicatorum Dianae Tifat(inae) a Cornelio Sulla ex forma Divi Augusti*". The sanctuary was administrated by: *magistri Fani Dianae, pr(aefecti) o pr(aetores) iure dicundo montis Dianae Tifatinae*. In the Imperial age, the cult spread in the provinces, as witnessed by inscriptions found in Gallia and Pannonia. Today, Sant'Angelo in Formis is no longer the small, remote church in the Work Lands (the ancient *Campania Felix*, today corresponding to the province of Caserta), yet its architecture and frescos are highly evocative of its glorious past and the flourishing artists in XI-XIII century who achieved the best figurative expression of the strict Byzantine religious observance.

It is one of the most famous basilicas of the Mediaeval age. It stands on a knoll dominating the plain of *Capua*. It was built on the ruins of the Temple of Diana Tifatina and still retains the vestiges of this building. It achieved its moment of greatest splendour when the famous abbot Desiderio da Montecassino, in 1073, rebuilt it in its present style. In short, the church became a rich and powerful convent.

The facade is preceded by a portico with five arches and the Basilica has three naves divided by fourteen columns. The external portico and the interior are frescoed all over the walls. The apsidal basin is painted with a Benedictine "Christ enthroned" surrounded by symbols of the Evangelists and angels; between them stands Abbot Desiderio with a square nimbus in the act of offering the temple. The central nave is decorated with "New Testament stories" matched on the right by the "Old Testament stories".

The Archaeological Museum of Ancient Capua

The Archaeological Museum was inaugurated in 1995 in a building set up in the area occupied in the Middle Ages by the Tower of Sant'Erasmo, where Robert of Anjou was born in 1278. Tradition claims that the tower was built on the Capitoline temple of the Roman city. The building was originally the residence of the Sveva king and was later also home to Angevin and Aragon monarchs. In its current appearance, with the large square courtyard, it was used in 1864 to breed stallions and rear horses sold all over southern Italy. This explains the delightful collection of coaches, owned by the former Horse Breeding Institute. The Museum illustrates the history and artistic culture of the city in Etruscan, Samnitic and then Roman times, through to the end of IX century A.D. It

Left: archaic antefix from Capua, with a Gorgon's head. Santa Martia Capua Vetere, Campania Provincial Museum. Above: ornamental bronze fibula, from Capua. Santa Maria Capua Vetere, Archaeological Museum.

Roman mosaic (I century B.C.) with birds drinking, from Capua. Naples, National Archaeological Museum.

is organised into ten halls exhibiting materials dating from X-I century B.C. with splendid examples of bronze jars, burial treasures and painted architectural terracotta.

Hall 1 has finds from the Bronze age (XVI-XIV century B.C.) from a small necropolis: modest burial treasures with clay jars and arrow tips.

Halls 2 and 3 are dedicated to the Iron Age, with burial treasures of IX-VII century. The most ancient relics are the globular and double-conical cinerary jars, *askoi* and salt-cellars. The goblets with birds, displayed alongside local products, were imported and testify to contacts with the Greek world during the first half of VIII century B.C. Many imports document trade with other peoples. In short, some objects are of Etruscan origin, such as the bronze basins with pearl-finished edges; others are of Greek origin, such as the trilobate *oinochoi* and the *kotylai*, while others still came from the Danube area, such as the amber.

Locally made pottery on the other hand is in clay and has particular forms, such as the "capeduncola", or imitated imported materials; quality in any case is very high. Production from end VIII to first half VII century B.C. became standardised, in any case witnessing the high quality of life of the population.

Hall 4 is dedicated to the so-called Oriental period, characterised by massive imports of proto-Corinthian or Corinthian ceramics and the assimilation by local peoples of the Greek life style. This took place in Capua and its territory also through the mediation of the Etruscans, as witnessed by *bucchero* vases, also produced locally, and the Etruscan-Corinthian *aryballoi*. A Ionic jar and a cauldron with mobile handles belonging to the same burial treasure are also extremely interesting. Numerous objects highlight flourishing crafts output in Capua during VI century B.C. For example, the archaic furnace where roof tiles and exposed architectural antefixes were made must have been extremely active.

Halls 5 and 6 highlight the coroplastics of *Capua*, that achieved high levels in the production of votary statuette and architectural palmette antefixes, with a Gorgoneion head and the face of Acheloos. The larger-than-life head from Triflisco is very evocative.

Hall 7 moves on to the Archaic period (VI-V century B.C.), when the Etruscan civilisation achieved its greatest splendour. Imported ceramics are more numerous compared to previous periods: Ionic goblets and Attic jars with black and red figures and mythological scenes of high quality, such as the *hydria* with killing of the Minotaur and the *stamnos* with the scene of the Lenee. Local production on the other hand standardised on decorations with or without black figures.

Hall 8 highlights the domination of the Samnitic peoples over the Etruscans at the end of V century B.C. Male burial treasures always have weapons, while female tombs have numerous gold nicknacks and figurative jars. The tuff box tombs have decorations and images of the deceased. The Hall also has a reconstruction of a chamber tomb with a life-size fresco of the deceased.

Hall 9 is dedicated to the Roman period. The are interesting centurial headstones, used to mark the boundaries of land-holdings, and in this case testimony of the expropriations inflicted by the Romans to the detriment of the Capuans as punishment for supporting Hannibal. In the Roman age, *Capua* was a centre famous for the production of perfumes, wheat, bronzes and ceramics. The city continued to prosper, as witnessed by numerous dedicatory epigraphs on buildings, fragments of frescoes and tuff sculptures. The funerary steles – simple or with typical decorations of the Hellenistic period, such as garlands, shields and weapons – handed down the "portrait" of the deceased.

Hall 10 has finds from recent excavations conducted in the sanctuaries of the area. The most famous it the Sanctuary of Diana Tifatina, where the singular continuity of the holiness of the area is witnessed by the presence of the Mediaeval Basilica of Sant'Angelo in Formis. This sanctuary revealed fragments of sima with lion heads and other architectural elements, as well as votary medals. Another temple in the area, on the other hand, revealed much pottery with red figures, votary terracotta and miniature jars. The statue of *Mater Matuta*, unfortunately headless, and a sphinx, both in tuff, are of great interest.

Capua Museum

The Campania Provincial Museum of Capua, inaugurated in 1874 in Palazzo Antignano, was defined by Maiuri as "*the most significant of the Italic civilisation in Campania*". The building was already founded in IX century and it is famous for its splendid Catalan portal with the shields of the Antignano and d'Alagno families.

The exhibition begins in the courtyard with a rich series of funerary steles, including a large protome with the personification of *Volturnus amnis*, the patron god of the city, found in the Amphitheatre and currently placed on a tall column in oriental granite. The "Lapidarium" has the richest collection of epigraphs from Campania. It was arranged by German archaeologist Theodor Mommsen who prepared the catalogue in 1873 while waiting for the compilation of the *Corpus Inscriptionum Latinarum*. The most evocative and precious finds include the so-called "Mothers of Capua" found in 1845 at Fondo Patturelli: hundreds of tuff statues, with seated mothers holding one or more swaddling children in their arms. These rough sculptures have geometrical shapes and realistic features and represent one of the most important documents of popular art in Campania: "*These statues of mothers, cut and squared off as if by axes striking cubic blocks of grey tuff, seated, rough, serious and imposing on chairs, shrouded and stiff in their front-on pose and the hieratic act of offering, all bearing in their arms the sweet weight of maternity – swaddling babes in twos or fours and, thanks to the propitiatory Damusa, even twelve, like so many chil-*

dren in Aracoeli – equally seem to be images of mother-goddesses. Strolling among them in the half-light of these rooms is like reaching the end of a holy street, thronged with offerers, or the hidden and mysterious entrance to a temple". So wrote Amedeo Maiuri in *Passeggiate Campane* (1950). The figure has been identified as *Bona Dea*, patron of mothers ready to give birth, or *Mater Matuta*, the protectress of female fertility. Chronologically, the sculptures cover an arch of time between VI and II century B.C.

The archaeological collections also include terracotta; production in Capua was famed all over the ancient world for beauty and enormous variety. There are architectural terracotta (acroters, antefixes, slabs, various kinds of roof tile), small models of temples, tiny sculptures and plaques used in part as clay cladding of temples and in part as votary items. Most of these objects were found in the temples of Dea Madre and Diana Tifatina. The most ancient date back to VI century B.C. and have zoomorphic subjects, such as how protomes (busts) of gryphons and horses, small figures of men and children, etc.

The exhibition of bronze works from Capua – famed in Antiquity – is arranged in three sections: ornamental bronze (fibulas, rings, bracelets), everyday objects (keys, mirrors, door hinges, writing instruments, belts, etc.) and lastly figurative bronze works with Greek and Campanian statuettes datable between V and III century B.C.

Ceramics include examples from the proto-historic age, decorated with simple engraved lines, as well as Etruscan (*bucchero* vase, VI century B.C.), Attic (VI-V century B.C.) and Italiot and Campanian (IV-II century B.C.) objects. The Museum also has the letters exchanged by its founder, Gabriele Iannelli, and Theodor Mommsen.

BENEVENTO

Archaeological map
of Benevento.

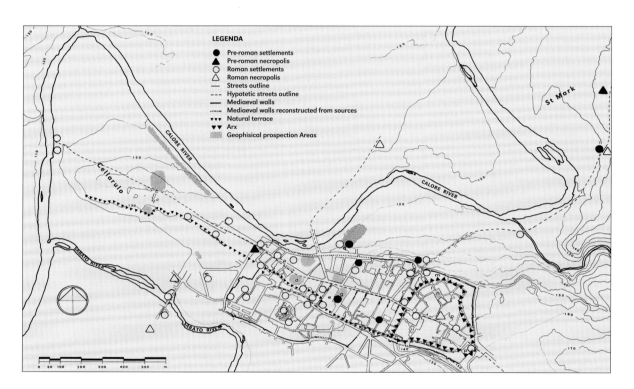

Archaeological map
of Benevento.

"*The Samnites initially pushed their raids as far as Via Latina and the territory of Ardea; subsequently, after sacking Campania itself, they became very powerful. The Campanians, accustomed to despotic government, soon submitted to their command. The Samnites were entirely annihilated in several stages, especially by Sulla, the dictator of the Romans, who realised, after putting down revolts by the Italics in many battles, that the Samnites were the only remaining united community, even daring to march against Rome; inasmuch he fought them in the fortified towns, killed many in battle (having given orders to take no prisoners) and the others – three or four thousand men who had laid down their weapons – were taken to the public prison in Campo Marzio. Three days later, having sent soldiers, they all had their throats slit and proscriptions did not cease until everything bearing the Samnite name was destroyed or banished from Italy. Those who complained of such brutality were told that experience had taught that no Roman would be able to live in peace while the Samnites were alive. And in short, although not entirely eliminated, their cities today are reduced to villages, such as Boviano, Isernia, Panna, Telesia, bordering with Venafro, and others still of which none is worthy of being considered a city. These details must be mentioned within due limits since they deal with the glory and power of Italy. In any case Benevento, like Venosa, have maintained their importance*".

Strabo, *Geographia* V 4, 11

History

Benevento was founded in IV century B.C. in an area inhabited since the Eneolithic age. A centre of Samnitic origin, it became a Latin colony in 268 B.C., after the war against Pyrrhus, when the name was changed from *Maleventum* to *Beneventum*. A base for Roman expansion in the south, Benevento remained loyal to Rome during the Second Punic War. In 90 B.C., with the promulgation of the Lex Iulia, it became a municipality and colony for veterans after 42 B.C. Emperor Trajan promised to develop a section of the Appian Way to connect the city with Brindisi.

Archaeological excavations have highlighted numerous monuments of the Roman age, today in part incorporated into or even inside modern buildings: sections of wall, the road layout at right angles on the two decumanums, the arch in honour of Trajan, the theatre commissioned by Emperor Hadrian and inaugurated in 126 A.D., the Arch of the Sacrament (II century A.D.), the Forum and remains of a baths building.

The Arch of the Sacrament is one of the few remains of the vast monumental Roman area. Not far from Piazza Duomo, it dates from the period after Trajan. Supported by brick pillars each of five metres in diameter, it has niches on both sides.

Theatre

The Roman theatre is one of the most imposing buildings for performances preserved in southern Italy. Built under Hadrian and extended by Caracalla 200-210 A.D., its location has always been known in that the plan of the building is perfectly legible even in the most ancient historical cartography, since it was preserved from within the outlines of the houses built on top since the Middle Ages. The date of the building is uncertain although, on the basis of an inscription with a dedication to Hadrian and analysis of building techniques, it is usually attributed to the Age of Hadrian. Nevertheless, certain considerations based on the study of the graphic survey and the observation that the dedication is re-used on the stage as a support element for the colonnade in front seem to suggest a date in II century.

The building measures about 90 metres in diameter and could contain about 20,000 spectators. There were three surrounding orders of 25 arches; most of the first order and the structures of the second order still stand, as well as the cavea, orchestra, part of the stage and three staircases behind the stage. The theatre is home today to summer performances.

Trajan's Arch

The monument symbolising Benevento is the fine commemorative arch with a single barrel-vault (15.60 × 8.60 metres) in white marble, built by Trajan to commemorate the opening in 114 A.D. of the extension of the Appian Way from Benevento to Brindisi that ensured faster connections between Campania, Puglia and the rest of Italy with the main ports serving the Orient – Brindisi and Taranto. It is the largest example of historic Roman reliefs in II century A.D. and the most complete depiction handed down to us of a Roman triumph, that of Trajan over the Dacians in 107 A.D.

The face towards the city (the present-day Via Traiano) narrates scenes in relief of the good government of the *princeps* and works of peace; the face overlooking the countryside (the present-day Via del Pomerio) depicts military scenes and Imperial policy in the provinces. The arch inside the barrel-vault is decorated by the sacrifices made by Trajan to

Trajan's Arch at Benevento, dating from II century A.D.

open the road and assign foodstuffs to Italic cities. Each pillar has three reliefs, with one on the attic, next to the commemorative epigraph, and two adjacent to the barrel-vault, separated by low panels with Victories killing bulls ("tauroctone") and figures of amazons; those facing the interior – from bottom to top and right to left – are an *adventus* of Trajan; his welcome by the Senate, the Roman People and the equestrian order; Trajan at the Forum Boarium, the traditional place for food administration of the Roman people; Trajan proceeding to the italic *dilectus*; the new arrival of Trajan and his welcome by the Capitoline Triad. The opposite facade depicts – from bottom to top and right to left – the concession of *civitas* to veterans settled in border colonies; the *receptio in fidem* of barbarian princes; the creation of provincial colonies; the provincial *dilectus*; the submission of the Dacians; the homage of provincial rural divinities. The attic and the frieze have high reliefs depict the triumph over the Dacians.

The architrave has the customary frieze and very high reliefs with triumphal scenes. Inside the barrel-vault, Trajan is depicted on the left between the lictors making sacrifices probably for the inauguration of Trajan's Way and, on the right, the institution of the *alimenta* (symbolised by the loaves on

the centre table), in the presence of lictors, personifications of Italic cities and peoples with children held by hand or seated on shoulders. While the reliefs on the pillars are by no means exceptional (the figures are rather heavy and banal), the reliefs inside the barrel-vault – despite lacking that accomplished sense of space seen in the panels of the arch of Titus in Rome – are of much higher quality in their search for a crowded yet never monotonous or over-loaded composition.

There seem to be close relationships with the large Trajan frieze in the Arch of Constantine, so that it is by no means unfounded to attribute the task to the urban workshop directed by the "Master of the Deeds of Trajan".

Trajan's arch was subject in recent years to restoration work that cleaned the marble surfaces blackened by smog and consolidated certain damaged reliefs. Set into the city walls, the arch became a gateway for access to the city and, in view of its dimensions, was named Porta Aurea, an appellative still found in the nearby Church of Sant'Ilario at Porta Aurea.

The Temple of Isis

In 1904, the Convent of Sant'Agostino along the north perimeter of the city revealed numerous fragmentary Egyptian and Egyptian-like sculptures from a Temple to Isis, built under Domitian 88-89 A.D. Although topographical surveys over the last decade have revealed a brick structure in a building adjacent to the convent, it was not possible to identify the exact location of the temple. It was possibly set up near this area – the ancient *pomoerium* – since, by law, international cults could not be welcomed inside the city.

The sculptures and inscriptions belonging to the sanctuary are today exhibited in the Samnium Museum and are *unique*, since they form the largest and best set of Egyptian sculptures ever found outside Egypt. Mention can especially be made of the statue of Domitian dressed as a pharaoh together with numerous sculptures of imperial figures, priests, sphinxes, hawks, divinities, obelisks, lions and architectural fragments. The core on show in the Museum is joined by the statue of the Apis ox found in 1629 and today standing at the start of Viale San Lorenzo at the crossroads with Via Torre della Catena, popularly nicknamed the "Bufala", and the obelisk raised in 1597, under Pope Sixtus V, now standing in the grounds of the Cathedral.

North side

West side

South side

With the advent of Christianity, the goddess Isis was demonised and became a "witch" – probably the origin of the legend of the witches of Benevento, that from the Middle Ages to our own times have inspired the figurative arts, literature and music. Inasmuch, the witches would be none other that the adepts of the original cult of Isis, transformed over the years into a demonical cult. Local tradition also suggests that Longobard Duke Romualdo, after his conversion to Christianity by Bishop San Barbato, uprooted the evergreen walnut where the witches met after bathing in the Sabato River. There are effectively many references to the original cult of Isis; for example, adepts worshipped the "golden viper", perhaps the *ureus* snake of Egyptian tradition, used purifying water, perhaps the holy water of the Nile, a fundamental element in the cults of Isis, and smeared their bodies with a possibly hallucinogen ointment.

Samnium Museum

Charles-Maurice de Talleyrand, foreign minister of Napoleon made Prince of Benevento by the French Emperor, had the idea of setting up at Benevento in 1806 a museum to house "the paintings, statues, inscriptions and other monuments of Antiquity", beginning with the collection of objects, especially headstones and reliefs, already in the College of Jesuits. The Museum did not come to fruition and many of its items were dispersed and occasionally found again. It was therefore the first municipality following the Unification of Italy to take the merit for the foundation of the new Samnium Museum, with events beginning in 1865 that culminated with the inauguration in 1873. Since 1929, the Museum has been housed in the Santa Sofia complex and was set up again after destruction suffered during the Second World War.

The Museum with two halls emphasises a theme-based layout. Exhibits range from pre-Roman culture in the ancient Samnium area to Greek and Magna Graecia civilisation in V and IV century B.C. and Roman works such as the Dancer, a Roman copy of a Greek original of V century B.C.; the Discobolos (the Discus Thrower), a Roman copy in green basalt of Policletus and the Athena, another Roman copy of an original by Praxiteles. The museum also displays burial treasures from the Samnitic necropolis of Caudium and the sculpture complex from the Sanctuary of Isis. The Museum also has important relics from the Longobard necropolis of Benevento of VI-VII century, including weapons, tools, jars, knick-knacks, garments and gold coins from the Longobard mint with images of the dukes and princes of Benevento.

Drawing of the friezes in Trajan's Arch at Benevento.

POMPEII

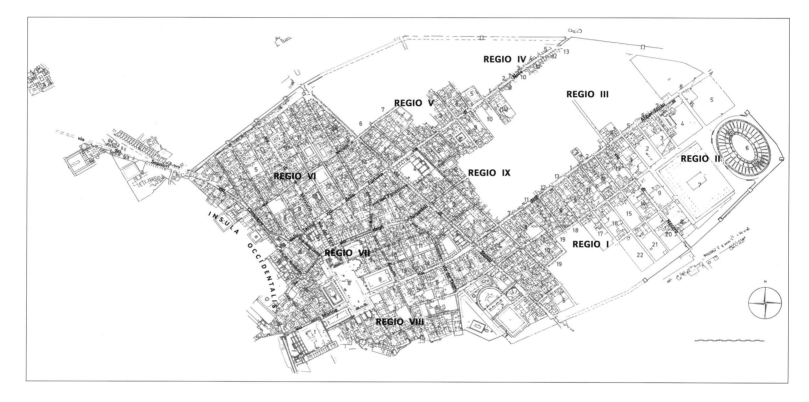

Map of ancient Pompeii.

Opposite page: the Forum.

"*The Oscans occupied Neapolis and nearby Pompeii where the River Sarno flows, followed by the Tyrrhenaeans, the Pelasgi and then the Samnites. Even they were expelled from this place. Pompeii, on the River Sarno, used to import and export goods, is also the port of Nola, Nuceria and Acerra ... Mount Vesuvius rises above these places, entirely inhabited by wonderful cultures except on the peak. The peak itself is mostly flat but entirely sterile, with an ashen appearance; it has cavities with fissures, opening on to sooty rocks on the surface, as if devoured by fire. One may suppose that this place once burnt and had craters of fire that then became extinct, having used up all burning material. Perhaps this is also the reason for the fertility of the land hereabouts, as in Catania, where they say that the surface covered by the ash thrown out of the fires of Etna made the land particularly ideal for growing vines. The soil in short is rich in good substance and burnt earth that also produces fruit. Inasmuch, when the earth is over-abundant with substance it is also likely to catch fire, like every sulphurous substance, and after it has dried and doused, it is transformed into ash that is also good for agriculture*".

Strabo, *Geographia* V 4, 8

History

About 800 years before Christ, the city of Pompeii was founded on a peak at the feet of Vesuvius. A small town, Pompeii was often obliged to submit to various conquerors. Thus, in VI century, the Greeks, who dominated the Gulf of Naples from *Cumae* to Sorrento, established the cult of Apollo in the Forum square and dedicated a Doric temple to Athena and Hercules in the Triangular Forum. The Etruscans who traded in the hinterland of Campania were also interested in establishing dominion over the city, in view of its position near the coast.

At the end of V century B.C., the Samnites invaded the plain of Campania and also conquered Pompeii. During IV century, the city was completely rebuilt and extended, the town plan was harmonised and the walls achieved their maximum development. Although rarely involved in the great events of history, the city became progressively Hellenised since the Samnitic patricians were fond of Greek culture and art. This Hellenisation found its expression in architecture and public works, such as the Temple of Apollo, the Basilica and the Triangular Forum, as well as private buildings, such as the House of the Coloured Capitals, the House of the Faun and the House of the Silver Wedding.

In III century B.C., Rome, after defeating the Samnites, forced Pompeii – like many other cities in Campania – to become its ally.

In the early I century B.C., the Italic allies – who suffered disproportionate oppression compared to the rights they enjoyed – demanded Roman citizenship. When all their petitions were rejected, they rebelled and the "Social War" (from *socii*, allies) began. Pompeii was also involved. The outcome was that in 89 B.C. the city was taken by Roman troops commanded by dictator Lucius Cornelius Sulla who, in 80 B.C., set up here a colony of veterans with their families. The city lost its autonomy as an Italic municipality and was officially renamed *Colonia Cornelia Veneria Pompeianorum*.

This saw the onset of a rapid process of Romanisation. The city soon took on the typical appearance of a Roman city and took up Roman political organisation, language, cults and customs. Romanisation also emerged in the appearance of the city: the Amphitheatre, the Odeion and the Baths were built, the Temple of Jupiter was converted to the cult of the Capitoline Triad. The middle classes of Pompeii, hard-working and good traders, exported their products everywhere, even to India: wine, oil, vegetables and an exquisite fish sauce *garum*.

In 62 A.D., Vesuvius made its presence felt with an earthquake of 9 on the Mercalli Scale. Almost all the public buildings collapsed and many people were killed. The people of Pompeii remained without water, their homes in ruins and prey to speculators. Emperor Vespasian sent a prefect from Rome, Titus Suedius Clemens. He restored order, re-developed the land registry and launched major reconstruction projects. Work was intense everywhere and the people of Pompeii began to recover serenity and hopes for the future, yet this illusion would only last another 17 years...

Discovery and excavation

The eruption in 79 A.D. buried Pompeii under a stratum of pumice, ash and stones up to six metres thick. As the centuries passed by, the city remained only a vague memory. The area was generically named "Civita", that is the "ancient city".

Few know that archaeology was born precisely in Pompeii about 200 years ago. Excavations began in 1748 on the orders of Bourbon King Carlo. The first excavations involved the theatre area. The finds were initially transferred to the Royal Palace in Portici and as of 1787 to Naples Museum.

The casts of Pompeians

Giuseppe Fiorelli invented in the 1800s the system for recovering the casts of the dead and objects in wood. He observed that organic substances, having been buried for centuries, had decomposed, leaving in the land their negative form, which he used as a "matrix". Fast-setting chalk was poured to reproduce the entire "mould".

The casts bear witness to the final agony of the Pompeians: the House of the Cryptoportico revealed a family caught late in the garden with a mother attempting to protect her daughter; in Regio I, a husband attempted to protect his pregnant wife with his body and a slave with the link of the chain on his foot that kept him tied. The most ancient excavations also revealed a swaddling baby and a crouching man protecting his face with his hands against the volcanic ash.

The Home

The Pompeian home is an exemplification of the Roman home in the Republican and early Imperial ages (I century B.C.-I century A.D.). Subsequent

evolution is exemplified, on the other hand, by the buildings in Ostia.

Homes are characterised by almost total closure towards the exterior. All light came through the interior courtyards. These homes had a first floor (*coenacula*), at times with balconies and foreparts jutting into the street (*maeniana*).

The first room at the entrance (*atrium*) was a large environment with a roof having a central aperture (*compluvium*). Rainwater fell into a basin below (*impluvium*) and flowed hence to a tank to supply houseshold needs. The roof of the atrium was supported by four columns (*atrium tetrastylum*) or by wooden beams (*atrium tuscanicum*). There was also a colonnade atrium, known as the Corinthium atrium (*atrium corinthium*). The atrium displayed the safe (*arca*) with the family treasure, the small temple (*lararium*) with portraits of forebears (*imagines maiorum*) and statues of the family's household gods (*lares familiares*).

The atrium was surrounded by small and dark bedrooms (*cubicula*). The presence of the bed is often indicated by a niche or a variation in the pattern of the mosaic, like a mat beside the beds.

The Romans ate reclining, so that the dining room (*triclinium*) had beds arranged in horseshoe fashion around the table. The servants served food on trays from the open side. In Summer, meals were taken in open-air tricliniums, placed beneath arbours or close to bubbling fountains.

The axis of the atrium led to the lounge (*tablinum*), where the owners welcomed guests.

There was no precise location for various utilities. They were usually placed near the peristyle, more rarely to the side of the atrium. The kitchen has a brick cooking top where a fire could be lit; a cavity underneath was used at times to store coal and wood. The latrine stood adjacent to and sometimes even inside the kitchen.

The garden (*peristylium*) was the green lounge of the home, adorned with flower beds, fountains, basins and statues spouting water. Between the columns in the portico (*intercolumnia*) there hung masks or discs of marble decorated with Dionysian figures (*oscilla*), that fluttered in the wind.

Pompeian painting

Pompeian paintings were based on the fresco technique, exactly as prescribed by Vitruvius in his *Architectura*. The standard paints are mostly coloured earths. Red and yellow are ochre, green was prepared from a "green earth"; white is calcium carbonate prepared from chalk; sky blue (*coeruleum*) is an artificial blend; black (*atramentum*) is made from glutin mixed with coal or burnt wine lees. The most common colour was red, famed as "Pompeian red"; for interiors it was made from cinnabar and, for exteriors, from earths rich in iron oxides.

Painters included the "maestro-designer", background painters (*parietarii*), figure painters (*imaginarii*) and workshop assistants.

It was German archaeologist August Mau (1840-1909) who first identified four decorative modes in Pompeii in wall decorations, now known as the "four Pompeian styles". They were studied and identified in Pompeii but in reality they were used all over the Roman world.

The "first style", that lasted from II century B.C. to about 80 B.C. (Samnitic age), is also known as the "structural style" since it imitates with simple cladding in painted stucco, that is with relatively modest means, the structure of the palaces of Hellenist monarchs involving expensive blocks of marble.

The "second style", that developed between 80 and 20-15 B.C. (Republican age), is also known as the "architectural style". The introduction of perspective, that completely disguised the actual walls of the room (*trompe-l'-oeil*), created the illusion that other, more sumptuous architectural spaces stood all around.

The "third" style, that developed in the Augustan age, saw decoration become flat and eliminated the illusion of other settings opening around the room. The painted wall was divided horizontally and vertically into three sections, as well as arranged in coloured squares and rectangles. In its later stages, the third style lost its elegance and became mannered, with obsessive filling with minute motifs in the "calligraphic" style. The third style also included Egyptian motifs, the expression of a fashion – "Egyptomania" – that was a phenomenon of Antiquity comparable with "*chinoiserie*" popular in the West in XVIII century.

The "fourth style", that developed between 45 and 79 A.D. (age of Claudius, Nero and Vespasian), is also known as the "fantastic style". This style was used to decorate the palaces of Nero (*Domus Aurea*) and Vespasian in Rome. The fourth style comprises panels set into perspective views with slender architecture. In short, this style saw the return of spatial illusion in walls with fantastic architec-

ture. For this reason, the fourth style was often associated with the fanciful and unbridled personality of Nero. The themes that appear in these paintings often narrate unhappy stories. Telling sad tales obviously had a moral intention, as in the contemporary literary works of Seneca.

The Forum

The *Forum* was the centre of the religious, political and economic life in the city and inasmuch was closed to traffic and no private buildings overlooked it. The square, always subject to town planning works and celebratory constructions, today emerges as the sum of various phases.

The square has a very elongated rectangular shape (143 × 38 m) that does not maintain the Vitruvian standard of 2:3 proportions that would have enabled the population better enjoy public events. This apparent anomaly may reflect a Greek tradition.

The north side was occupied by the Temple of Jupiter, that was converted into a *Capitolium*, set between two commemorative arches – as also appears in the relief of the *lararium* by C. Caecilius Jucundus – originally clad in marble and replete with fountains. The niches of the east arch had statues of Nero and Drusus, as suggested by a fragment of an inscription; the arch supported an equestrian statue. The other arch seen to the west was attributed to Tiberius.

The ancient tuff paving was replaced by new finishing with large slabs of travertine, sacked after the eruption together with the statues, some of which also equestrian, dedicated to imperial figures and illustrious Pompeians. The Curia stood

opposite the temple with administrative and political offices, such as the College of the Decurions, the Office of the Duumvirates and the Office of the *Ediles*. The long sides were home, on the east side, to the electoral seat (*Comitium*), the market (*Macellum*) and the buildings for imperial cults ("Eumachia Building", "Temple of Vespasian" and "Temple of the Public Gods"); the west side, on the other hand, had the Weights and Measures Office (*Mensa Ponderaria*), the Granaries, the Latrine and the Prison.

The Temple of Apollo

The Temple of Apollo was one of the most ancient temples in the city. Finds of Greek and Etruscan

pottery by Amedeo Maiuri using stratigraphic assays on the west side of the podium indicate that the cult was practised since VI century B.C.

By II century B.C., it was the most important place of worship in the city. The temple, in the Italic style, stands on a high podium. It was surrounded on three sides by a portico with Ionic tuff columns. In the Augustan age, nine apertures on the side facing the Forum were enclosed. The columns were stuccoed and converted into the Corinthian style after the earthquake in 62 A.D.

The portico held bronze statues of Apollo the Archer and his sister Artemis (the originals are in the National Archaeological Museum in Naples). The first base after the entrance has an inscription engraved in Oscan with the name of Consul Lucius Mummius, who in 146 B.C. defeated Corinth and subjected Greece. One cannot inasmuch exclude that some of the statues that decorated the portico came from his booty and arrived in Pompeii through auction sales.

The portico was decorated at the time of the fourth style with Nilotic friezes and scenes of the Trojan War, such as "Achilles and Agamemnon" and "Hector aided by Athena", as attested by 1800s documentation.

In front of the temple there stood a column with a clock (*meridiana*), an allusion to the solar nature of Apollo, and an altar of the Republican age (little after 80 B.C.), with a dedication in Latin by the quattuorviriums. One of these, Marcus Porcius, was a supporter of Sulla; two others, of the *gens Cornelia*, were relatives of Sulla. Inasmuch, they were representatives of the first colonial aristocracy (*homines novi*).

The threshold of the cell has a copy of an inscription in Oscan, with bronze lettering, today in the Naples Museum: "The quaestor Oppius Campanus ... promoted the building ..., approved by the assembly, with money offered to Apollo". The cell, decorated with perspective cube mosaics (*scutulatum*), housed the statue of the god, never found again, and an *ómphalos* in stone, symbol of the umbilicus of the world venerated in the Sanctuary of Apollo at Delphi.

The Basilica

The Basilica was a gigantic building with three naves (55 × 24 m) with the entrance on the southwest side of the Forum. It dates to II century B.C. (130-120 B.C.) and is the most ancient example of this architectural style common throughout the Roman world.

The broad entrance vestibule (*chalcidicum*) was probably used for public announcements.

The interior was made up of an enormous square with a roof supported by 28 brick columns, at least 11 metres high, forming three naves. The wall decoration in the interior involved large slabs of painted stucco imitating large blocks of multi-colour marble (first Pompeian style). The walls support semicolumns in stucco with two orders: Ionic below and Corinthian above. The upper floor was connected with the second floor of the portico in the Forum. The rear of interior was home to the imposing, austere facade of the *tribunal*. The seat (*sella curulis*) of judges administering justice stood on a podium about 2 metres high; the base in front of it had a bronze equestrian statue. Access by magistrates and defendants was by a wooden staircase that was then immediately removed to avoid riots between family relatives and the accused. The building was therefore used both as a tribunal and as an indoor forum. In this way, when bad weather affected the main Forum, the Pompeians could withdraw to the Basilica to continue their business.

The Eumachia Building

The Eumachia Building (VII 9, 1) was a large wholesale market for fabrics near the Forum. It was built little after 22 A.D. by Eumachia, priestess of Venus, who inherited a major wool business on the death of her husband. An inscription on the architrave of the portico reads: "*Eumachia, daughter of Lucius, public priestess* (of Venus) *built at her own expense, in her own name and that of her son Marcus Numistrius Fronto, the vestibule, the inside gallery and the porticos and dedicated them to the Concordia Augusta and to Pietas*". The building was a kind of commercial centre where decoration was intended to exalt the imperial family that, through its efforts, ensured the well-being of traders. The facade had statues of Aeneas, Romolus, Caesar and Augustus with respective *elogia* engraved on slabs of slate. The entrance portal was decorated by a stupendous cornice in marble with garlands of acanthus, birds, insects and various small animals, intentionally recalling the decorations of the Ara Pacis in Rome.

On the right of the entrance there was a small room with a jar perhaps used as a latrine, rich in ammonia, and therefore used to bleach fabrics. These fabrics were sold on stalls set up around the central courtyard, while the corridor with rear windows was used as a storeroom. The apse at the base had a statue of the Concordia Augusta with the face of Livia. The corporation of cloth washers and dyers (*fullones*), that nominated Eumachia as their patron, dedicated a statue to her at the rear of the apse; today, a chalk copy is exhibited, whereas the original is in the National Archaeological Museum of Naples.

The House of the Faun

The House of the Faun (VI 12, 2) was one of the largest and finest in Pompeii. Its area of about 3,000 square metres occupied an entire town

Opposite page: statue
of Apollo citharist, House
of the Citharist, Pompeii.
Naples, National
Archaeological Museum.

block. It was excavated in 1830-1832 and named the House of Goethe, in honour of August von Goethe, son of the famous poet, while the modern name derives from a statuette of a faun in bronze, dancing and perhaps playing a double flute, in the centre of the *impluvium*.

It was built in the Samnitic age (III-II century B.C.) The facade was in the first style with mock masonry blocks. The mosaic in the entrance had a short inscription to welcome guests: "*have*", "welcome!". The entrance corridor (*fauces*) is overlooked by two small temples in stucco with four small Corinthian columns standing on pedestals in red porphyry. The decoration of this house is one of the most important examples of the so-called first Pompeian style.

The numerous figurative mosaics, with tiny tesserae measuring only about three-five millimetres per side – today in the National Archaeological Museum of Naples – bear witness to the refined culture of the owners.

In 1831, the floor of the exedra opening out on to the first peristyle revealed an enormous mosaic (5.82 × 3.13 metres). The mosaic represents the decisive battle between Alexander the Great and Darius III of Persia at Gaugamela (331 B.C.), although it is also traditionally identified with the battle of Issos (333 B.C.).

Around the second *atrium* there was a services quarter with cabinets, jar stores, utilities in terracotta and safes. This area, evidently a stable, revealed the skeletons of four people and two oxen. It was used as a *latrina*, while in others the *suspensurae* and the interstices indicate a heating function; it was the kitchen oven and also heated the bathroom. The *triclinium*, underneath the flooring, has some rooms of a III century B.C. home brought to light by stratigraphic excavations performed in 1961-1965 by German archaeologists.

The House of the Vettii

The House of the Vettii (VI 15, 1) illustrates the level of luxury achieved by the rich merchant middle classes in Pompeii by I century A.D. In the entrance, there was a painted *Priapus* which, its penis on the dish of a set of scales using a bag of coins as a counterweight, seemed to say: "It's worth its weight in gold!".

The atrium without columns ("Tuscanic" type) had two wooden arches with the family treasures. The tablinum was suppressed to make more room for the garden, overlooked on the other hand by three large rooms set up as picture galleries.

The "Ixion Room" had architectural decoration with paintings of unhappy love. These depicted the loves of *Pasiphae*, wife of *Minos* and Queen of Crete, for a fine bull, that in reality was Zeus. The Queen had *Daidalos* build a wooden cow, which the artist is showing to her in the painting, where she would hide for amorous encounters. This bestial union gave birth to the Minotaur, the monster half-man, half-bull.

Ixion's painting depicts the punishment of the young man for his passion for Hera. Inasmuch, husband Zeus tricked him by sending him a cloud resembling the goddess who seduced him; moreover, he was also punished for his bad intentions by being bound to a wheel that never stopped moving.

The last painting narrates the abandonment of Ariadne on the island of Naxos by Theseus. The Athenian prince, who escaped from the Labyrinth after killing the Minotaur thanks to the expedient of the red thread devised by Ariadne, promised to take the young girl to Athens as his bride. However, when Theseus arrived in Naxos he abondoned her. The story in any case had a happy ending, since – despite being cast off by a prince – the young girl later married a god, Dionysus, who in fact also appears in the painting.

The "Room of Penteus" had three episodes of the Theban saga: the "Torment of Dirces", the "Torment of Penteus" and "Hercules as a young boy strangling the snakes". The depiction of the torment of Dirces found its maximum expression in the "Farnese Bull", today in the National Museum of Naples, a masterpiece already famous in ancient times as the work of sculptors Apollonios and Tauriscos of Rhodes. The painting depicts Queen Dirces bound by her stepsons Anfion and Zetos to a bull to drag her to the top of Mount Citeron, in Beotia, as punishment for mistreating them and their legitimate mother, Antiope. After this, Anfion and Zetos founded Thebes and its walls with seven gates built thanks to the magical music of Anfion, whose lyre-playing could even make stones dance. The painting with Penteus shows the Theban king stoned by Bacchants, including his wife, since he had banned the orgiastic cults of Dionysos in Thebes. The same theme was the subject of Euripides' famous tragedy, the "Bacchants".

The painting with Hercules shows the hero, only eight months old, strangling the snakes sent out of jealousy by Juno, since he was born of the union between Zeus (symbolised by the eagle) and Alcmena, fleeing in fear behind her husband Amphtryon.

The decoration of the *triclinium* was without doubt among the finest in all Pompeii. The walls, in the fourth style, had red panels divided by decorated bands on a black base. The centre of the panels had pairs of Bacchants and flying heroes (Paris, Theseus, Hippolyte). The *predella* had paintings of long friezes on a black base with cupids, in the company of *Psichai*, depicted as florists, perfumers, couriers, goldsmiths, dyers, bakers and vintners. The inserts underneath the perspective views depicted scenes from Greek myths, such as the contest between *Apollon* and *Python* for supremacy over the sanctuary of Delphi; Orestes and Pilades in Tauris; Agamemnon, Iphigenia and the hind of Diana.

The kitchen had an erotic annex where the man of the house took his female slaves. The most enchanting part of this rich mansion was the garden, laid out as a green lounge. Surrounded by a peristyle, it was arranged with flower beds adorned by bronze and marble statues.

The Stabian Baths

The Stabian Baths (VII 1, 8) were the oldest in the city. The name derives from the disposition of the building at the crossroads between the Street of Plenty and the Stabian Street. Built in II century B.C., they were extended after the arrival of the Roman colony, renovated in the Imperial age and restored after the earthquake in 62 A.D. When the eruption took place, restoration work was still underway and inasmuch the baths were never properly used.

The main entrance on the Street of Plenty gave access to the gymnasium, surrounded by a colonnade portico; this had an outside pool (*natatio*) preceded by a huge area used as changing rooms and a hall for personal washing (*destrictarium*). The external facade of rooms and was decorated with paintings and stuccos in the fourth style, today almost entirely vanished but known from water-colour engravings of XIX century; one of these has an aedicule depicting a Satyr offering wine to Hercules, who is already rather drunk.

A chamber was interpreted as the room of the administrator (*balneator*), while another room was the *sferisterium* for ball games. Behind these two rooms there were small chambers for individual bathing,

perhaps left over from the older baths dating back to IV century B.C.

The baths were divided into male and female sections, separated by a single heating system (*praefurnium*). Each section was divided sequentially into *frigidarium*, *tepidarium* and *calidarium*. These rooms were inside large barrel vaults, decorated with painted stuccos.

Access to the male sector was through an elegant chamber on the right of the main entrance. It is still roofed today by a barrel vault faced with stuccos, medallions and octagons containing figures of nymphas, erotic figures (erots) and tritons, all elements associated with water. This gave access to the *frigidarium* that given its circular shape must originally have been a sauna (*laconicum*) and to the changing rooms (*apodyterium*). The *frigidarium*, today almost entirely vanished, was actually superbly decorated with a starry dome and river gods set into large windows overlooking the gardens. The changing rooms (*apodyterium*) had a long bench with niches for stowing clothes. Bathers then moved to the *tepidarium* and the *calidarium* to complete their visit. Their ruined status, following the earthquake in 62 A.D., provides a better understanding of how heat circulated in the gap in the walls and under the raised floor.

The female sector, smaller but better preserved, was accessed from a corridor on Stabian Street and another corridor on Vicolo del Lupanare. The latter entrance had the wording in black "*Mulier*" that is "Women".

The Theatre

The Theatre of Pompeii could host about 5,000 spectators. It was built as early as the Samnitic age, II century B.C., but was renovated many times. It current design dates from renovation in the Augustan age thanks to the munificence of Marcus Holconius Rufus and Marcus Holconius Celer. We even know from a rare inscription the name of the architect "*Marcus Artorius M. l. Primus architectus*".

The interior, underneath the curved cornice of the building, had drilled blocks housing the poles that supported a sun-blind (*velarium*), operated using ropes

and winches. The seats for spectators were in the *cavea*; the wider seats at the bottom (*ima cavea*) had comfortable chairs (*bisellia*) for important personalities. For example, in the last row of the *ima cavea*, the place of the *bisellium* of Marcus Holconius Rufus was marked by an inscription in bronze letters "*To Marcus Holconius Rufus, son of Marcus, duovirium with jurisdictional powers for the fifth time and for five years for the second, military tribune by popular vote, flamen of Augustus, patron of the colony, by decree of the decurions*". Two circle boxes (*tribunalia*) at the side of the stage, that is above the orchestra entrances (*vomitoria*), were also reserved for major figures.

The stage had an architectural facade with three doors and two storeys, imitating Hellenistic royal palaces. The area, marked by an apsidal niche in the centre and two rectangular niches at the sides, was clad with slabs of marble and decorated with columns and statues. Behind the stage, the *postscaenium* had changing rooms for the actors. The chorus danced and sang in the orchestra pit.

During the intervals, the audience met in the large square portico behind the stage, known as the "Gladiator Barracks" because it was used for this purpose in the last years of the city. Here, last century, processional garments were found with gold embroidery and the bronze weapons of the gladiators: fifteen helmets, fourteen greaves, four belts, sword hilts and a shield; moreover, a group of eighteen skeletons found here included a bejewelled lady perhaps visiting a young hero. Iron clamps were also found, used to immobilise the ankles of reclined slaves.

The Amphitheatre

The amphitheatre of Pompeii is the most ancient of those known in the Roman world. It was built after the foundation of the colony (80 B.C.) on the initiative of the duoviriums Caius Quintius Valgus and Marcus Porcius, who also commissioned the *Odeion*. After the earthquake, it was restored by duoviriums Caius Cuspius Pansa, father and son. It was built in a peripheral site to avoid blocking city traffic during performances. The monumental external staircases provided access to the "cavea" where there were seats for spectators. It could welcome up to 20,000 spectators. Most of the terraced seats and the upper gallery, reserved for women, are still extant. The gladiator fights, known as *ludi*, were held in the arena.

Cheering for these performances also often broke out into bloody riots, as in 59 A.D. between Pompeians and Nocerins: dozens of Nocerins were killed and, following the disorders, the Rome Senate decreed "disqualification" for ten years from the Pompeii arena. This decision was withdrawn in 62 A.D., following the earthquake that devastated all citizens. The event was depicted in a famous Pompeian painting, today in Naples Museum. The painter captured, with the freshness of popular reporting, the games building with a bird's-eye view to include all exterior and interior details. The painting thus depicts the tondo of the amphitheatre with the external facade, comprising arches and two high ramps, the *velarium* that shaded spectators from the sun and the rioting supporters outside and inside the arena.

The Villa of Mysteries

The Villa of Mysteries was excavated in the early XX century and has become the most famous building in Pompeii. The first building dates to II century B.C., but subsequently underwent many renovation projects. The period of greatest splendour lasted from the foundation of the Roman colony to the Augustan age. In early I century B.C. it was decorated in the fashion of the "second style". A majestic frieze was painted in the main hall with almost life-size figures ("megalography"). The building is a four-sided block standing on a square cryptortic forming the base (*basis villae*); it stood on a slope and the terrace offered a view of the gulf. The entrance, on the east side, was exactly opposite the present access.

The first part was the production sector, with a handling courtyard giving access on the one hand to the wine cell and, on the other, to the kitchens. The large cellar had two presses, one of which was in wood with a carved head of a goat, the sacred animal of Dionysos, the god of wine. The wine, squeezed with these presses and left to ferment in jars in the garden, was then stored in amphora.

This was followed by the noble area where the owner and his family lived, with bedrooms, dining rooms, lounges and a panoramic, semi-circular terrace.

In the hall adjacent to a bedroom, the owners commissioned the famous "megalography" paintings depicting the "mysteries" used to name the complex, with the initiation of a young girl to the mysteries of marriage in accordance with the precepts of the cult of Dionysos.

The frieze shows an older lady taking part in the ceremony and making sure that everything is perfect. The small Dionysos, accompanied by two priestesses, sings a hymn written on a scroll of papyrus. In the meantime, others are preparing gifts, such as country cake, holy water for ablutions and an olive branch for asperges. Silenus plays the lyre, while two small satyrs accompany him with Pan pipes. Aura descends from the sky wearing a wind-blown cloak. Aside in a corner are the old Papposilen and two small satyrs: the young man sees the mask at his shoulders reflected in the water of a goblet and thus understands what he will be like when old. In the middle Dionysus supervises the scene, drunk, lain in the lap of Arianna or Venus, the patron goddess of the city.

At their side, the priestesses make ready to reveal a large wooden phallus placed in a country basket. The young girl initiate seeks refuge in the lap of a priestess, while she is whipped by a winged god; by withstanding the pain she will show that she is by now an adult and ready to be married. Alongside, her companions dance and play tambourines in the hope of distracting her and alleviating her pain. On passing the test, the young girl makes ready for the wedding ceremony; a maid is doing her hair, while an erot expressly sent by Venus offers her a mirror.

Mozart in Pompeii: "I saw neither scorpions nor spiders!"

The excavations of the Temple of Isis, 1700s gouache by Pietro Fabris.

In the "Magic Flute", Mozart included on stage the choir of the initiates of the cult of Isis. Mozart and Schikaneder, his librettist, were especially inspired by an article by Ignaz von Born about Egyptian mysteries, published in 1784 in "Mason's Journal", and by a novel by Jean Terrasson about the initiation of Prince Sethos ... yet did Mozart ever visit a temple of Isis, ever climb the staircases, see the statues, priests, snakes, musical instruments and paintings? ... yes, in Pompeii. In May 1770, Wolfgang was 14 and travelling with his father Leopold to Naples. They had already visited Verona, Mantua, Milan and Rome. Leopold wrote to his wife: "... *the streets of Naples have been unsafe for two weeks. The brigands killed a merchant. Soldiers were sent from Rome and there was a full-scale battle. It seems that the brigands withdrew to the borders of the Kingdom and, if what people say is true – that they also killed a courier of the King travelling to Spain – then Naples will use all its power to exterminate them. In any case, I will not move from here until I know for sure that the situation has settled ...*". The young Wolfgang added in this letter a reassurance for his mother: "*I have seen neither scorpions nor spiders*". Poor Mozart, how he must have been excited in his imagination by brigands and scorpions!

They reached Naples on the evening of the 14th. He wrote shortly after to his sister Marianne, who had remained with their mother in Salzburg: "*Naples is very attractive but as noisy as Vienna and Paris; I think it is even more undisciplined than London*".

On the 16th, Leopold wrote to his wife: "*We are determined to see everything. On the 13th, St. Anthony's day, we left by coach for Pozzuoli at five in the morning. We arrived just before seven and took a carriage to the Bay of Nero's Baths, the grottos of the Cumaean Sibyl, Lake Averno, the Temple of Venus, the Temple of Diana, the Tomb of Agrippina, the Elysian Fields, the Dead Sea with Charon, the 'Piscina Mirabile' and the Centocamerelle. On our return, we saw Monte Nuovo, Monte Gauro, the port of Pozzuoli, the Colosseum, the Solfatara, the Astroni, the Grotto of the Dog and Lake Agnano, and the grotto of Pozzuoli with Virgil's tomb; just imagine, it took eight minutes to walk all along it! Today we lunched at Certosa di San Martino; we enjoyed the landscape and tasted all the specialities of the place. From Monday, we will visit Vesuvius, Pompeii and Herculaneum (the cities they are now excavating) with their finds, Caserta and Capodimonte ... In order to see all these marvels we also have to carry a torch with us, since many things are underground ...*".

Seventeen years later, another illustrious German visitor, Johann Wolfgang Goethe, described these underground visits to ancient Herculaneum by torch light (*Travelling in Italy*, 18 March 1787).

On 18 and 20 May, Leopold and Wolfgang visited The Royal Palace at Portici, where the King's Art Collection and the finds from Pompeii and Herculaneum were jealously housed prior to being transferred to the present-day National Museum.

On 19 May, Leopold wrote to his wife Marianne: "… *yesterday we went to Portici to present ourselves to Marquis Tanucci* (the Borbon prime minister). *It rained a lot and the air was fresh. We had to wear our splendid summer clothes with gallons. Wolfgang's is pink mohair, known in Italy as the colour of fire, with a sky blue lining and silver embroidery. Mine is cinnamon … with silver embroidery and an apple green lining. They are two fine outfits that in any case will resemble two old spinsters when we return home to you*".

In the evening, wearing the same clothes, they visited the Hamiltons, in Palazzo Sessa in Via Cappella Vecchia, where they met the flower of Neapolitan culture. Leopold: "*Yesterday evening we visited the English ambassador Hamilton, who we had already met in London. His wife* (the first, Catherine Barlow, 1747-1782) *is a delightful person and plays the piano wonderfully well; she trembled for having to play in front of Wolfgang*". Thanks to the description of these garments, it was possible to recognise the Mozarts in a painting depicting them in Naples at another concert, at the House of Lord Fortrose.

When Leopold at the end of June had to think of returning home, he was actually rather reluctant to do so. He had learned to love the life of Naples, despite acknowledging its negative aspects: "*… the crowd of beggars, a repellent common people forgotten by God, the bad manners of the children, the incredible lack of discipline even in church …*". This was how he wrote to his wife on 9 June, announcing their departure on the 20th. Wolfgang was also very happy: "*I am lively and happy as ever. I love travelling. I have even seen the Mediterranean. A kiss for mother and a thousand kisses for Nannerl!*".

… yet we are going back to Pompeii. The Mozarts arrived there by coach, travelling along the Via Regia delle Calabrie (the present-day Naples-Portici-Pompeii national road). Access to the excavations at the time was through the Great Theatre. We are informed about what Leopold and Wolfgang may have seen in 1770 by the first guide to the excavations, by Frenchman François Latapie, written just six years later. The guide, in short, has a ground plan showing the buildings that were then visible. One of the most important was the Temple of Isis, excavated only five years prior to the arrival of the Mozarts. They initially passed through the large courtyard surrounded by the porticos behind the Theatre, that in the last years of the city was converted from a *foyer* into the "Gladiator Barracks". Here, they were told about the finds of the helmets and armour they had just seen in the Portici Royal Palace. The guides gleefully told them about the discovery, three years earlier, of the skeleton of a lady with splendid jewels, a lover furtively visiting her hero of the arena!

From the theatre, where only the upper steps had been excavated, the Mozarts would have enjoyed the view over the sea before moving on to the Greek temple. Latapie later describes the Temple of Isis, excavated between 1764 and 1766, as "*… a small building, but also one of the best preserved of the city*".

Mozart composed "The Magic Flute" 21 years later, in 1791. The traditional scenario for the opera, wherever it is performed – be it Berlin, Paris, La Scala in Milan or San Carlo in Naples itself – seems as if fixed in a stereotype, resembling a painting from Herculaneum that Mozart also saw in the Portici Royal Palace: the great priest of Isis in a tunic at the top of the staircase of the Temple amidst sphinxes, showing the faithful a gold vase with the holy water of the Nile; below, a huge choir of initiates, with shaven heads, makes sacrifice and sings hymns to the divinity; all around, in the garden of the sanctuary, Egyptian plants and birds.

How much of what Mozart saw in Portici and Pompeii, accompanied by the tales of the guides, was fixed in his young, imaginative mind? Is it possible that the fairy-tale character of the opera, its youthful joy and trust in humanity, reflect the impressions he gained in Naples?

Roman fresco (I century A.D.) from Herculaneum, with the Temple of Isis.

ERCOLANO

*Map of the city
(after M. Pagano-U. Pastore).*

*Opposite page:
Suburban Baths, atrium.*

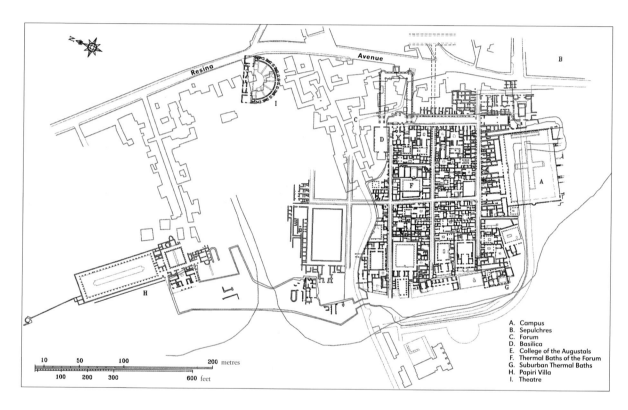

A. Campus
B. Sepulchres
C. Forum
D. Basilica
E. College of the Augustals
F. Thermal Baths of the Forum
G. Suburban Thermal Baths
H. Papiri Villa
I. Theatre

"Immediately after Neapolis there is the fortress of Herculaneum, standing on a promontory stretching out into the sea blown by the Libeccio wind that makes the place more healthy".

Strabo, *Geographia* V 4, 8

Herculaneum in Antiquity was a small coastal city in Campania almost half-way along the coast road linking *Neapolis* and *Pompeii* and the much more important cities of *Nuceria*, *Stabiae* and *Surrentum*. The city stood on a rise about 12 high metres overlooking the sea and its small port enjoyed the natural anchorages provided by two river inlets mentioned by Sisenna (4 fr. 53), an historian of I century B.C.: *"a fortified city with mod-* *est walls on a promontory rising from the sea between two streams"*.

Unlike Pompeii, Herculaneum seems to have been a more peaceful town, especially devoted to sailing and fishing, as shown by the large quantity of nets, hooks, ropes and sailors' tools and recently also by the find of two boats. At least in the part so far excavated, there were no deep grooves left by waggons in the large basalt slabs of the roads

View of the "Sacellum" of the Augustals.

by intense and noisy traffic, as poets complained even in Antiquity. These hints and the generally more original character of decorations and architecture give the impression of a more lordly and refined city.

Herculaneum – even in the vicissitudes of excavation – especially boasts its private buildings and their large variety of shapes and types. The home in Herculaneum seems to be freer and more evolved, that is more inclined towards new designs than in Pompeii. Although Pompeii saw the kind of old patrician home, designed in accordance with the old outlines for Italic residences, gradually become more fragmented, after the earthquake in 62 A.D., into merchant and rented houses, with consequent development of the upper storeys tending to gain in height what they could not achieve in terms of surface area, in Herculaneum this "modernisation" process of the Italic and Hellenistic home seems to have been more rapid, per-

haps because of the influence that a city as large as *Neapolis* exerted on its neighbours.

Inasmuch, Herculaneum still had Samnitic homes, that in the Roman age stood boldly on another storey above the peak of the compluvial roof (House of Tramezzo di Legno); homes of the merchant class that abandoned any link with the conventional outlines of Italic homes, replacing the atrium with the well-lit and well-ventilated courtyard of modern homes and the original single *domus* with several unrelated tenants; noble homes, but with complete transformation of the portico of the Hellenistic home into enclosed porticos with large windows like huge corridors; and, lastly, the large block in the eastern quarter (*Insula orientalis II*), already reflecting the type of home of the Imperial age with several quarters and several storeys as in Ostia.

Moving progressively into the heart of the city towards the Forum, homes in Herculaneum gained new designs that increasingly reflected the classes, life-style and customs of its citizens. In a city that did not suffer like Pompeii from the levelling current of industry and commerce, the contrast between rich, lordly homes and popular housing is stronger and deeper than in Pompeii. A single "block" (*insula*) often sees two or three rich and large homes occupy most of the area, while the rest are modest houses set into narrow sites with several upper stories; at times, associated as they are with workshops, they manage – depending on the changing fortunes of the owner – to insinuate and expand themselves between different buildings to the detriment of pre-existing noble residences.

The city, standing as it did close to the sea, was designed to enjoy the view; inasmuch, many of the finest mansions of the upper classes in Herculaneum were especially built to look out over the enchanting panorama of the gulf, as shown by their disposition along the edge of the promontory and the use in their interiors of typical elements of villa architecture, such as verandas, terraces with siesta rooms (*diaetae*) and belvederes overlooking the gulf (House of the Mosaic Atrium, House of the Deer, House of the Gem, House of the Relief of Telefos). For example, in the form in which it has come down to us, the House of the Mosaic Atrium involves the juxtaposition of a home with an atrium and one with a terrace; in short, it has three quarters distinguished by their structures and decorations: the atrium quarter, the viridarium quarter and the terrace quarter.

The House of the Deer also emphasised the development of the part enjoying the view over the sea. This explains the modest entrance, that was merely "utilitarian": a small staircase leads to the upper floor with a gallery for the servants, a winding corridor leads to the services quarter (kitchen, latrine and cupboards), while the triclinium is entered from the front and the garden from the left. The triclinium, enjoying a free view over the sea, resembles a reception hall, with floors with marble inlays and austere paintings on a black base as shiny as basalt. The cryptoportico, built for strolling in the shade, was designed as an art gallery with sixty paintings depicting cupids and still lifes (of these, twelve are still on site and eighteen in the Naples National Museum). The sculptures – the satyr with a wineskin, Hercules drunk, the marble goblet and two deer attacked by hunt-

ing dogs (now being set-up in the Museum) – come from the garden, where they were on show amidst the flower beds. The entrance to the garden is surmounted by a fronton in paste glass with the head of Ocean in the centre and a frieze with cupids on tritons on the sides. The garden had a table with lion paws and Baroque capital with marbles inlay on slate, perhaps from an aedicule since destroyed. There was a summer triclinium in the centre of the garden that was originally roofed. The terrace (*solarium*) has two rest rooms (*diaetae*) opening on to a pergola with flower vases.

These were sumptuous homes, furnished with precious multi-colour inlay floors (*opus sectile*) made from highly-prized Oriental and African marbles, fine painted decorations and works of art. Homes such as the House of the Relief of Telefos, with a panoramic lounge clad with marble, are striking in their decorative luxury and the "luxury" of the architectural design.

Fresco with Hercules, Nexus and Deianira, Sacellum of the Augustals.

Alongside these noble mansions, Herculaneum has also revealed more humble homes, built for modest families of craftsmen and divided into small rental quarters; one example, the House of the Trellis, remains unsurpassed in the miraculous conservation of its poor building technique, wooden frame and trellis.

The better conservation of the upper floors and the survival of the ceiling and roof beams, the window frames, doors, staircases, partitions, beds and common utensils gives the house a sense of completeness not found in Pompeii. It was thereby often possible to re-position the sturdy support architraves and beams of the ceilings, refit and even use the ancient hinges of a door, climb to the upper floor of a home on the original steps of a small wooden staircase, today protected by slabs of glass.

Numerous finds of wooden artefacts – another exceptional characteristic of Herculaneum – with precious and rare examples of ancient furniture (beds, wardrobes, a cradle, etc.), as well as full-scale machinery in the workshops (a dyer's press, winches, fames, etc.), means that Herculaneum, much more than Pompeii, moves visitors with the humanity of this house and what suddenly appears of its furnishing in its most intimate corners.

Precisely the better forms of *urbanitas* in Herculaneum also mean that decorative painting here, in general, seems to be more accurate and refined than in Pompeii. Such painting was defined as "Pompeian" since it is traditionally linked with the name of Pompeii, yet it includes in reality the precious heritage of paintings discovered in three cities buried by the eruption in 79 A.D., and thus also those of Herculaneum and Stabia. This is an essentially craft phenomenon, but of considerable artistic quality, as demonstrated – in Herculaneum itself – by the megalographs of the Basilica. At the current status of excavations, paintings in the first and second style are rare, while decorations of the third and fourth style predominate, typically characterised by expensive colours such as sky blue.

The execution of ornamental details is very rich and accurate, that without doubt made these decorations much more expensive. The most common decorative motifs are curtains and embroidered fabrics. The most common subjects, on the other hand, are deer and does – as well as narrations of the feats of Hercules, the god considered to be the legendary founder of the city. Paintings in Herculaneum were based – as in Pompeii – on the fresco technique, exactly as prescribed by Vitruvius in his *Architectura*.

The first style in Herculaneum appears in the Samnitic House, the House of the Wooden Sacellum (V 31) and House IV 6. The second style is seen in the House of the Hotel, House IV 33 and the Villa of the Papyri. The finest examples of the third style are the decorations of the Caupona (House number IV 16), the House of the Carbonised Furniture, the House of the Large Gate, the House of the Tuscan Colonnade and the Gymnasium, where the painted walls in Hall III also have Egyptian motifs, the expression of a fashion – "Egyptomania. The fourth style, like the third, was also very common; the best examples are the decorations of the House of the Tramezzo di Legno, the House with the Mosaic Atrium, the House of the Deer, the House of the Carbonised Furniture, the *tablinum* in the House of the Bicentenary, the House of the Large Gate, the House of the Tuscan Colonnade and the apsidal hall of the Gymnasium (today in the Naples National Museum).

The Villa of the Papyri

Standing in a north-west suburb of the city, the Villa of the Papyri, already surveyed by tunnelling between 1750 and 1761, was partially excavated between 1996 and 1998. The villa, extending for 250 metres parallel to the coastline, has a residential quarter and a long garden with a pool and belvedere. The dimensions of the building are very impressive: a large peristyle 100 metres long by 37 metres wide, with 25 columns on the longer sides, and a pool 66 metres long.

The name derives from the finds of almost two thousand *rotuli* (scrolls) of carbonised papyrus, essentially written in Greek. Patiently unrolled and deciphered, they include Epicurean texts in Greek. They are conserved today at the International Centre for the Study of Herculaneum Papyri in the Naples National Library. The papyri were joined by splendid finds of mosaic floors, important fragments of frescoes and, especially, entire sculptural cycles in marble and bronze today in the National Archaeological Museum of Naples.

The owner was perhaps Lucius Calpurnius Piso Cesoninus, father-in-law of Caesar. He was an important figure, with a distinguished military and political career as a follower of Augustus; he was a

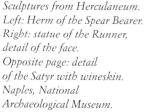

Sculptures from Herculaneum.
Left: Herm of the Spear Bearer.
Right: statue of the Runner,
detail of the face.
Opposite page: detail
of the Satyr with wineskin.
Naples, National
Archaeological Museum.

friend of literary figures and philosophers, who were frequently guests in his villa. He chose and exhibited numerous sculptures in accordance with a precise decorative plan. Herms were placed around the pool depicting Hellenistic monarchs and Greek literary figures. All around, statues of nymphs, does and satyrs accentuated, on the other hand, the demonic character of the garden. A statue of Athena, goddess of war and patron of culture, stood in the middle. The building was faithfully replicated in the United States by magnate John Paul Getty in his villa at Malibu.

Excavation in the 1990s highlighted the atrium area of the villa with a colonnade terrace overlooking the sea, where mosaic floors and pictorial decorations in the second style were found. The terrace in the north-west sector turned up a female head resembling the Greek amazons. Excavations have also highlighted, in the corner opposite this terrace, a female statue wearing a peplum (*pe-plophoros*) found more or less intact.

The presence of the second style suggests that it

was built between 60 and 40 B.C. The most important results emerging from the recent investigation have helped define the three-dimensional reality of the building. The conventional hypothesis suggested a villa standing on a slope overlooking the sea supported by a massive embankment. On the other hand, as many as four architectural levels adapted to the slope have emerged with an overall theatrical effect.

Recent excavations also revealed a large building with halls, embankments and a bath area identified as a *natatio calida* following the model of the suburban Baths. The colonnade courtyard revealed a small carbonised boat and the skeleton of a horse. Later, the rooms in the interior were excavated where a neo-Attic relief in Greek marble was found set into a painted wall. The scene has a nude satyr with a *pedum*, sitting on a rock, drinking from a small jar. Opposite him, a female figure is taking water from a leonine protome fountain in a *rhyton*. On the right, a small satyr with a nebris is pouring from a *oinochoe* into a goblet.

OPLONTS

Plan of the Villa of Poppea at Oplontis.

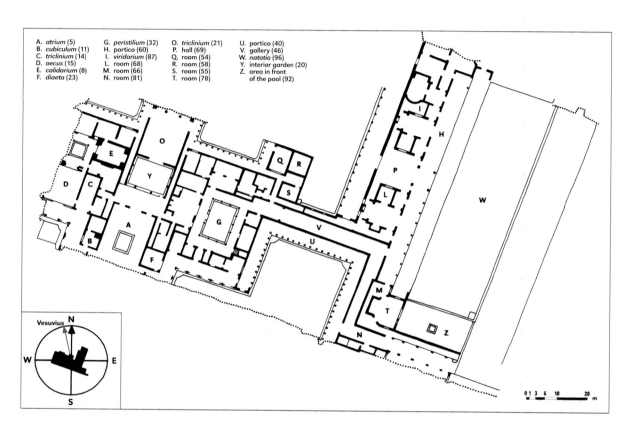

A. *atrium* (5) G. *peristilium* (32) O. *triclinium* (21) U. portico (40)
B. *cubiculum* (11) H. portico (60) P. hall (69) V. gallery (46)
C. *triclinium* (14) I. *viridarium* (87) Q. room (54) W. *natatio* (96)
D. *oecus* (15) L. room (68) R. room (58) Y. interior garden (20)
E. *calidarium* (8) M. room (66) S. room (55) Z. area in front
F. *diaeta* (23) N. room (81) T. room (78)   of the pool (92)

"Nero then married Poppea, who he loved more than all the others, yet he nevertheless also murdered her with kicks because, pregnant and ill, she had bitterly reproved him one evening for returning home late from a chariot race".
Svetonius, *The Lives of the Twelve Caesars*, Life of Nero VI 35

In the 1970s, excavations were conducted in ancient Oplontis, near Torre Annunziata, not far from Pompeii, in a huge villa with sumptuous decorations, that turned out to be that of Empress Poppea, wife of Nero.
Judging from the building technique and the decorations, it was built around mid-I century B.C. Already some decades beforehand, the Gulf of Naples, that Cicero nicknamed "*crater ille delica-*

tus", saw important property investments by the Roman aristocracy, with the creation of *otium* (leisure) villas, rustic villas, nurseries, baths, etc. These considerations, together with the exceptional dimensions of the villa, suggest that it was owned by a Roman and not a local figure, nor even the Samnitic aristocracy, by then expropriated of its assets by the creation of a colony in Pompeii by dictator Sulla in 80 B.C.

The villa is certainly an impressive monument: an area of 130 metres in length and 110 in width with 3650 square metres of inside areas (excluding pergolas, pools, gardens, etc.). The complex comprised two separate bodies: one to the west, the older built mid-I century B.C., with a structure inspired by the *domus* with an atrium; the other, to the east, of the age of Nero, focused around a *natatio*.

Not only the dimensions but especially the architectural principles applied in the composition of the building volumes and the green areas make this building one of the most significant known to

to the east of the *natatio*. A long avenue runs alongside the basin and is flanked on the east side by thirteen statue bases; a tree, probably a plane, grew behind each of these. This row of trees and statues formed an open gallery which could be seen in full against the background of the Lattari Mountains by guests strolling under the marble portico along the swimming pool. The sculptures disseminated in the area probably created a gymnasium setting, in complete assonance with the Hellenising trends of Roman culture.

The marvels of the garden of this quarter are by no means exhausted since the set-up of area 92 must

us from the Roman world. The exploration of the gardens, that accompanied excavations, showed that the two parts were inter-related, and the architect was undoubtedly also a *topiarius*, that is a designer of gardens. Nor should we overlook the function performed in this context by the sculptures, arranged in accordance with precise decorative intentions, and the garden paintings, mostly painted on the walls of the royal gardens to amplify the effects of illusion. The villa in short is an admirable fusion of every component in Roman architectural and decorative culture.

The most important garden was probably the one

also be mentioned; it was overlooked by the windows of the elegant *diaeta* 78, with walls in marquetry wood, from which the owner could show guests a fine marble basin-fountain made in Greece, decorated with figures of Pyrrhic dancers, neo-Attic *imitationes* of an original base today on show in the Acropolis, Athens. The more mischievous would have rather glanced at the sculptural group of the Satyr and the Hermaphrodite with their erotic play reflected in the water from the edge of the pool.

The Poppei Villa at *Oplontis* is a splendid example of a Roman *otium* and *luxuria* villa where all

View of the "atrium" of the Poppea Villa at Oplontis.

Rear partition of the "diaeta" (hall), Villa at Oplontis.

the elegance of architecture, garden art, painting and sculpture of the time were cleverly exploited for the leisure of the owners. It is sad to note that perhaps its greatest advantage is no longer evident today – the view of the sea and the mountains, lost for ever because of surrounding constructions.

The decoration in the second style of the atrium is one of the largest handed down to us. It transforms the royal environment into a sumptuous Hellenistic palace; the prospectus has three doors – as in theatrical settings (*scaenae frons*) – but the more southern gate is replaced by the royal en-trance. On a low black wainscot, the building is represented for about two thirds by the central part around the *impluvium*.

The central body has a podium interrupted by a medial opening flanked by columns, decorated with bosses and lightning bolts framed by rhomboids, and two small pillars. Here there is a staircase with a torchlight. At the top, there is a sumptuous door, the *valva regia* of theatrical scenery, decorated with bosses on cornices, banded squares in the lower panels and winged victories in the upper inserts. The door top is protected by a shelf with strips, denticular cornice and modil-

lions with the head of a gryphon. Above this, there is a painting with an architectural landscape.

At the sides of the door, there are two symmetrical niches with red-brown walls; inside, two shields are hung on each side with female heads in relief (*imagines clipeatae*). The flooring of the niches has two silver cists with gilt bronze covers and a crown embellished with gemstones. At the sides of the niches, there are two progressively foreshortened aedicules with Ionic columns on the front and strips on the edges. The base part, painted in cinnabar red, is enclosed at the top by two cornices on which a theatrical mask stands. The floor-

ing supports two silver incense burners with decorated bases crowned with a perforated globe.

On the right of the central body a significantly foreshortened depiction of one of the two lateral partitions of the building. Another door, similar to the previous one, opens on to a steps in front of which there is a tripod in gilt bronze with wild animal paws. On the sides of the staircase there are two wings with four Tuscanic columns in alabaster. The Doric epistyle has metopes with pateras alternating with bucrans. The iron beams placed between the columns have rows of typical golden Macedon shields with a star. The Tuscanic colon-

Rear partition of the "diaeta" (hall), detail.

plinth, a pink band and three courses of isodomic work. The median zone has uprights (orthostates) decorated with holy landscapes in monochrome yellow. At the top, there is a band of imitation marble, a red cornice with white trusses and modillions with stylised paws and, lastly, an upper area with slabs of multi-colour marble framing blue tiles with erotic figures (erots).

The hall as such is decorated, on the other hand, with complex architectural scenery with sanctuaries. A band with a black base supports a straight podium with mirror-like finishes in red-brown and green between bands of yellow frames. The building above stands on a green platform in turn supported by a slightly withdrawn yellow base on the podium. The central element is the *columnae caelatae* with a gilt drum decorated with flowering plants with red and blue buds and Ionic capitals with male heads. The jutting epistyle supports two white statues of protruding sphinxes. The chamber of the propileum opens on to a gate with a double wooden door with handles having leonine heads and a fretwork fronton with women and flowers; the red doors are surmounted by two golden gryphons, while a gilt shield with festoons hangs from the architrave.

Behind the gate and a low curtain wall, there is a *tholos* with a conical roof which houses a statue of a divinity wearing a diadem – Juno. Beyond the *tholos* there is the interior portico of the sanctuary. The sides of the central, slightly withdrawn *propylon* have two niches flanked by three columns in Numidian yellow marble with an arched roof. The niches reveal behind a lowered curtain a series of small Ionic pillars linked by iron bars. The span of the roofing arch is only embellished with a festoon of leaves, although *imagines clipeatae* are suspended from the architrave with busts of divinities: the one on the left is corroded, while the one on the right, on the other hand, has a bust of Vulcan-Haephestus, recognisable by the helmet and tongs. Between the central propileum and the side niches there are two short walls in brownish red against which lean two incense burners in gilt bronze with lion paws. The upper part, on the parapet, has two silver fountain basins. Other elements include a torchlight placed in front of the central gate and two multi-colour birds hopping on the base. The wall is enclosed at the top by a band, set between two jutting cornices and decorated with a frieze of weapons.

nade is followed by a short wing standing on a green base with a wall in cinnabar red, marked off by Corinthian corner strip and an Ionic epistyle. Lastly, on the north end of the wall, standing on a black wainscot, there is a white pillar that sets off the entire scene.

Some fragments, never re-positioned during restoration, indicate that the upper order of the wall was painted with architecture against a sky background. The paintings are accompanied by white mosaic flooring with a perspective meandering band around the impluvium.

In the triclinium, in keeping with a recurrent fashion, architectural, mosaic and pictorial decorations separate the royal quarters into an antechamber and an inner room; the painted wall is distinctly divided into two parts by a Corinthian strip with scrolls and gryphon heads near the mosaic threshold. The antechamber is decorated by an enclosed wall with a high wainscot comprising a black

The white mosaic floor has black perimeter strips; a multi-colour perspective meandering threshold marks the passage between the vestibule and the dining room, while perspective multi-colour rhomboid flooring was placed in the middle between the triclinium beds.

The *oecus*, unfortunately not yet completely excavated, has one of the finest and most evocative walls of the second style. The composition depicts a sanctuary of Apollo, marked off at the extremities by two strips. Alongside these, converging in perspective towards the centre, are two arms of a portico with red pillars enclosed at the bottom by balusters and freely open to the sky at the top; antelope skulls are hung from the pillars. Above the architrave there is a green isodomic wall with a shelf having "S-shaped" modillions supporting a row of shields.

The *propylon* as such stands at the back of these wings, comprising four Corinthian columns standing on two blocks of a podium with marble inserts of various colours. In the centre, between the podiums and the median columns, the second floor of the back partition has a gate with a door with Ionic strips surmounted by a round arch. The lower half has a small door with a partly open iron gate. Beyond this, one glimpses against the background of a lush garden, a high cylindrical based crowned by festoons of leaves in turn supporting a gigantic tripod in gilt bronze decorated on the rim with precious stones and a frieze of fret-worked stars. The lateral *intercolumni* of the *propylon* are enclosed in the lower part by a low wall; a large red architrave horizontally links the central arch and the lateral walls; behind there is an imposing portico with two storeys; the lower order is Tuscan and the upper order Ionic. This wall has numerous isolated decorative elements, alluding to the function of the complex. At the bottom, in front of the door to the sanctuary, a torchlight is lain on stones; on the podium, in the inter-column, there are two laurel branches, while two birds hop next to the bases of the central columns. The lateral *intercolumni* have two theatrical masks standing on trusses and next to these, placed on a lowered curtain, there are two majestic peacocks. Lastly, at the top between the lateral columns and the red architrave, there are two insets (*pinakes*) with foreshortened hatches, with marine or lake landscapes and buildings. The mosaic flooring of the same period comprises multi-colour marble flakes set in "basket" style.

Overview of the sculptural group depicting the Satyr and the Hermaphrodite, Villa at Oplontis. Opposite page: detail.

The sequence of small gardens, aligned with the interior of the rectangular body overlooking the *natatio*, is one of the most refined elements of imperial architecture progressively added to the main core of the villa dating from the Republican age. The play of perspective in the gardens linked with each other through broad axial windows is accentuated by gardens painted in the wall decorations. The enclosed walls, to the east and west, are also imagined as standing against pairs of windows painted within a red back partition. Above the wainscot, enlivened by bunches of flowering plants, the uprights of the windows are clad with ivy; in the light of the windows, against an unrealistically yellow background, there are views of the gardens with trees, shrubs and statue-fountains, such as the female centaur with a square basin offset by a companion with a circular basin, while the fountains in the adjacent panels have two sphinxes. The north wall has a neo-Attic marble basin with a huge winged monster in relief; a peacock poses superbly on its edge, while other birds flit between the branches of the central tree and between the shrubs to the side in the background.

The skilful dissimulation of the service passages is equally astonishing – as a continuation of the corridor so that the comings and goings of servants would not disturb the enjoyment of the delightful scene. In this regard, it must be mentioned that the graffiti on the walls of the villa are mostly in Greek, that demonstrates cultured servants, perhaps oriental, appropriate to the needs of a luxurious noble residence.

STABIA

"Stabia was a fortified city until 30 April 89, when, during the social war, commander Lucius Sulla destroyed it; since then, is has become merely a resort".

Pliny the Elder, *Naturalis Historia* III 9, 70

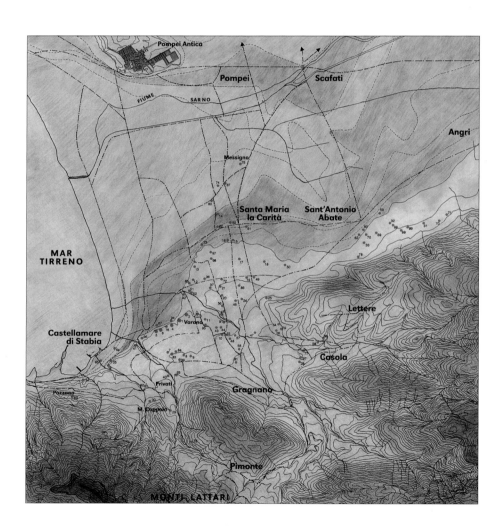

*Archaeological map
of Stabia.*

The city of Stabia extends on the southern border of the Gulf in an inlet at the feet of Monte Faito, 1,100 metres high. It is located mid-way between Vesuvius and the island of Capri, 5 km from Pompeii and 18 from Sorrento. The city was once one of the most important places in Campania, as a commercial centre, with a port and resorts. It was Oscan, Greek, Etruscan, Samnitic and ultimately Roman. Finds of tombs from the iron age document its antiquity. The name "Stabia", that must be Oscan, was connected with the Latin word *stabulum*, "stables".

The military port of Nocera against the Romans during the Sannitic Wars, the city was besieged and forced to capitulate in 308 B.C. In III century B.C., Rome, after defeating the Samnites, forced many cities in Campania to become its ally.

In the early I century B.C., the Italic allies – who suffered disproportionate oppression compared to the rights they enjoyed – demanded Roman citizenship. When all their petitions were rejected, they rebelled and the Social War began. Stabia was also involved. The outcome was that on 30 April 89 B.C. it was taken by Roman troops commanded by dictator Lucius Cornelius Sulla. The Romans, given the strategic position of its port, decided to raze it to the ground.

Archaeological testimony of the existence of an urban centre prior to 89 B.C. is provided by the find of a section of the Sannitic walls about 200 metres from the Villa of San Marco, as well as the discovery of homes decorated in the so-called "first Pompeian style" in the Bottoni estate. The city was subjected to Nocera and, having in any case lost its administrative autonomy, essentially became a mere resort, as mentioned by Pliny.

This saw the onset of a rapid process of Romanisa-

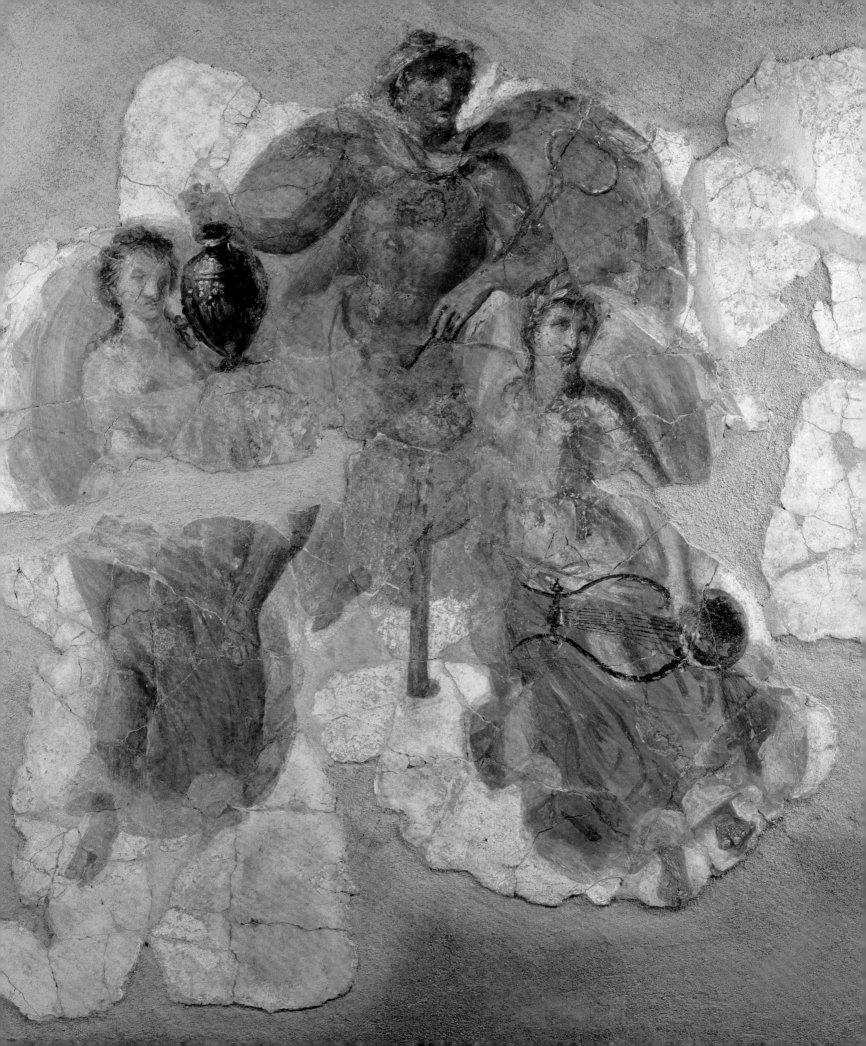

Stabia, Villa of San Marco,
"Planisphere of the Seasons".

Previous page: Stabia,
Villa of San Marco,
"Hermes Psychopompos".

tion until ancient *Stabiae* was buried together with Pompeii and Herculaneum by the eruption of Vesuvius in 79 A.D. It was precisely at Stabia that Pliny the Elder died, in the attempt to aid his friend Pomponianus by ship, after it proved impossible to land at Herculaneum.

The villas

Stabia was already famous in Antiquity for its healthy climate and the presence of mineral springs, mentioned by Pliny the Elder (I century A.D.), Columella (I century A.D.) and the medical doctor Galen (II century A.D.). These conditions, together with the beauty of the landscape, must have encouraged wealthy Roman society to build panoramic villas at Stabia. Cicero (*Family Letters* VII 1, 7) wrote to his friend M. Marius, who owned a villa at Stabia, and complained that he

was obliged to suffer the boredom of the city while his friend enjoyed the spectacular scenery of the gulf: "*yet I do not doubt that you opened a panoramic window in your bedroom overlooking the port of Stabia and thus spent the morning ... enjoying that enchanting sight*".

The most important archaeological monuments are the luxurious Roman *otium* villas along the edge of Varano hill, built there for a better view of the Gulf. Access could be gained from the top or from below, so that the slope descending to the sea had ramps, tunnels, grottos decorated with mosaics and rest areas, seeming from afar to be an architectural complex of great scenic impact. The largest are the Villa of Ariadne and the Villa of San Marco, although as many as six have so far been identified. The hinterland, on the contrary, had more than 40 rustic villas testifying to capillary occupation of the territory and intensive exploitation of the countryside, producing wine, olive oil, vegetables and fruit.

The villas were already excavated by the Bourbons in 1749-1762 and 1775-1782. The Bourbons transferred to Naples most of the finest figurative paintings and often those left on site were deliberately damaged with picks to discourage thieves. The sumptuous complexes were brought to light as of 1950 thanks to an enthusiastic local historian, Libero D'Orsi.

The Villa of San Marco was already excavated between 1749 and 1754. The most ancient core dates to the Augustan age, although the complex was substantially extended in the Claudian age. The markings on the roof tiles may suggest that the building was owned by a certain *Narcissus*, a slave freed (*liberto*) by Emperor Claudius (41-54 A.D.). The majestic building was designed as a leisure villa (*otium*). The atrium had an impluvium and a monumental domestic altar (*lararium*); the service areas were arranged around it. The bath area was built in a triangular space between the edge of the hill and the entrance area; it had a small atrium with a small pool for ablutions on cold water. The large pool (7 × 4.75 m) in the *calidarium* was heated in the middle by a bronze boiler ("*samovar system*") of which only the decorations on the base of the basin remain; the boiler was taken by Sir William Hamilton and loaded on the ship *Colossus* that in 1798 was intended to carry to London part of his collection – only it sank off the English coast.

The villa had a garden shaded by two rows of plane trees planted by a long pool, enclosed towards the hill by a nymphaeum decorated with stuccos depicting Neptune, Venus and athletes. A series of small rooms (*dietae*) enjoyed superb views of the garden. The first room, decorated in the latest fashion – the so-called fourth Pompeian style – has six splendid figures: Perseus with winged feet holding the decapitated head of Medusa, Iphigenia as a priestess holding the archaic statue of Athena (the "Palladion") and a torchlight, a devotee, a muse seen from behind with a lyre, a nude figure and a woman opening a pyx. The ceiling is painted with a Nike holding the palm of victory. The adjacent room is painted, in the centre of the imitation vault, with the story of Europa kidnapped by the bull. The last room, architecturally the most sumptuous, has a scene with

a young man lying on a triclinium with a concubine at his feet.

A second large peristyle to the south was surrounded by porticos supported by twisted columns, that fell during the earthquake in 1980. The ceiling of the portico was decorated with paintings depicting the "Planisphere of the Seasons", the "Apotheosis of Athena", the muse "Melpomene", "Hermes Psychopompos" and the "Chariot of the Sun with Feton" (today in the Stabian Antiquarium).

The *calidarium* of the villa revealed a painting with a scene of building work (today in the Antiquarium), while the *frigidarium* – found on a table with silver lion paws – two oxydian goblets with Egyptian divinities in coloured stones and gold profiles (today in the National Archaeological Museum of Naples).

Stabia, Villa of Ariadne, the so-called "Flora da Stabia" (Proserpine).

Egyptian goblets in oxydian from the Villa of San Marco at Stabia. Naples, National Archaeological Museum.

The Villa of Ariadne was already excavated between 1757 and 1762. Built on the slopes of Varano hill, it covers an area of about 11,000 square metres. The name was inspired by the finding of a painting with "Ariadne abandoned in Naxos", but it is also known as Villa Varano, after the hill on which it stands. The most ancient core dates to mid-I century B.C. and includes the atrium, the peristyle and the adjacent rooms.

Its antiquity is witnessed by the two small rooms on the exterior, on the sides of the entrance to the atrium, that had decorations in the so-called second Pompeian style imitating architecture. This core was extended in the next century with a banquet hall having a view over the sea and an enormous gymnasium (104 × 81 m), today buried, with more than one hundred columns. The circuit of the gymnasium measured exactly two stadiums, the measurement prescribed by Roman architect Vitruvius for the porticos of such buildings.

The part of the villa standing over the edge of the hill was supported by a terrace decorated with blind arches and pinnacles. One of the arches revealed a charcoal drawing of a ship.

The paintings in the large triclinium depicted stories dear to Venus, the goddess of love: *Ariadne* (after whom the villa is named), was abandoned by Theseus on the island of Naxos in the arms of sleep (*Hypnos*) and then escorted by Dionysos accompanied by a cupid carrying a torch; "*Licurgos and Ambrosia*"; "*Hyppolite*" informed by his wet-nurse of the love of his step-mother Fedra for him and, in the antechamber, "*Ganymed*", kidnapped by the eagle and carried before the throne of Jupiter.

A small room near the triclinium is decorated with an original cladding of "tiles" painted with female figures, erots and birds. The ceiling of a small panoramic room near the atrium revealed a "portrait of a couple" in a rhombus, where the figures are characterised by the fashionable hair-dressing typical of the Julian-Claudian period.

Other finds include a bronze boiler shaped like a tower and a gold ring with a garnet and an engraving of Apollo, both today in the National Archaeological Museum of Naples. The stables also revealed the remains of two agricultural waggons in 1981.

The paintings on the other hand include the famous "*Flora*" that was accompanied by three other paintings with "Leda and the Swan", "Medea" and "Diana Huntress"; as well as figures of priests of Isis and the famous painting with "Venus selling the cupids". This painting was so famous in XVIII century that abbot Galiani in 1767 wrote from Paris to Minister Tanucci: "*I've seen more than ten homes with copies of that painting of a woman selling cupids like chickens here* (in Paris)".

The Antiquarium

Although currently not in use, the Stabian Antiquarium, close to the "Libero D'Orsi" Lyceum, has interesting testimony of the life in the city from VI-II-VII century B.C. to the late Renaissance. The most ancient core comprises rich burial treasures from the necropolis discovered around Castellam-

*Paintings in Stabia.
Side: sea nymph.
Bottom: seated woman.
Naples, National
Archaeological Museum.*

mare, especially at Santa Maria delle Grazie. Between VIII and VI century, local black clay pottery prevailed, joined in the early VI century by heavier *buccheros* imitating Etruscan products. The inside of a smaller *bucchero* goblet made in Campania has one of the most ancient Etruscan graffiti inscriptions found hereabouts. During VI century, imported pottery made in Greece (Chalcis and Corinth) made its appearance, as well as local imitations. As of mid-VI century, pottery with black figures and black paint began to appear, not only imports but also local imitations (Ischia).

The most conspicuous core is made up of paintings and stuccos from the Roman villas. These paintings belong to the Roman decorative fashions of the Julian-Claudian and Flavian ages, better known respectively as the third and fourth Pompeian styles. One particular complex comprises stucco panels from Petraro (Gragnano), still under execution during the eruption in 79 A.D. The statue of the "Shepherd", one of the glories of the museum, was found in 1967 in the Fusco estate, less than 100 metres from the Villa of Ariadne, in a building today buried under illegal constructions.

Items surviving in Stabia after the eruption in 79 A.D. include a milestone installed in 121 A.D., under Emperor Hadrian, on the eleventh mile of the Nuceria-Stabiae road, and a sarcophagus with "Apollo and Athena with Muses" (where Julius Longinus was buried, commander of the decurions of Misenum), found in 1879 in the necropolis under the present-day Piazza Municipio.

Vesuvius

The volcano

Vesuvius reaches 1281 metres above sea level. The crater is elliptical and measures 550 × 650 metres; it is 330 metres deep. The base rectangle measures 10 × 8 kilometres. The "magmatic chamber" may stand 5 km below ground.

The volcano has two peaks: Monte Somma is what remains of the ancient crater or "caldera", while Vesuvius as such is the more recent part. The volcano is defined as "Plinian" (after the description of Pliny the Younger), or "explosive" (since every cycle of activity starts with an explosion), or "catastrophic". Depth surveys, down to 1,350 m below ground, indicate an age of about 300,000 years, yet the volcano may in any case be much older. Probably, Monte Somma, when it was still active, was higher than today – perhaps even 2,000 metres above sea level. The most ancient documented eruption seems to have taken place 22,000 years ago, while the Great Cone or Vesuvius was probably formed about 14,000 years ago. The eruption of 79 A.D. is the first historical-

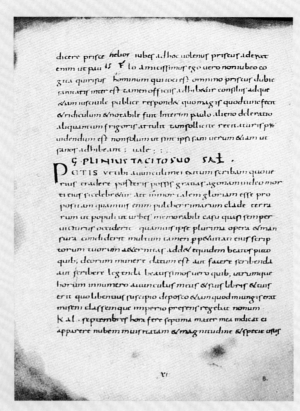

ly documented event, thanks to the chronicles of Pliny and the testimony of Pompeii and Herculaneum. The eruption in 1631 saw the onset of the modern history of the volcano, that came to an end in 1944. Between 1631 and 1944, at least 19 important eruptions were recorded, with an average of one every 16 years.

The most famous eruption, in 79 A.D., rose 15-30 kilometres high and spread by up to seventy kilometres – as far as Agropoli, south of Salerno. The eruptive mass had a volume of three cubic kilometres. The height and type of burial of the ancient cities varied in relation to their distance from the crater: more distant towns were struck by "volcanic rain", while nearby centres were buried under magma. So, Pompeii – about 12 km from the crater – was buried under about 5 metres of ash, pumice and lapillus, while Herculaneum, 7 km distant, was submerged under 20 metres of pyroclastic flow, commonly known as "tuff".

Given the enormous pressures and high temperatures, the volcano also produced 240 mineralogical varieties. They are now the main part (about eighty examples of crystallised forms) of the Vesuvian Collection in the Mineralogical Museum of the University of Naples; many of these are named after famous Neapolitan scientists – such as "cotugnite" (after doctor Cotugno), "tenorite" (after botanist Tenore), etc.

So why have people continued to live in the shadow of Vesuvius – a volcano – for at least one hundred thousand years, always fearing new earthquakes and new eruptions? Is it truly only a sense of resignation? This question may well be solved by geo-archaeology, a new discipline studying the relationships between the history of the earth and the history of mankind, enriching archaeology as such with lively scientific debate. The answer, all told, is rather simple: natural resources. In short, a volcano – at times the sudden cause of death and destruction – may also be for many generations an endless source of wealth: land rich in minerals and inasmuch unusually fertile (ensuring even five harvests a year), the incredible variety and abundance of building materials, the plentiful streams flowing without sinking into ash beds, spa and mineral waters and – last but not least – the beautiful landscapes that only in such volcanic areas are so detailed and various.

Yet what would the plains of Campania be like today without this large and threatening volcano that also produces such fertile land? Vesuvius is the origin of a favourable eco-system for human settlement, the reason for such dense inhabitation that has characterised the Gulf since Antiquity. The Romans defined all this in very simple terms: *Campania Felix*.

The eruption of 79 A.D.

The Pompeians had just begun to rebuild their city, seriously damaged by an earthquake (9 on the Mercalli Scale) in 62 A.D., when they heard a tremendous explosion in the morning of 24 August 79 A.D.
Vesuvius had suddenly re-awoken, hurling into the air a column of smoke at least 15 kilometres high. Suddenly, that cloud fell to earth, blanketing the sea and hiding Capri from sight. A dark, thick night fell. It resembled the last night of the world.
Scientist Pliny the Elder, then admiral of the fleet at Misenum, tried to provide aid with his ships but they were repulsed – first by the seaquake and then by the rubble blasted into the sea by the volcano. He changed course towards Stabia where, obese and unwell, he died from a heart attack.
The soldiers sent by Titus to bring aid excavated the volcanic material to restore the roads and found intact bodies, still wearing clothes and jewels, often joined in a final embrace. They resembled an entire population fallen into deep sleep rather than dead victims. The few survivors only saw the sun again after three days, hidden as if by an eclipse. When the haze finally disappeared, the landscape at the feet of Vesuvius was utterly changed. Everything was covered by a black cloak. From Naples to Sorrento, no homes, no trees, no people were to be seen … Pompeii was buried under a stratum of pumice, ash and stones up to six metres thick.

The "form" of Vesuvius

An eruption as powerful as the one in 79 A.D., issuing so much material spread all over the surrounding area (up to 300 sq. km.), undoubtedly modified the "shape" of the volcano itself.
Debate over the appearance of Vesuvius prior to 79 A.D. has continued for more than a century, since we do not possess exact direct testimony. The debate essentially focuses on this question: was Vesuvius prior to 79 A.D. a volcano with one peak (Monte Somma alone) or, as it appears today, with two peaks – Monte Somma and Vesuvius? In other words, which eruption formed the Great Cone?

Probably, Monte Somma, when it was still active, was higher than today; the rim of its crater has been lowered by meteorological and tectonic action. Obviously, the collapse filled the base of the crater, raising it to create the characteristic "caldera" of its basin. This "caldera", after a lengthy period of stasis, initially saw the formation of a small new eruptive crater that progressively formed the Great Cone.

Attempts to re-construct the ancient shape of Vesuvius prior to 79 A.D. refer to several ancient paintings. One from Herculaneum, today lost but handed down to us as drawing, has a view of the coastline with a mountain formation in the background resembling Vesuvius seen from Naples. It must be mentioned, however, that these Pompeian landscapes are generic and never realistic views, and inasmuch are not very reliable.

Another famous painting, from the *lararium* of the "House of the Centenary" in Pompeii and today in Naples Museum, shows us Vesuvius with Bacchus. Those who claim that Vesuvius had a single cusp use this fresco as proof.

A painting in the Catacombs of San Gennaro in Naples, the Saint revered in popular religion as the master of the volcano, depicts the Saint against a background of a mountain with two peaks, identified as Monte Somma and Vesuvius. In conclusion, it is possible that the Great Cone or Vesuvius was formed by an eruption prior to that in 79 A.D. but was enlarged by the eruption in 79 A.D. and developed actively in I-VI century A.D.

A dozen or so known eruptions between I and XIII century A.D. raised the cone of Vesuvius by about 600 metres, creating its present-day shape.

Changes along the coastline

The masses erupted by the volcano in 79 A.D. – more than three cubic kilometres – caused the coast to advance by more than one kilometre between Naples and Stabia, so that some towns lost forever their relationship with the sea. For example, a boat was found in Herculaneum in front of the "Terme Suburbane", that clearly suggests that the southern border of the city was delimited by the beach, that today stands at Granatello.

The lagoon port of Pompeii, that probably stood in the modern Bottaro area, was buried and the coastline advanced by about 1500 metres. Pompeii therefore completely lost its port and maritime vocation.

Inasmuch, the coastline underwent significant variations from the Roman age to our own times especially because of volcanic phenomena – joined by human modifications of the territory especially since early XX century, such as quays, port installations, road, land-fills, etc., thereby denoting a general trend for advancement.

THE LETTERS OF PLINY THE YOUNGER

The first letter (Epistulae IV 16)

"Dear Tacitus, you asked me to tell you about how my uncle died ... He was at Miseno in command of the fleet. On the ninth day before the calends of September (24 August), towards the seventh hour (1.00 p.m.), my mother told him she had seen a very large and unusually shaped cloud ... they couldn't tell from which mountain it came (only later was it known to come from Vesuvius). It was shaped like a pine. It rose upwards like a trunk and then widened out like a crown. I think that it was raised by a current of air and then fell because of its own weight. It spread out, partly white, partly dirty and spotted, because of the earth and ash it carried ... My uncle ordered that a "liburnica" be prepared for him ... He was leaving home when he received a note from Retina, the wife of Cascus, frightened by the danger since her villa stood at the feet of the mountain and there was no escape except by sea. She begged him to save her from that terrible situation ... He ordered the quadremes to take to the sea and went on board himself to take aid to Retina and many others, since the coast was densely populated given it amenable climate ...

The ash was already falling on the ships, hotter and denser as they drew nearer. Pumice and black cobbles also fell from the sky, baked and crushed by flames. All of a sudden, a shoal appeared in the sea and the beach

became inaccessible because of the rocks spewed from the mountain. He hesitated for a moment but, when the pilot suggested they should return, he shouted: "Fortune helps only the brave, set course to Pomponianus!" He lived in Stabia, on the other side of the gulf. There, Pomponianus had already loaded his baggage on to ships and was ready to set sail as soon as the adverse wind settled. For my uncle, on the other hand, the wind blew favourably and he was able to disembark. He embraced his frightened friend, comforting and giving him courage. To calm his fear, he reassuringly asked to take a bath. After his bath, he sat at table for dinner. He was happy ... or pretended to be so. In the meantime, Vesuvius sparkled everywhere with great fires and high columns of flame. The dazzle was all the more intense in the dark night. To calm the terror of everyone present, he repeated that fleeing country folk had forgotten to douse the fires in their abandoned farms. Afterwards, he retired and slept deeply. The heavy and noisy breathing from his large body was heard by those standing guard at the door to his apartment. Yet he was awakened, since the courtyard in front of his apartment was so full of ash and lappilus that, if he had remained in the room, he would never have got out again. He rejoined Pomponianus and the others unable to sleep. They discussed whether it was best to remain in the villa or in the open. The house, in short, shuddered with frequent and violent earthquakes ... They tied cushions over their heads held tightly by cloths to protect themselves against the falling stones ... They decided to go to the beach to see the offered an escape. The sea was very heavy and contrary. He laid a canvas on the beach and laid down. He asked for cold water and drank avidly several times. He was roused by flames and an intense odour of sulphur ... He stood up with the help of two slaves, but collapsed immediately to the ground, since he could not breathe because of the dense smoke that suffocated his delicate and easily inflamed throat. When day came – the third since we had last seen him – his body was found intact, covered by the last tunic he had worn: he seemed more to be asleep than truly dead ...".

The second letter (Epistulae VI 20)
"From Caius Pliny to Tacitus:
*The letter I wrote to you about the death of my uncle saw you ask for more descriptions of the events that I
also suffered at Miseno, where I had remained ... In previous days, the earth had shook but we were not too
frightened since earthquakes are frequent in Campania. Yet that night the earth shook with such particular violence that we had the impression that everything was not so much shaken as turned upside-down ...*
*Day had broken an hour beforehand but the light was still uncertain and languid. The nearby houses were shat-
tered. It was only then that we decided to leave Miseno. We were followed by an endless mass of people who
pushed ... The waggons, even if standing on absolutely flat land and wedged with stones, shook and never remained still. We saw the sea retreat, almost as if pushed away by the earthquake. The coastline had advanced
and a great many fish had been washed up on the beach. To the east, there was a black cloud slashed by long
tongues of flame, bolts of lightning and flashes. The ash was already falling in scatters. Behind us there rose a
thick, dense cloud that followed us and settled on the ground like a stream. We had just sat down on the edge
of the road when night suddenly fell on us. Women shrieked, children cried for help and men shouted. People
called for their parents, their sons, their wives. There were even those so frightened of dying that they called for
death. It was like the last night of the world ... the ash began falling again, dense and heavy. Thrown to the
ground, we jumped up and brushed off the ash, otherwise its weight would have suffocated us.*
*The cloud finally evaporated, becoming almost smoke or fog and the light of day immediately returned. The
sun also re-appeared, a livid sun as if in an eclipse. Everything was changed: there was a cloak of ash as deep
as snow. We returned to Miseno, had something to eat and passed an anxious night suspended between fear
and hope; yet the earth continued to tremble ...".*

RESETTLEMENTS AFTER THE GREAT ERUPTIONS

Immediately after the catastrophic eruption in 79 d.C., the progressive reconstruction of the roads was
joined by extensively documented testimony of resettlement in the area of Vesuvius between Naples and
Stabia in II-IV century A.D. In any case, volcanologists say that resettlement after major eruptions takes
about 200 years, the time needed for the reclamation of crop-growing land or *humus*. Such resettlement
must have been very slow, as villages gradually expanded over time. They developed along the roads or near
the sea and streams. The few remains, often built using "recycled" materials, suggest a much more modest
lifestyle compared to the luxury of the Vesuvian cities and villas prior to 79 A.D. They involve craftsman
workshops, farms, tombs with few burial treasures, etc. They are all the more evocative when we recall that
Procopius, in VI century A.D., climbing up to the crater, wrote that the flames could still be seen.
On the other hand, it is astonishing to see that almost two millennia passed before the area slowly but completely regained the social-economic status that had characterised it prior to the catastrophe in 79 A.D., an
evident sign that natural resources always affect the type and manner of resettlement. In short, the ancient
consular road that before the eruption linked Neapolis, Herculaneum, Pompeii and Nuceria, more or less
corresponds to the present-day "Royal Calabrian Road". Just as in Roman times it was flanked by residential villas, so in the 1700s it welcomed – given the enchanting landscape and mild climate – stupendous villas that earned the Portici-Torre del Greco section the nickname of the "Golden Mile". Parallel to the
road, above and below it, coastal and inland stretches also developed. The coast welcomed sumptuous *villae maritimae* for *otium*, while the foothills saw *villae rusticae* also involved in agricultural production. It
effectively had the same functional division of the territory as today, with a central residential band, an
agricultural band on the slopes of Vesuvius and a coastal band with resort mansions that then, as today,
could also be reached from Naples directly by sea.
Today, the maritime vocation of Herculaneum survives. Stabia has retained its port and spa economy, while
the Sorrentino coast, as in Antiquity, still attracts tourism. Pompeii, on the other hand, is an exception
since, with the loss of its port because of advancing coastline, has lost its maritime vocation to remain only an agricultural centre.

CAPRI

Capri: view of the island with the "Faraglioni".

History

The island of Capri has an area of 10 square kilometres and its highest point is Monte Solaro (589 metres). The resident population today is about 12,000 inhabitants. Geologically speaking, the island – made up of calcareous rock – is the extension of the Sorrento Peninsula. In very remote times, it was probably linked to firm land: excavation work in 1906 to extend the Hotel Quisisana brought to light bones of animals of the Quaternary Age that could never have reached Capri across the sea, such as elephants, rhinoceros, horses, bears, deer and hippopotami. The flint tips found in the Grotto of Ferns testify to the presence of man on the island as early as the end of the Palaeolithic Age. These finds explain the anecdote mentioned by historian Svetonius (*Vita Augusti* 72) whereby Emperor Augustus, visiting the island, collected "*bones of huge animals and the weapons of heroes*".

The Greeks, who since VIII century had founded numerous colonies on the coasts of Sicily and southern Italy, settled on the island in view of its strategic position at the southern entrance to the Gulf of Naples. Virgil (*Aeneid* VII 733 onwards) tells that Telon reigned here, King of the Teleboi originally from Acarnania.

Strabo (V 4, 9) recalls that "*Capri in ancient times had two small cities but later only one. The Neapolitans conquered this …*"; in this way he suggests that there were two settlements, later identified by historians on Mount Anacapri and the site of the modern town of Capri.

Capri was rarely mentioned until Augustan times. The Emperor Augustus was enchanted by the island and in 29 B.C. wished to make it his private estate for vacations, as mentioned by Svetonius (*Life of Augustus* 92): "*He took certain auspices and omens as infallible … In short, he was so de-*

lighted that on the island of Capri the antlers of a very old elk, by then drooping to the ground and languishing, had regained new life on his arrival, that he agreed with the city of Naples to exchange Capri with the island of Ischia".

Tiberius chose Capri as his residence during the final period of his reign (27-37 A.D.). Tacitus recalls that the Emperor built twelve villas here, each dedicated to a divinity of Olympus (*Annals* IV 67): "*At that time, Tiberius had settled (in Capri) between the gods and twelve impressive villas and whereas as he was at first engaged in the business of government he now degenerated into secret pleasures and*

Tiberius III 60): "*(Tiberius) had been on Capri only a few days when, suddenly, a fisherman offered him a large mullet, while he stayed in an isolated place; Tiberius, frightened by the fact that the fisherman had climbed up to him from the rear part of the island, through harsh and impenetrable land, rubbed the mullet into the fisherman's face. And since the poor man, while he was being punished, was pleased that he had not also offered a giant lobster he had caught, the Emperor ordered his face to be tormented with the lobster as well …*".

The island was also affected by the eruption of Vesuvius in 79 A.D., yet the imperial villas were

Tiberius' Leap at Punta della Campanella, in an 1800s painting by Hermann Corrodi. Naples, private collection.

deplorable idleness". The Emperor – after a lifetime of mourning, disappointed loves and warfare – preferred to govern the Empire from this island, in need of marvellous isolation. Tacitus (Annals IV, 67) also says: "*Caesar (Tiberius) … went into hiding on the island of Capri, three sea miles distant from the tip of the Sorrento peninsula. I am inclined to believe that such solitude especially pleased him because the coasts all around have no ports and offer haven only to small boats; nor could anyone land here without being seen by the guards …*". How much he wished to preserve this isolation emerges in a cruel anecdote mentioned by Svetonius (*Life of*

not seriously damaged and continued to be the summer residence of the Flavians. It was only from II century A.D., with the growing loss of interest by the imperial family in the island and the entire coast of Campania – except for the curing baths of Baia – that its fortunes declined. Interest would only be resumed about 1,600 years later, thanks to the "discovery" in the 1800s of the Blue Grotto.

The many villas and residences of modern times include the particularly evocative mansion of Swedish author Axel Munthe (1857-1949), who was the personal doctor of the royal family of Swe-

Villa Jovis, in a model
by C. Krause.

Opposite page:
the famous "Blue Grotto".

den. An enthusiast of archaeology and history of art, as well as fervent collector, with the income from a medical studio he owned in Piazza di Spagna in Rome he purchased in Anacapri in the early XX century the ruins of the Chapel of San Michele and the surrounding land where he built his villa; he later also purchased Castello Barbarossa, the 1500s fortresses of the Viceroy of Naples, the Guard Tower, the towers at Damecuta and Materita, as well as the residence of the Bishops of Capri. The villa, built from 1896, stood on top of one of the twelve villas built by Tiberius; remains of Roman paintings and mosaics are to be found more or less everywhere. Here, the good doctor created a rich and elegant collection of works of art. Although the author leads us to believe in his most famous book, "The History of San Michele", that many were found on his own land, in reality most of these objects came from the Antiques shops in Rome and Naples. So, the superb Egyptian sphinx in syenite granite at the end of the belvedere claimed to have been found in the sea at Capri, was actually purchased from an art merchant in Via Margotta. Donated on his death to the Swedish state, the Villa today welcomes students, artists and scientists to strengthen cultural relationships between Sweden and Italy.

Villa Jovis

"Gigantic vaults of cisterns, some intact, others cracked and open as if to receive and enclose in their vacuous depths a blue inlet of sky; open underground mouths that mark with violent shadows the bluish rocks and the earthy grey of the disintegrated walls; a long corridor that by ramps, steps and infills arrives below the highest summit of the mountain and the small white church on top, leads to a group of rooms with an unusual ground plan and disposition, enclosed at the base by a semi-circular wall standing over the extreme edge of the rock; and on the higher declivity of the mountain, a shapeless mass of ruins scattered between rocks and vineyards, buried between the green and gold of gorse bushes and red poppies, was all that remained of the most sublime, most ethereal Imperial Villa of Capri, which tradition and legend claim as the favourite residence of Tiberius: palace, stronghold and fortress of his island city."

This is how Amedeo Maiuri described Villa Jovis in September 1931. In short, the villa – commissioned by Tiberius – resembles an impenetrable fortress standing on the promontory opposite Punta della Campanella, in a dominant position over the strait known as "Bocche di Capri". It was explored under the Bourbons, while systematic excavations were performed by Maiuri in 1932-1935.

The building that came to light covered an area of 7,000 square metres; nevertheless, the original complex probably also embraced woods, gardens and other buildings. The rooms were arranged around a central core comprising impressive cistern architecture, with a quadrilateral layout divided into four naves in turn divided into smaller rooms. The overall capacity was as much as 8,000 cubic metres of water, a quantity absolutely necessary for the requirements of an imperial palace built on an arid island. The building stood on terraces to offset the slope.

The entrance to the *palatium* had a vestibule with four columns in "cipollino" marble, followed by a second accordance service vestibule. On the south side, there was a bath area with the canonical sequence of *apodyterium*, *frigidarium*, *tepidarium*, *calidarium* and *praefurnium*. North of the vestibule, there was access to the servants' quarters with kitchens, service areas and store rooms. The complex was dominated on the east side by the leisure areas, while to the north there was the

residential quarter accessed only by passing in front of the quarters of the Praetorians, the body guards of the Emperor.

A long corridor led to a complex made up of a triclinium, with lounges and rest areas, in front of which there was a "loggia" (*ambulatio*) measuring about 300 Roman feet (92 metres). The *ambulatio* opened out on one side on to a terrace overlooking the sea known in local tradition as "Tiberius' Leap" – where the Emperor had people disagreeable to him thrown, as mentioned by Svetonius. To the west, on the edge of the mountain, there was a tall building identified by Maiuri as an astronomical observation tower, the *specularium* of

Trasillo, the astrologer that the superstitious Emperor always wanted by his side. Recently, on the other hand, Clemens Krause has suggested that it was the base of a large lighthouse used to send and receive messages from Rome. A smaller tower, used as a lighthouse, stood further south, commissioned by Tiberius and that perhaps collapsed a few days before his death. Rebuilt in the Flavian age, it was clad with bricks and retained its function as a lighthouse until XVII century.

The villa remained an imperial residence until II century A.D. and became the refuge of a hermit in the Middle Ages. The chapel of Saints Christopher and Leonard was then built here, subsequently ex-

Statue in marble of "Poseidon", from the depths of the "Blue Grotto". Capri, Museum of the Certosa di San Giacomo.

panded into the present-day Church of Santa Maria del Soccorso, the patron saint of sailors.

The Sea Palace

Among the numerous architectural remains found on the island, the Sea Palace, despite repeated sacking, is the only one that can be defined as an imperial villa. The villa extended along a strip of land 800 metres long between the present-day port area and the site known as the "Beach of Tiberius". It therefore stood between the sea and the promontory, reflecting the well-known design of sea-side villas characterised by panoramic architecture.

The villa was commissioned by Augustus and then restored by Tiberius. Excavated and pillaged by Austrian Norbert Hadrawa in 1790-1791, it was also significantly damaged during the French occupation in 1806-1815 when it was converted into a small arsenal and a small fort was built. The area today is completely built over with modern villas, so that the only remains of the ancient imperial residence are a few terracing walls, the cisterns and parts of the residential quarters all but lost amidst the vegetation. A large garden (*xystus*) surrounded by various rooms once stood on the site of the present football field. A ramp led to the quarters by the sea, opening at the centre on to a large exedra and nymphaeum overlooking the sea. There were several tanks below the exedra, used in antiquity for fish farming, as well as a small port.

Villa of Damecuta

Another villa built by Tiberius – according to Tacitus – stood at Anacapri, on the far western tip of the island in a panoramic position on the Damecuta promontory, the best part of the island for summer stays. The villa could be reached by land and sea. The area was converted into a military training field and a fort was built during British and French battles to take possession of the island in the early 1800s; moreover, remains found on the surface of the land were variously tampered with or re-utilised by local farmers who did not hesitate to destroy or sell parts of columns and slabs of marble. It was only in XX century when Swedish doctor Axel Munthe donated his huge estates to the Swedish State that the villa was systematically investigated (by Amedeo Maiuri in 1937).

We will never know the original extension of the complex; there are still a few structures along the rocky edge of the mountainside, such as imposing arched elements, a long panoramic "loggia" (*ambulatio*) overlooking the sea with remains of brick columns finished with plaster supporting the pergola and a belvedere resembling an exedra. Lower down, on the eastern side, there is the residential quarter with a number of lounges with traces of plasterwork on the walls and a small *cubiculum*, still retaining remains of the mosaic flooring; a nude torso of a youth was found here.

The main Damecuta villa also had an appendix – the smaller Gradola seaside villa. It was first excavated in the 1800s by American colonel J.C. MacKowen, who found columns and fragments of statues; new archaeological exploration was undertaken in 1998. The complex has only revealed several cisterns, a lounge area and a terrace. It is assumed that there was an interior connection with the Grotta Azzurra below through a passage sought in vain since the 1800s.

Painted pebble-stone, Paleolithic age, from Capri. Naples, National Archaeological Museum.

The "Grotta Azzurra"

The "Grotta Azzurra" – in Roman times a nymphaeum decorated with statues – is a natural cavity about one metre above sea level, so that the light penetrating from the outside through the water is reflected on the walls with a opalescent sky blue colour. "Discovered" in 1826 by German poet August Kopisch, it was later visited by a growing number of German and French artists, followed by English and Scandinavian colleagues. Mention need only be made, among others, of H.C. Andersen, A. Dumas, F. Nietzsche, R.M. Rilke, J. Conrad, I. Turgenev, M. Gorkji, G. B. Shaw, D.H. Lawrence, A. Munthe and C. Malaparte. Praised by poets and writers, immortalised by painters, it is the basis for Capri's modern fame as a tourist resort.

In 1964, a sensational discovery was made in the waters of the grotto: two statues, one depicting Poseidon (Neptune) and the other a Triton, cut off at the knees as if emerging from the sea. Today, these sculptures are housed in the Certosa Museum.

SORRENTO

View of Punta della Campanella.

Opposite page: "Sacrifice to the goddess Diana", relief in marble from the Villa of Capo di Massa Lubrense, near Villazzano.

"Not far from Pompeii stood Sorrento, a Campanian city, especially characterised by the Athenaion, that some call the Promontory of the Sirene (mermaids); the tip of the promontory is home to a temple dedicated to Athena, built by Ulysses. It is separated from the island of Capri by a short stretch of sea. On passing the cape, the small, deserted and rocky "Sirene" islands come into view. On the other side of the Sorrento promontory, there is a sanctuary with ancient votary gifts since the place was already venerated by local inhabitants. Here ends the gulf known by the name of Crater, delimitated by two south-facing promontories, Cape Miseno and Athenaion; the coast is entirely occupied by these cities, as well as villas and plantations close to each other, creating the impression of a single city".

Strabo, *Geographia* V 4, 8

History

Around VIII century B.C., the Eubaean Greeks settled in Campania arrived in the Sorrento Peninsula and set up a flourishing agricultural and commercial economy. They gave life to myths and legends of adventurous travellers, such as Liparos, son of King Auson, who was helped by Aeolus, King of the Aeolian Islands, to conquer Sorrento; or the Sirene (Mermaids) on the small Li Galli islands, known in ancient times as "Sirenusse"; and Ulysses, who supposedly founded at Punta della Campanella a sanctuary dedicated to Athena with a temple-lighthouse, the most important of the peninsula that they called

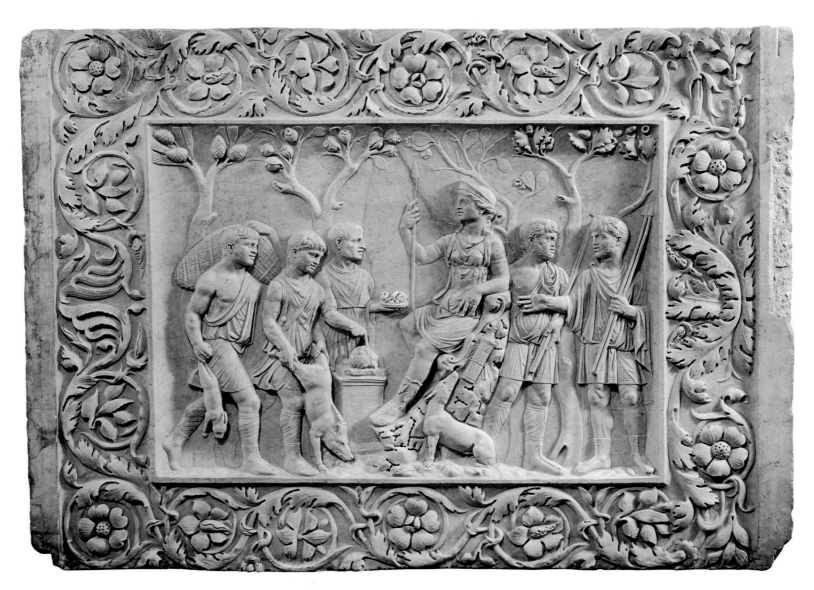

Cape Ateneo. The foundation of Sorrento dates back to the Greek age: and the modern city still today has traces of the orthogonal ground plan typical of Greek colonies. Later, Sorrento did not mint its own coinage and this suggests that it belonged to the Nucerina League together with Stabia and Herculaneum.

Standing on a sheer terrace overlooking the sea, it was already a famous resort for rich Romans who built here their sumptuous panoramic villas. In this period, many water tanks were installed along Via Minervia to supply the villas on the coast, whose spas and nymphaeums required huge supplies of water. The period of greatest splendour coincided with the ages of Caesar and Hadrian. Seaside villas – such as those of Agrippa Postumus and Pollio Felix – clearly show through the luxury

of their furnishings the calibre of visitors to the Peninsula from Augustus onwards, a status that grew even further with the presence of Tiberius in nearby Capri in 27-37 A.D. The Sorrento Peninsula also suffered destruction and abandon following the eruption of Vesuvius in 79 A.D.

The villas

The extraordinary position of Sorrento, its healthy climate and its rich vegetation immediately attracted the Romans – so that it was very likely, in the most panoramic points of the coastline where modern villas and luxury hotels stand today, that a Roman villa would also come to light. And, in fact, the park of the Hotel Excelsior Vittoria in the 1800s revealed structures identified with the Villa of Agrippa – son-in-law of Augustus, admiral of

the Roman fleet and promoter of the Pantheon in Rome – the villa mentioned by Svetonius in his Life of Augustus (27 and 74).

Again in the 1800s, the park of the Hotel Royal, in Via Rota, revealed about two and a half metres below ground a marble statue – 1.80 metres high – depicting a boxer, crowned with olives and standing on a tiny herm of Hercules; the inscription indicates that the artist was the sculptor Koblanos of the renowned school of Aphrodisia in Turkey. The statue is exhibited today in the National Archaeological Museum of Naples. Close by, in 1971 during the building of Villa Fonzoni adjacent to the Hotel Royal, a colossal female statue in white marble 2.60 metres high was found about three metres below ground, probably depicting Flora or Demetra. The statue perhaps stood in an exedra facing the sea; mosaics were also found in the vicinity. Unusually, the owner commissioned a copy of the statue prior to its removal, which still today stands life-size in the courtyard of the villa. The statue is exhibited today in the Archaeological Museum of Sorrento.

The Cape of Sorrento was home in Antiquity to a seaside villa (I century B.C.-I century A.D.) of which only ruins remain today. Known in popular tradition as "The Baths of Queen Giovanna", it included a *domus* higher up with essentially agricultural functions and a villa by the sea. The slope

was terraced, while the two sites were linked by ramps and tunnels. Inasmuch, the villa could be reached by land and sea. The architecture exploited the beauty of the landscape to the utmost.

The most evocative element is the natural basin, that the owners converted into a small port. Architecture and decoration were all designed to maximise *luxuria* and *otium*. The villa has been identified as that of Pollio Felix, a rich citizen of *Puteoli*, described by poet Statius in his *Silvae* (II 2). Cape Massa Lubrense, near Villazzano, in turn re-

vealed another Roman villa in the early 1900s. It also extended over the entire promontory, with various terraces sloping down to the sea. Finds here include two capitals in marble with palm leaves in the Pergamon style and four interesting marble reliefs, as well as a cornice with vegetal decoration that, given the excessive use of the drill, are dated to the age of Hadrian: the first de-picts a procession of satyrs, the second a triumph of Bacchus, the third a sanctuary of Cibele and the fourth a sacrifice to Diana, with the goddess seated on a rock with a group of hunters sacrificing a boar to her. The reliefs are displayed in Sorrento Museum.

In 1980, Massa Lubrense (Marina della Lobra), also revealed the remains of a villa with a sumptuous

Sculptures in marble from Sorrento. This page: "peplophoros", female statue. Opposite page: statue of a boxer. Naples, National Archaeological Museum.

nymphaeum with mosaics about 24 metres long and 2.70 metres high, with a large waterfall in the centre. Nestled into the mountainside, this architecture was the background for the *natatio* that, on the other hand, opened out towards the sea. Dated to the Julian-Claudian age, it is the most representative example of its kind in Campania. The nymphaeum alternates circular and rectangular niches in mock rock, entirely faced with multi-colour glass-paste mosaics depicting gardens with birds. The individual scenes, set against an Egyptian blue background, were linked by panels with twisted candelabra, festoons and masks. Materials of various kinds and origins were used: *Egyptian frit* for the blue, colourful limestones, sea sheels and hard stones. *Egyptian frit*, that Vitruvius called *coeruleum*, was prepared by baking together silica, malachite, calcium carbonate and sodium carbonate. The tesserae were probably produced in the workshops of Pozzuoli or Literno, perhaps using sand suitable for such processing found on the coast between Cuma and Literno. The nymphaeum was re-built in the park of the Piano di Sorrento Archaeological Museum.

The Temple of Athena at Punta della Campanella

The Temple of Athena at Punta della Campanella, with reference to the tradition mentioned by Strabo, was founded by Odysseus himself during his troubled return from Troy to Ithaca. Famous for its springs, it was probably a temple-lighthouse standing on the tip of the promontory, like the Athenaion of Lindos or the Temple of Poseidon at Cape Sounion, in Greece, where the cult of Poseidon was linked with that of Athena. Unfortunately, nothing remains today.

There was a recent discovery of a cliff inscription commemorating the building of the staircase, that led from the small port to the sanctuary, cut into the rock by the *meddices* of the Minervium. The Oscan inscription testifies to the control over maritime traffic by the Samnites in III century B.C. In translation, it reads: "*M. Gavius (son of) M. L. Pitachio (son of) M. / L. Apulius (son of) Ma, magistrates of the Sanctuary of Minerva / commissioned and utilised / this port*".

Excavation assays in Summer 1990 inside and near the Saracen tower have revealed, among other things, a large quantity of drinking goblets, none of which are intact. Verses by poet Statius (*Silvae*

III 2, 23-24) suggest that it was customary for sailors passing the cape and thus entering the Gulf of Naples to climb to the temple and, drinking toasts to the goddess, broke the goblets in her honour and threw them into a holy well (*bothros*): "*Laeva salutavit Capreas, et margine dextro / Sparsit Tyrrhenae Mareotica vina Minervae*". This is how Maccio Celer celebrated the goddess for having aided him during his return from Egypt. The votive offerings found in the sanctuary also included votary figurines in terracotta of a kind of Athena Parthenos, similar to those used in the Doric Temple in Pompeii and the Privati Sanctuary in Stabia.

As early as III century B.C., offerings began to decline – testimony of the loss of favour of the cult of Athena, that completely disappeared in the Republican age. This decline was such that, with the establishment of the colony of *Surrentum* in the Augustan period, the territory of the sanctuary was shared out among the veterans of the *princeps*. We know nothing of the destiny of the sanctuary of Athena at Punta della Campanella after it was abandoned. When Tiberius lived in Capri (27-37 A.D.), a building appeared on the promontory – perhaps a villa – that may be linked with the residence of the Emperor at Capri.

The Museums

The Sorrento Peninsula Archaeological Museum named after French archaeologist Georges Vallet is housed in the neo-classic Villa Fondi at Piano di Sorrento. The park looks down over the sea, above Marina di Cassano, in a panoramic position also embracing Vesuvius and the Gulf.

The Museum illustrates the development of the Sorrento peninsula from pre-history through to the Roman age. The prehistoric section illustrates the first settlements in grottos with animal bones, pulp ceramics and stone materials. It is followed by testimony of the Gaudo Culture (II millennium B.C.) with burial treasures from the tombs found at Trinità, near Piano di Sorrento. Then comes the Archaic section with a splendid marble head from Massa Lubrense and Doric capitals in tuff from Vico Equense.

The upper floor exhibits burial treasures found during excavations in the archaic and classical necropolis of Massa Lubrense (Sant'Agata sui Due Golfi, Deserto), Vico Equense (Via Nicotera) and Sorrento. Another section, dedicated to cults and

Top: *model of the
Villa of Pollio Felix
(Studio Romatre,
Arch. M. Travaglini, Rome).*

Bottom: *Sorrento,
Punta della Campanella,
Oscan inscription.*

inscriptions, has materials from the sanctuary of Athena at Punta Campanella, together with a copy of the Oscan inscription carved into the rock.

The urban development of *Surrentum* is illustrated by an archaeological chart and materials from the city and its necropolis; these include a "trapezophoros" in tuff with a male herm, a provincial transposition of cultured models, from a funerary communion found in a colombarium dating from the first Imperial age. The section dedicated to sea-side villas has marble reliefs and capitals from the Villa of Cape Massa, near Villazzano, and a model of the Villa of Pollio Felix. The park has a reconstruction of the mosaic nymphaeum from the Villa of Massa Lubrense at Marina della Lobra.

Another museum building – the Correale Museum – is home to a precious art collection. Donated to the city in 1904 by Alfredo Correale, Count of Terranova, it was opened to the public in 1924. The museum also has Greek and Roman archaeological finds from different parts of the peninsula. There is a very interesting sculpture in Parian marble of Artemis or Iphigenia riding a deer, a Greek original of the Classic Age, and the famous Sorrento base decorated with low reliefs depicting scenes dealing with the religious policies of Augustus. The base has portraits of Diana with a torch, Apollo with a tripod and cittern and Letus with the Cumaean Sibyl at his feet. The prophetess is surrounded by the Sibylline books placed on the Palatine by Augustus, so that it can be assumed that the monumental entrance depicted is that of the imperial palace – the *Domus Augusti* on the Palatine.

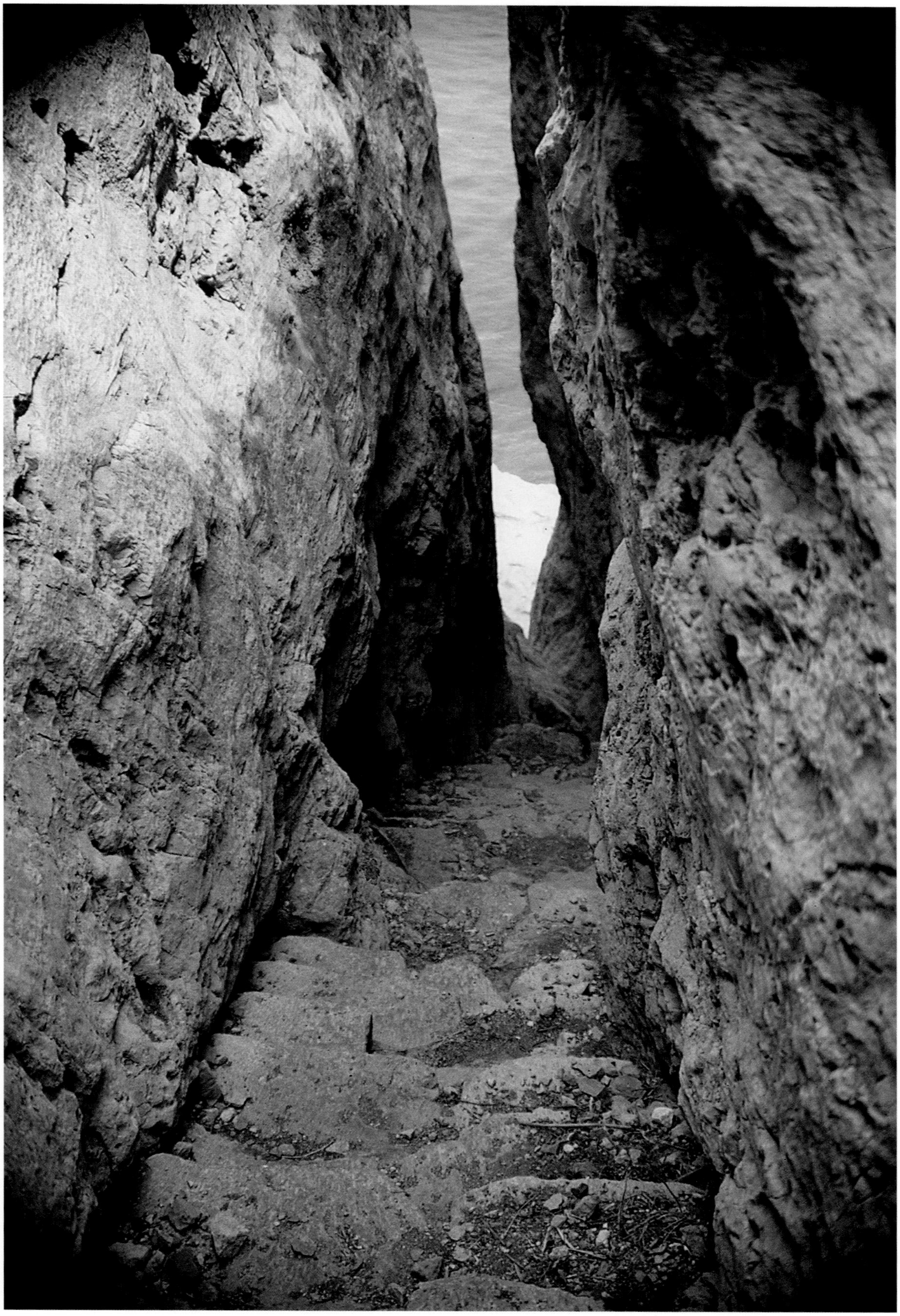

Sorrento, Punta della Campanella: the Samnitic Staircase.

Goethe, Vesuvius and the antiquities of Campania: "Et in Arcadia ego!"

The writings of Johann Wolfgang Goethe (Frankfurt 1749-Weimar 1832) during his visit to Naples and Campania essentially involve letters and notes, that were then incorporated in "*Italienische Reise*", published 29 years after his visit (in 1816-1817) and effectively part of his autobiography "*Dichtung und Wahrheit*" ("Poetry and Truth").

The topics of interest that emerge from these writings essentially concern: the fertility of the earth, Vesuvius, the happy and hard-working Neapolitans, meetings with eminent or unusual people (Hamilton, Filangieri, Venuti, Hackert, Tischbein, Kniep, Angelika Kaufmann, etc.) and, lastly, the "living" antiquities found all over the landscape – in Capua, Naples, Pompeii, Herculaneum and Paestum – rather than hidden in museums as in Germany.

Yet why did Goethe want to visit Italy? The decision was taken for various reasons, including sentimental ones, but in any case to fulfil his dream of youth – travelling in Italy – perhaps even to emulate a family legend: the "Travel" of his father Johann Kaspar in 1740, 47 years earlier. He explained it all himself: "*My father taught my sister Italian in the same room where I was obliged to memorise Cellarius. I finished my homework rapidly and, since I had to remain seated, I pretended to be reading but I was actually listening and easily learnt Italian, that seemed to me to be an entertaining deviation of Latin … He often told me that later I should go to Wetlar and Regensburg, as well as Vienna and, lastly, to Italy, but more than once he said I should see Paris first because, having seen Italy, other places are not as interesting. He often repeated this tale of the future course of my youth, since he also always finished with story about Italy and a description of Naples. Every time his characteristic seriousness and dryness seemed to dissolve and come alive, so much so that we children developed a passionate desire to visit this paradise as soon as possible*".[1]

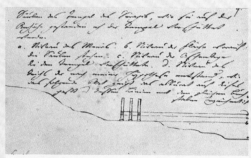

Inasmuch, making secret preparations, he left Carlsbad on 3 September 1786 on route to Brennero. He was 36 and remained away from Germany for twenty months. He arrived in Naples on 20 March 1787; he then left for Sicily, returning to Naples in May. His "Travel" ended in Rome in April 1788. Goethe stayed in Naples for fifty days in two stages – with an interval of forty days for his trip to Sicily – that is 25 February-29 March and 16 May-5 June 1787.

At the end of the 1700s, Naples was the Capital of a Kingdom and one of the main cities in Europe. Only a century later – at the height of the post-Unification crisis – Naples, on the contrary, became backward and scrounging.[2]

The letters of Goethe are a diary, a precise report about people and things that left a mark in his heart. In short, Naples and the Neapolitans left an indelible impression in his soul. "*I am also in Arcadia!*" he exclaimed, quoting the title of one of the famous bucolic paintings of Nicolas Poussin. In any case, this unitary relationship between nature, history, art and popular customs was precisely Goethe's fundamental discovery in Italy.

His evaluation is significantly positive, defending the Neapolitans against accusations of laziness since he found them to be a frugal and hard-working people; he confessed his vain search for the "*lazzarone*" (scoundrel) and saw no thefts or trickery on every street corner.

Opposite page:
"Portrait of Goethe in Naples"
wearing the Werther costume,
in a painting by Johann
Heinrich Wilhelm Tischbein.
Naples, San Martino Museum.

This page: Goethe,
the "Serapeo" of Pozzuoli,
sketch explaining the
phenomenon of Bradyseism.

[1] Johann Wolfgang Goethe, *Dichtung und Wahrheit* (Poetry and Truth), Zürich (Gutenberg) 1949, part 1, book 1, p. 31; see *Goethe's Werk*, Zürich (Artemis Verlag), vol. 10, p. 40.
[2] About a century later, Giustino Fortunato, the great historian of southern Italy, described the deterioration of Neapolitan society in a depressing picture of the city, the common people, the managerial classes, "camorra" criminality, public safety and gambling; everything was different, sadder and darker, compared to joyful city described by Goethe: Giustino Fortunato, *Ricordi di Napoli (Recollections of Naples)*, Milan (Treves) 1874; now see: Wolfgang Goethe, *Lettere da Napoli*, translated by Giustino Fortunato, with an introduction and edited by Manlio Rossi Doria, Naples (Guida Editori) 1989.

THE FIRST STAY IN NAPLES

Naples, Sunday 25th February 1787
At last! I have also arrived here happily and with good auspices … We at last reached Capua itself, where we had lunch. A delightful plain opened up before our eyes in the afternoon. The wide main road runs between green fields of wheat: the wheat is like a carpet and very tall. The poplars are planted in rows, with branches lopped at the top and vines clinging to their trunks. It is like this well into Naples. It is tidy, easily ploughed and well-worked land: the vine shoots are extraordinarily large and tall, the festoons stretched like fluttering nets from poplar to poplar.
Vesuvius always stands on the left, furiously smoking; I was thrilled to my very soul to see this delightful subject with my own eyes. The sky became increasingly clearer and the warm rays of the sun shone even into a narrow coach. We approached Naples in a truly pure atmosphere: and so here were are in an entirely different country … The Neapolitans believe they live in Paradise and have a very sad idea of Nordic countries: "always snow, wooden homes, widespread ignorance but plenty of money". That's what they think about us! The entire German people would be greatly edified (should they come to know).
Naples itself seems to be happy, frank and lively: an entire people moving 'en masse', the King[3] is hunting and the Queen is pregnant – things couldn't be better!

On Monday 26 February, Goethe took lodging in Naples in Largo del Castello, near Castel Nuovo, not far from the sea, in the Locanda of Cavalier Moriconi, where "*the lively decorations of the hall, especially the vaults and the arabesques in a hundred compartments, clearly suggest the vicinity of Pompeii and Herculaneum*".[4]

Tuesday 27th February 1787
… We went towards evening to the Grotto of Posillipo…[5] my father came to mind, emotionally, who treasured indelible impressions of what I was seeing today for the first time … one might say that he would never have been entirely unhappy, because he always remembered his time in Naples.[6]

Thursday 1st March 1787
A trip by sea as far as Pozzuoli, fine excursions by coach, delightful walks in the most marvellous place in the world! Under the purest sky, the precarious land. Ruins of an inconceivable splendour, cursed and frightening: boiling water, caves exhaling sulphur, volcanic mountains that hinder vegetation, bare and sad spaces. Yet the

[3] The famous "big-nosed King", Ferdinand IV, the Bourbon monarch of Naples. After the second restoration, he was 're-named' Ferdinand I, King of the Two Sicilies (1759-1825). His Queen was Maria Carolina of Austria, the thirteenth daughter of Francis I and Maria Teresa of Austria; she bore 17 children.
The King, succeeding in 1759 at only eight years old his father Carlo, who had to take the Crown of Spain, could by no means reign and a regency was set up under Tuscan Bernardo Tanucci (1688-1783), formerly Minister of Justice under Carlo and now Prime Minister. In 1768, still only 17, Ferdinand married Maria Carolina.
In 1767, Sir William Hamilton, the English Ambassador to Naples, wrote to Lord Shelbourne: "*Unfortunately, for himself and his people, he has not had good tutors nor officials capable of being a model for his rank. Despite all this, he is loved by the Neapolitan people … Since it was decided to keep him away from nobles of his own age, he had to seek company among servants and the lower classes …*".
In a letter in 1769 that Leopold Mozart wrote to his wife, Wolfgang Amadeus, then 14, added "*The King has received the grossest Neapolitan education. At the Opera he always sits on a bench so that he seems to be a little taller than his companion. The Queen is attractive and kind and greeted me cordially at least six times on the 'Molo' promenade*". Mozart must have heard the stories then circulating about the King, who even set up a market stall to sell the fish he had caught at Castellammare. He once received his father-in-law, Emperor Joseph II, with a loud fart, adding "*Dutiful homage to your health!*". Joseph II elegantly replied "*Although disgusting he is not entirely revolting … he wash-es his hands and doesn't stink*". One could hardly expect from such an apostle of Nature any efforts on behalf of archaeology. On the occasion of a visit to Pompeii, he had pavement blocks removed so that the royal coach could pass. Nor did he provide funds for excavations. Hamilton complained that nothing more was being done at Herculaneum and that in Pompeii "*instead of focusing on the town gate, found five years ago, they are excavating here, there and everywhere without any research criteria and then bury everything again*".
[4] This Locanda (inn) no longer exists. It stood more or less by the entrance to the Galleria Umberto I on the side of Via Municipio and an inscription recalls the location: V. Spinazzola, *Il Viandante di Volfango Goethe e la casa che Goethe abitò a Napoli*, Naples, 1903, pp. 9-15; B. Croce, *Volfango Goethe a Napoli*, in Aneddoti e ritratti, Naples 1903, p. 7; F. Torraca, *Per una lapide che ricorda la dimora di Volfango Goethe in Napoli*, Naples 1903, (from a speech made on 6 May 1903); B. Croce, *Volfango Goethe a Napoli*, in Anecdotes and profili settecenteschi, Palermo 1914, pages 97-162, particularly page 99; see B. Croce, *Aneddoti di varia letteratura*, Bari 1954, vol. 3, page 16 ss.
[5] The grotto had already been described in Antiquity by Strabo and Seneca and also visited by the young Mozart on 16 June 1770 (see the section on Mozart in this book).
[6] Goethe's father, Johann Kaspar, aged 30 and before having a family, had visited Italy and even wrote a book about the country in Italian: J.K. Goethe, *Travelling in Italy in 1740*, edited by A. Farinelli, 2 volumes, Rome, 1932; *Reise durch Italien im Jahre 1740* (übersetzt von A. Meier), München 1986.

vegetation elsewhere always flourishes, penetrating where it can into every corner, rising above everything that is dead around lakes and streams, even lining with the finest oak woods the walls of an old crater.[7]
In this way, it thrusts here and there between the events of Nature and history … In the meantime, Man, living there, revels in joy and we also did the same … I noticed many things. When I return to this topic,[8] the chart will be of great help to me, as it was during the visit, as well as rapid sketch by Tischbein …

Saturday 3rd March 1787

Yesterday, although it was foggy and the peak was hidden behind clouds, I climbed Vesuvius. We travelled by coach to Resin, and then on mule-back climbed the mountain amidst vineyards; I crossed at the feet of the lava poured in 1771, on which a thin yet extensive musk had already formed … Leaving the small hut of the hermit on the left[9] I finally reached the cone of ash, that is very difficult to climb … We reached the old crater, today filled in; we found lava poured two months, fourteen days and even five days ago, that had already cooled. We climbed on top, flanking a recent volcanic hillock: it smoked from all parts. Since the smoke flowed away from us, I wanted to climb to the crater. We had taken just fifty paces in the midst of vapours that were so dense that I could barely see my shoes. Holding a handkerchief to my nose was no help; I could no longer see the guide; walking was unsafe on the detritus issued from the volcano: I thought it sensible to turn back and enjoy the spectacle on a better day, when the smoke was not so dense. In any case, I have at least learnt how difficult it is to breathe in such an atmosphere … In any case, the mountain was very peaceful: no flames nor rumbles nor stones thrown into the air as over the last few days. I have examined it now, to inspect it properly as soon as the weather is better.
The lava I saw was already mostly known to me. However, I discovered a phenomenon that seems to me to be very significant and I want to examine it better, consulting experts and collectors. It is the stalactite lining of a volcanic fumarola, that was formerly vaulted but now split, rising in the middle of the ancient crater today filled in. I think this hard, grey stalactitic stone was formed by the sublimation of the lighter volcanic exhalations, without the aid of humidity and without melting …[10]
I have already seen enough men of every kind, fine horses and marvellous fish. As regards the position of the city and its sumptuousness, as often described and celebrated, I have no other word to add. Here, it is often said: "see Naples and then die".

Tuesday 6 March 1787

Rather unwillingly but a faithful companion as ever, Tischbein went with me this morning to Vesuvius … We left in two coaches, feeling that we would not survive the clamour of the city if only one of us drove the horses …
The road, passing through the last suburbs and market gardens, seems already to indicate something plutonic.
Since it hadn't rained for some considerable time, the evergreen leaves, the terraces and the cornices were coat-

---

[7] The Astroni Wood at Agnano.
[8] Goethe, famed for his inventiveness even in the field of Natural History, was the first to attempt an explanation close to the truth, as indicated in his notebook (Tagebuch on 19 May 1787), later incorporated into his essay A problem of architecture and natural history in 1823. Berlin has a sheet of paper with two of his sketches outlining his explanatory hypothesis for the phenomenon of the Serapeo columns, where only the middle section was affected by lithophagus molluscs ("Temple of Serapis at Pozzuoli", pen and ink on ivory paper, 265 × 190 dated 19 May 1787; Berlin, Staatsbibliothek, Härtel Collection Corpus VIb year 1978, n. N35, s.i., p. 108). The notes explain the symbols used in the sketch. The back shows the columns in their current state, after excavation; the front (bottom) the hypothesis that local volcanic phenomena may have created a hollow filled with sea water ("e-f"); inasmuch, the molluscs left in the basin would have clung to the columns ("section cd"). It is astonishng how this is close to the exact answer to the question, while his contemporaries still thought of fluctuations in sea level. A century went by before the exact answer to the problem was found – the lifting and lowering of ground level: Charles Babbage, Observations on the Temple of Serapis at Pozzuoli near Naples,

London, 1847, and Charles Lyell, Principles of Geology, London 1847 (1st edition).
The legend of the drawing is annotated (Diaries, Pozzuoli, 19 May 1787): "… and [the sea] formed a small pool e-f of depth c-d. Now, the lower part of the columns c-b was covered and none of the aquatic creatures could reach it – on the contrary, they became readily affixed to the parts of the columns underwater and made holes about the size of a finger. The columns are in Greek cipollino marble and attract crustaceans as an excellent meal … as can be seen now that it has returned to light.
N.B.: There is still some powder, at a certain height the columns are clean and intact around the temple. And there would be even more to say about Solfatara, Monte Nuovo, etc. Yet I am sure of one thing: volcanic effects find their causes deep below ground; in this case, I mean below the level of the sea. Yet this is still too generic and requires a broader discussion that I have time for or have so far achieved": in: Porzio – Cause Picone 1983, pages 40 and 94 with plate 92.
[9] The hermit was a talkative and helpful Frenchman who had lived up there for about fifteen years. The hut was still there in 1839 where the Royal Observatory was built and later became an inn.
[10] See Rovereto 1942.

---

ed with a thick, grey powder; as well as anything else where it could settle. Only the bright blue sky and the splendid, lively sun indicated that we were still among the living.

At the feet of the steep slope, an old and a young man appeared before us, both stocky.[11] The former hauled me, the second Tischbein. I say they hauled us because each of the guides wore straps that travellers hang on to; and so strapped they use hammers and their feet to climb the slopes.

This is how we reached the plateau near the cone. The remains of Monte Somma stand to the south.

A glance at the place to the west refreshed us, like a good bath, after all the effort and our tiredness. We walked around the crater, that smoked continually and threw stones high into the air. When the space allowed us to keep at a good distance, it was a majestic and sublime sight. First of all, there was a great explosion that reverberated from the depths of the abyss; then thousands of large and small stones were thrown into the air, shrouded in clouds of ash: most of them fell back into the vortex. The stones pushed to the sides fell with a strange noise down the slope of the cone: the heavier stones fell to the ground first, bouncing down with a dull thud, followed by the smaller stones and lastly the shower of ash. All this was repeated at regular intervals, that we could easily measure simply by counting. Yet the space between the cone and Monte Somma is rather narrow.[12] Many stones fell around us, making our march rather unpleasant. Tischbein became increasingly irritated on the mountainside: the monster, not content merely to be horrible, was also rather dangerous. Yet since real risks can be appealing and encourage men to challenge them, in a spirit of contradiction, so I wondered whether it would be possible to climb the cone and reach the crater and return again in the interval between two eruptions. I asked the guides beneath a protruding crag opposite Monte Somma where we had stopped to eat our provisions in safety. The younger guide offered to accompany me in this bold enterprise. We protected our heads with linen and silk kerchiefs and held ready with our hammers, as I grasped his leather belt.

The stones still crackled all around us and the ash fell in showers, while the sturdy young man pulled me up the scorching slag. And thus we found ourselves on the edge of the immense abyss; the smoke was blown away from us by a light breeze, that nevertheless engulfed the chasm for some time, fuming through a thousand fissures. There was a brief pause and the dense steam revealed a glance here and there at the crevassed rocky walls. The view was neither instructive nor pleasing but since nothing could be seen I hung on to try and discover something. We had forgotten about calculating the time; we were on the crest of a monstrous vortex. All of a sudden there was a rumble and the formidable eruption blew up in front of us; we instinctively huddled, as if this gesture could save us from the falling stones: the stones were already crackling around us and without thinking that a new pause would come – so happy were we to be unharmed – that we ran down to the base of the cone while the ash was still falling, covering our heads and shoulders.

I was greeted and criticised in a very friendly manner by Tischbein and, after regaining my breath, I was able to dedicate special attention to the old and new lava flows. The older guide could exactly identify their various ages. The older ones were already covered by ash and flattened out; the more recent flows, especially those poured slowly, had a singular appearance, since they had dragged hardened masses to the surface again for some time and thus often came to a halt, yet – once again swept up by the river of flame – they took on the strangest and weirdest shapes, like those found in glaciers. This agglomerate of molten matter even included large blocks which, from the piece I collected, entirely resembled primitive rock. The guides said that this was old lava from the deepest base sometimes issued by the volcano.

Wednesday 7th March 1787

This week Tischbein[13] carefully showed me and explained a great many art treasures in Naples. He is a fine admirer and painter of animals and had already told me about Palazzo Colobrano[14] and its bronze head of

---

[11] Bartolomeo Madonna and his son Raimondo. Bartolomeo, nicknamed "the Cyclops of Vesuvius", was a guide between 1760 and 1790 to scientists and tourists; Raimondo, on the other hand, was the guide of Alexander von Humbold and Gay Lussac (1805).

[12] This is the Horse Atrium, the valley between Vesuvius and Monte Somma.

[13] Wilhelm Tischbein (1751-1829) portrayed "*Goethe in the Roman countryside*", the most famous portrait of the author. The painter lived in Rome between 1783 and 1787. Goethe stayed with him 1787-1788 in the building now home to the Goethe Museum (18 Via del Corso). From 1789 to 1799 he was the director of the Naples Academy of Fine Arts and later settled in Germany until his death. Tischbein painted a portrait of Goethe with Vesuvius in the background, today in the San Martino Museum, Naples.

[14] Palazzo Carafa, a magnificent building of the Neapolitan Renaissance (1466) in Via San Biagio dei Librai (also known as Spaccanapoli).

a horse.[15] *We went there this morning. This precious relic stands upright in the courtyard, opposite the main door, in a niche above a fountain and is truly astonishing. What an impression this head must have made when it was still joined to its body! Overall, it is much larger than the horses in the church of St. Mark. Closer inspection of its parts better reveals its admirable character and strength. The fine forehead, the puffed nostrils, the attentive ears and the bristling mane: such vigour, such power!*
We then observed a statue of a woman placed in a niche above the main door. Winckelmann says it depicts a dancer ... It is extremely attractive and delicate; the missing head has been skilfully replaced: in any case, it by no means seems to be re-worked and would deserve a better location.[16]

The colossal horse's head in bronze from Palazzo Carafa at Spaccanapoli, today in the National Archaeological Museum.

Friday 9th March 1787
Today we visited the Prince of Waldeck, in Capodimonte,[17] *where there is a large collection of paintings and medals, etc.; it is not very well laid out but there are several valuable objects ...*[18] *Everything that reaches us in the North in bits and pieces – coins, gemstones, vases and even truncated lemon trees – has an entirely other effect in mass here, where such treasures are common: the rarity of works of art at home makes them all the more precious; here, on the other hand, one learns to value only what is excellent. Etruscan vases are now very expensive but thet are undoubtedly fine and beautiful.*[19] *Few travellers leave without buying one ... and I fear I have also been seduced.*

Sunday 11th March 1787
... I went with Tischbein to Pompeii. We enjoyed the magnificent views all around us – already known to us in a thousand drawings – but only now seen wonderfully together as a whole. Pompeii is surprisingly small. Narrow, albeit straight streets, some of which with pavements: small, windowless houses, with rooms lit only through the doors opening on to the atrium and the peristyle; even the public works, such as the bench near the gate of Herculaneum, the Temple and a villa in the suburbs are more like doll's houses than real buildings.[20] *Yet these rooms, galleries and corridors are embellished with delightful paintings: the plain walls had a real painting in the middle, today damaged: the corners and edges had delicate and delightful arabesques, from which airy figures of young girls and nymphs stood out at times, while elsewhere wild animals and pets leapt from rich garlands. The entire city is like this. Even in its present state of abandon, initially under stones and ash and then excavated and sacked, it reveals, among all its people, a taste for the arts and painting, of which today not even the most fervid admirer has any idea, nor even the sentiment and the need. If we consider the distance between Pompeii and Vesuvius, it is evident that the volcanic material that buried the*

---

[15] The original of this colossal horse's head was transferred in 1809 to the National Museum. Some experts suggest that it is part of an ancient bronze horse that first stood in the Temple of Poseidon and was also linked with the legend of the horse sung by Virgil. In reality, it was a gift of Lorenzo il Magnifico to his tutor, Diomede Carafa, Count of Maddaloni, who thanked him in a letter dated 12 July 1471 *"for the gift of the bronze head of a horse"*. Vasari in the first edition of *Lives of the most excellent painters, sculptors and architects* claims in his biography of Donatello that the head is ancient, yet in the second edition he attributes to him and adds "it is so fine that many people think it is ancient".
The antiquity of the statue is still open to debate: U. Pannuti, *Intorno alla cosiddetta Testa Carafa nel Museo Nazionale di Napoli*, Römische Mitteilungen 95, 1988, pages 129-157 (an ancient work, perhaps restored by Donatello); E. Formigli, *Der sogenannte Carafa-Kopf. Technische Untersuchung eines grossen Pferde-Kopfes*, Thetis 3, 1996, pages 137-145 (Renaissance work in view of the internal screws).
[16] The statue, known as "The Dancer" or "The Nymph", is now in the Vatican Museums (Masks Room). It is a classic Roman sculpture copied from an original of III century B.C., also mentioned by Winck-

elmann (*Geschichte der Kunst des Altertums*, V 3, 6). A year later, the statue was involved in an episode that Goethe narrated in every detail in the third part of *Travelling in Italy* (*Notes* April 1788). In short, it was taken to Rome by a merchant in 1788, offered for sale to Goethe and then sold to Pope Pio VI, who installed it in the Room of the Pio Clementino Museum: S. Adamo Muscettola, *Rediscovered Memories of Ancient Naples*, Prospettiva 53-56, 1989, pages 236-244; *Eadem*, *Naples and its Antiquities*, in F. Zevi (editor), *Neapolis*, Naples 1994, pages 95-109, especially pages 104-105.
[17] The Royal Palace of Capodimonte, unfinished at the time. The building, designed by Medrano, was begun in 1738 but only completed in 1829.
[18] The prestigious Farnese Collection, today in the Naples National Museum.
[19] In the 1700s "Greek" vases were known as "Etruscan".
[20] The bench near the gate of Herculaneum was used by Priestess Mamia; the Temple is the one dedicated to Isis and the Villa may be that of Diomedes, at the end of the Street of Tombs, excavated between 1771 and 1774.

city could not have been thrown by an explosion or carried by the wind; it seems more likely that the stones and ash remained suspended in the air for some time, like clouds, until they finally fell on the doomed city. A mountain village buried under snow perhaps gives a good idea of what probably happened.

Here and there, from the buried streets and ruined buildings, occasional bare walls protrude, when the hill, sooner or later, was cultivated with vineyards and gardens. So, more than one landowner, ploughing his land, undoubtedly made the first significant "harvests". Inasmuch, many rooms are empty; in the corner of one room, a pile of ash was found hiding small tools and art objects.

The singular and almost pitiful impression of this mummified city drifted away once we sat under a pergola in a poor hotel to eat a frugal meal, refreshing ourselves under the blue sky, the splendour and the light of the sea, in the hope of meeting again here to enjoy the place shaded by green vine leaves.

Near Naples, I noticed for the second time those small homes (the "bassi") – perfect copies of the Pompeian houses. We were allowed to visit one, which we found to be very clean and tidy: cane chairs with elegant fabrics, a gilt chest of drawers painted with flowers in various colours. So, after all these centuries and so many events, the same climate inspires the inhabitants to the same habits and customs, tastes and inclinations.

Tuesday 13 March 1787

… On Sunday, we went to Pompeii. Great catastrophes have happened all over the world but very few have resulted in so much pleasure to posterity. I can't think of any that are more interesting. The homes are small and narrow but decorated inside with fine paintings. The gate of the city[21] is very fine, followed by the necropolis:[22] the tomb of a priestess is a semi-circular bench, with a stone espalier, with a large inscription.[23] Beyond the espalier, our eyes ranged over the sea and the setting sun. Magnificent, truly worthy of thought! … Over the last few days, I have also studied the products of Vesuvius: it is quite another thing to see them all together. In truth, I should dedicate the rest of my life to observing them; by making many discoveries, I could help expand human knowledge. Please tell Herder that I am studying botany every day: the principle is always the same but it would take a lifetime to complete it. Perhaps I may be able to develop the main outlines.

Caserta, Friday 16 March 1787

… Naples is a paradise; everyone lives in a kind of exaltation and oblivion. This is even happening to me; as soon as I recognise myself, I find I am quite the opposite. Yesterday I said to myself: either you were crazy until now or you have become crazy! From here, I visited the ruins of ancient Capua and everything related to them.[24]

One has to come here to learn about vegetation and how to cultivate the land! The flax is already flowering and the wheat is already tall. There is a huge plain around Caserta: the fields are so close to each other and so carefully cultivated that they resemble flower-beds in a garden. Everything is well-ordered by poplars overgrown with vines;[25] and, despite the shade, the soil even produces the best cereals …

Caserta, Friday 16 March 1787

While it is a pleasure to study in Rome, here one wants only to live … it is a wonderful sensation for me to be surrounded only by people intent on enjoying themselves.

Hamilton, the English Ambassador, after such lengthy study of Nature has reached the peak of all natural and artistic joys in a beautiful young woman.[26] She is with him now. She is English, twenty years old, exceptionally beautiful and has a fine figure.[27] He makes here wear Greek garments that suit her perfectly; and she, letting her

---

[21] The Gate of Herculaneum.

[22] The Necropolis, known as the Gate of Herculaneum.

[23] This was a very elegant type of holy arts comprising a hemicycle bench, known as the *schola* or *exedra*, made up of slabs of grey tuff; the sides were decorated with the feet of gryphons. It is the tomb of Priestess Mamia, as witnessed by the inscription "*Mamiae P. f. sacerdoti publicae locus sepulturae datus decree decurionum*". Goethe then wrote: "*A marvellous place, made to heighten thought*". Princess Maria Amalia of Weimar had Tischbein portray her sitting majestically on a similar tomb – a copy that she installed in the Weimar parks.

[24] Goethe must have seen, in these times, the amphitheatre, the Arch

of Hadrian and the tombs along the Appian Way ("La Conocchia" and "Le Carceri").

[25] This is the so-called "maritata" vine that grows upwards to create a characteristic "green wall" between the poplars – a technique also used in ancient times in the Capua countryside to produce "*Falernum*" and "*Faustianum*"; see Pliny, *Naturalis Historia* XIV 34. The advantage is that the vine is well-ventilated and that the land below can be used to grow other crops; the drawback is that the lymph – having to reach so high – is weakened.

[26] Sir William Hamilton (1730-1803) English ambassador in Naples since 1764, collector and historian of archaeology and volcanology.

[27] Miss Harte-Emma Lyon (1763-1815), the famous courtesan of hum-

hair down and taking two scarves, changes her attitudes, gestures and expressions so often that it is all like dreaming. What a thousand artists would be delighted to make, she achieved to perfection, in a marvellous variety of movements. Standing, kneeling, sitting, lying down, serious, sad, facetious, exultant, coy, seductive, threatening, troubled: one expression follows the other, changing continually. Every expression is made and changed in the folds of her veil and so many different hairstyles. In the meantime, her old husband devotedly holds the lamp. He glimpses in her all the beauties of ancient statues, the fine profiles on Sicilian coins, even the Apollo of the Belvedere! In short, it is unique entertainment ... We have already enjoyed two evenings in this way ...

Naples, Sunday 18 March 1787

We could no longer postpone our visit to Herculaneum and the Portici collection. That ancient city, standing at the feet of Vesuvius, was buried by the lava of several eruptions, so that the buildings are now sixty feet below ground.[28] They were found by excavating a well, at the base of which a marble floor was found.[29] What a shame that the excavations were not made systematically by German miners since there is no doubt that random and furtive work has ruined many important items! Seventy steps descend through a grotto where one can admire, in the torchlight a theatre that once stood in the open air and where visitors are told about what was found and then taken away ...[30]

We then entered the Museum with good letters of introduction and received a warm welcome; but we were not allowed to make any drawings.[31] Perhaps this is why our observation was more attentive and returned us to the past more intensely, since these objects were all around us, within the grasp of their owners for their use and enjoyment. These small homes and rooms of Pompeii now seemed even smaller to me – yet, at the same time, larger; more cramped, because I imagined them filled with so many precious tools; yet larger, because these tools not only served necessity but, embellished and artistically decorated in the most ingenious and delicate ways, they brightened and soothed the soul, in a manner that a more spacious home could never achieve.
For example, there was a beautifully modelled bucket with a truly elegant upper edge; seen at close hand, this edging was raised on both sides and the two semi-circles were joined to make a handle so that it could be carried with the greatest comfort.[32] The oil lamps, depending on the number of wicks, are decorated with masks and vine shoots, so that every flame illuminates a work of art. High, delicate bronze candelabras we used to hold the oil-lamps; while, on the other hand, the oil-lamps had to be hung and embellished by every kind of ingenious and imaginative figure that must also delighted everyone as they moved in the breeze. Hoping to return, we followed the caretaker around the rooms and, time permitting, we found things that both entertained and instructed us.

Naples, Tuesday 20 March 1787

The latest news is that a stream of lava, invisible from Naples, erupted and flowed down towards Ottajano, encouraging me to visit Vesuvius for the third time. We reached the feet of the mountain with my two-wheeler and horse and as soon as we jumped down our usual guides appeared. I didn't want to do without them both: I took one out of habit, the other out of trust and both to feel more at ease.

---

ble origins, the lover and then the wife (married in 1791) of Sir William Hamilton. She later became the lover of Admiral Horatio Nelson and, on the instigation of Queen Maria Carolina, had a pernicious influence on his cruel repression of the Neapolitan revolution in 1799. She died in poverty in Calais, after being imprisoned as a debtor. She remained famous in Naples for her performances in the ancient costumes of Herculaneum – "*Les attitudes de Madame Hamilton*" (see the essay on Hamilton in this book).
[28] The city of Herculaneum is buried under about 20 metres of tuff (eruption in 79 A.D.) and of about 7 metres of lava (subsequent eruptions).
[29] This refers to the chance discovery of the theatre by a farmer (Enzechetta) digging a well and despoiled by Colonel Prince d'Elboeuf around 1709. History of the first despoliations: V. Papaccio, *Marbles of Herculaneum in France. History of certain distractions of Principe E.M. d'Elbeuf*, Naples 1995. In 1738, the Bourbon King Carlo I temporarily halted this disgraceful action by commissioning a series of explorations in tunnels that lasted until 1777.

[30] Theatre of Herculaneum: M. Pagano, *Il Teatro di Ercolano*, Cronache Ercolanesi 23, 1993, pages 121-156; U. Pappalardo, *Nuove testimonianze su Marco Nonio Balbo ad Ercolano*, Mitteilungen des Deutschen Archäologischen Instituts, Rome, 104, 1997, pages 285-297; German version: *Der Patronus von Herculaneum: Marcus Nonius Balbus*, in J. Mühlenbrock-D. Richter (editors), *Die letzten Stunden von Herculaneum*, Haltern Exhibition Catalogue, Mainz 2005, pages 171-181.
[31] A wing of the Portici Royal Palace, built by King Carlo in 1738, was home to the Herculaneum Museum and its finds from Pompeii and Herculaneum (later transferred to Naples): A. Allroggen Bedel-H. Kammerer Grothaus, *Das Museum Ercolanese in Portici*, Cronache Ercolanesi 10, 1980, pages 175-217; Italian translation: *The Herculaneum Museum of Portici*, in M. Gigante *et al.*, *The Papyrus Villa*, Naples 1983, pages 83-128.
[32] The bucket he sketched may be the one today in the National Museum of Naples (probably, inv. Nr. 73146).

*Pompeii and Vesuvius,
watercolour by Goethe.*

When we reached higher up, the old man stayed with our cloaks and provisions; the young man followed and we boldly climbed towards a dense steam, erupting from the mountain below the crater: we flanked the crater and then descended easily until, beneath the clear sky, we saw the lava bubbling from an awful cloud of smoke.

One may hear something spoken of a thousand times yet it is only by seeing it that its distinctive character is revealed. The lava was ten feet wide at most: yet the way in which it flowed over the gentle, uniform slope was rather surprising; as the lava flows, it cools at the sides and on the surface, forming a channel that becomes continually enlarged, since the molten material hardens on top of the torrent of fire that pushes the slag floating on the surface uniformly to right and left. Then, little by little, a bank rose over which the lava continued to flow quietly, like the rustling of a windmill. We walked at the side of this rather high embankment; the slag rolled regularly at the two sides as far as our feet. We could see, from below, the tongue of fire through gaps in the channel; we also managed to observe it higher up as it continued flowing.

The brightness of the sun seemed to dull the flowing flame; nothing except a little smoke rose into the pure air. I wanted to get closer to the point where the lava issued from the mountain. The guide assured me that it was close by and made up of an arch and a ceiling, where he had already been several times. To see and verify it all, we climbed the mountain to reach this point from behind. Fortunately, a strong breeze blowing across the site kept it clear … excepting the steam from a thousand crevices that fumed around us.

Lastly, we reached the vault, hard and distorted like tack-bread but it was so broad that we could not see where the lava emerged. We took another twenty paces but the ground become increasingly hot: an unbearable, suffocating vortex of steam hid the sun. The guide – who had gone on ahead of me – returned, pulled me back and we fled the infernal boiling.

After the view restored our eyes and wine our throats, we followed the cone to see other details of the summit of this Inferno emerging in the midst of Paradise. I again closely examined several crevices, the true ducts of the volcano – they do not so much smoke as continually and violently exhale fiery air. I observed that they were entirely lined by a stalactitic material resembling bells and nipples along the whole channel. Their irregularity allowed us to gather many of these suspended products, removing them easily with our walking-sticks and some hooks. I had already seen merchants – using the name "lava" – selling these examples and now I was delighted to have discovered that they are a volcanic soot, deposited by fiery sulphurous exhalations often enclosing volatile minerals.

A truly splendid sunset and a wonderful evening restored me on our return; yet I felt how prodigal contrasts confuse the senses. The terrible in the beautiful, the beautiful in the terrible cancel each other out and generate a sensation of indifference. Certainly, the Neapolitan would be quite a different man should he no longer feel caught between God and the Devil.

Naples, Friday 23 March 1787

My relations with Kniep[33] have now been settled in a very practical manner. We were together in Paestum and he proved to be, on the outward and return trips, an avid drawer. There are some rather fine sketches …[34] This is what we agreed upon. As of today, we will live and travel together, without him having any other concerns

---

[33] Christoph Heinrich Kniep (1748-1825), an artist Goethe met in Rome, who accompanied him on his travels to Naples and Sicily. After Sicily, he settled in Naples where he became a Professor at the Academy of Fine Arts.

[34] See Weimar, Goethe-Nationalmuseum inv. 1235 - Porzio - Cause Picone 1983, fig. 82, page 39 and page 88: this is probably the so-called "Basilica".

*than drawing, as he has done over the last few days. All the sketches will be mine ... he will draw a certain num-
ber of subjects for me, up to an agreed figure. His skill and the importance of the views collected in accordance
with my decisions will govern the rest ...*

The second stay in Naples

Naples, Thursday 17 May 1787 (To Herder)
*Here I am again, my dears, safe and sound. I had an easy and short trip around Sicily; when I come home, you
will be able to judge how I lived and what I saw ...
There is nothing else that appeals to me here, since I went again yesterday to Paestum ... In a separate sheet enclosed herein, inasmuch, I especially describe my tour of Salerno and Paestum. It will be the last and, I imagine,
the finest picture I will bring with me back North. The Temple of Neptune[35] is preferable, in my opinion, to
everything else to be seen in Sicily ... Allow me to express my thoughts briefly in these terms: the ancients represented existence and we the ordinary effect; they painted what was horrible, we paint horribly; they what was
pleasing and we only in a pleasing way. This is the reason for exaggeration, mannerism, affectation and pompos-
ity; since when one seeks effect and writes for effect, one never feels that it is sensitive enough ...*

Naples, Sunday 27 May 1787
*... Hamilton and his attractive English lady are unceasingly amiable. I lunched at their home and, towards
evening, Miss Harte gave a fine performance of her music and singing. On the insistence of friend Hackert ...[36]
Hamilton allowed into his secret sanctuary of art objects and antiquities. It was rather jumbled: artefacts of different epochs placed at random, busts, torsos, vases, bronzes and every kind of embellishment in Sicilian agate,
even a shrine, as well as engravings, paintings and everything else he had managed to buy. I opened the broken
top of a long chest on the floor out of curiosity and saw two magnificent bronze candelabra. I showed them to
Hackert and asked him in a whisper if they came from Portici. He nodded that I should say no more. In short,
they might have been lost on the way from the excavations at Pompeii ... it is precisely because of such fortunate
purchases that Hamilton only shows his hidden treasures to intimate friends ...
I also saw with surprise an upright chest, painted black inside, surrounded by a magnificent gilt frame; the space
was too wide to serve a standing person and this was how we were told it was used. This lover of the arts and
young girls, not content to see, as if a mobile statue, the attractive image of his English lady, also wanted to admire an incomparable painting; and so, wearing clothes of various colours with a black base, she not unrarely imitated in this gold frame the ancient frescoes of Pompeii and modern masterpieces.[37] It seems that the epoch of
such happy experiments is over: in any case, it was difficult to move the appliance and place it in the light. So we
were not allowed to enjoy this spectacle ...
If I may say something that a good-mannered guest should never dare, I must admit that our attractive and delightful Miss Harte[38] seems to me not to have a soul, that she may undoubtedly offset with her fine figure, but
she has a dull voice and dull conversation, lacking in sentiment. Her singing is equally lacking in warmth and
fascination. And, in general, this is what happened in these cold images. There are beautiful women everywhere; yet those with deep feelings and a fine voice are very rare: rarer still are those with these qualities and
an attractive figure.*

Naples, Monday 28 May 1787
*Pliny, in Section V of the his Natural History,[39] feels that only Campania is worthy of a detailed description.
"This region is so delightful", he says, so amenable, so blessed, that the work of nature is manifestly evident.
Since this air is so vital, this sky so sweet and always salubrious, these fields so fertile, these hills so open and*

---

[35] The so-called Temple of Poseidon in Paestum.
[36] Philipp Hackert (1737-1807), from 1786 a painter at the Court of
Naples under Ferdinand IV: J.W. Goethe, *Philipp Hackert*, in
Goethes Sämtliche Werke. Propyläen Ausgabe, vol. 20, München,
1963, pages 204-327; Italian translation: G. Vasale, *J.W. Goethe,*

Philipp Hackert (Italian and original text side-by-side), Bari 1996.
[37] This is part of the prestigious collection that later formed the British
Museum (also see the essay on Hamilton in this volume).
[38] Also see the essay on Hamilton in this volume.
[39] In fact, it is in section VI.

sunny, these forests so peaceful, these woods so dense, these trees so richly varied; and so many excellent mountains, and broad fields and abundant vineyards and olive groves, and flocks of sheep with noble fleeces, and big-shouldered bulls; there are so many lakes, such a wealth of rivers and springs irrigating everywhere, so many beaches, so many ports! And this same land, everywhere, opens its breast to trade and, almost avid in coming to the aid of men, extends its arms to the sea! I make no mention of the geniality, customs and vigour of these peoples, who have dominated so many countries with language and hands. The Greeks, so used to boasting, made such an honourable assessment of this country that they even named a part of it Magna Graecia ..."

Friday 1 June 1787, evening
My visits of thanks were equally interesting and enjoyable; various things were presented to me that I had so far neglected or postponed. Venuti[40] showed me some hidden treasures; I once again admired and revered his Ulysses,[41] priceless albeit, mutilated. As a last kindness, he accompanied me to the Capodimonte chinaware factory, where I sought to impress in my memory, as far as possible, the Hercules,[42] and I satiated, once again, my eyes with Campanian vases.
Sincerely moved and taking farewell in the most friendly manner, he then confided to me that he was upset I would not be able to stay with him for a certain time. My banker, who I had found at table, did not want me to leave. Everything would have been fine and good had not the lava fascinated my imagination. While I was busy settling payments and packing the baggage, night fell ... and I raced to the Quay. From there, I saw the fires and all the lights and their reflections flickering even more in the heavy sea, and the full moon in all its magnificence to one side of flaming Vesuvius and, lastly, the lava that wasn't there the day before yesterday and yet followed its grim and scorching road. I would have liked to arrive up there but the preparations would have taken too much time and I'd not have arrived before morning. I did not want to miss, through haste. the spectacle I was enjoying: I remained on the Quay until, despite the comings and goings of the crowds and the disputes over which direction the lava stream would flow, I felt my eyes close to sleep.

Naples, Saturday evening, 2 June 1787
... I had already promised to visit Duchess Young, who lives in the Royal Palace.[43] I had to climb many staircases and walk along many corridors, the last of which were full of crates, wardrobes and all the other vexing clutter of a royal cloakroom. In a high, sombre chamber, I found an attractive young lady of graceful and refined conversation ... born in Germany ... We were on the upper floor. Vesuvius stands right in front: the lava flow, already reddening after the sunset, began to gilt the smoke accompanying it; the mountain resounded, surmounted by a thick and immobile cloud, and different agglomerates, with every new eruption, were struck by flashes that lit up the reliefs; from there down to the beach, a strip of flames and fiery vapours; and all the rest, the sea and the earth, the cliffs and the fields, visible in the dusk, in a peaceful transparency, in a magical calm. All this, seen at a glance, as the moon rose behind the volcano, almost as if completing a stupendous painting, could not but astonish me. The eye embraced everything in a single glance and, although it wasn't possible to examine every detail, the overall impression was never lost. Although our conversation had been interrupted by such spectacular sights, afterwards it became very intimate. We were looking at a text that a thousand years and more would not suffice to comment. As the night deepened, so the village seemed all the more illuminated. The moon shone like a second sun; the columns of smoke and their luminous masses were perfectly distinguishable: actually, a more powerful telescope revealed, at the black base of the cone, the scorching stones thrown up by the volcano.[44]

---

[40] Marquis Domenico Venuti (1745-1817), son of Marcello, the first Director of Excavations at Herculaneum. He directed (1781-1799) the Capodimonte Chinaware Factory that, under his guidance, moved towards a neo-classic taste.
[41] It is not possible to identify this statue, even though described – albeit ideally – in a letter of Heinrich Meyer in 1789.
[42] The Farnese Hercules, a famous Roman sculpture, the original of which is attributed to Lisippus, found in 1540 in the Baths of Caracalla in Rome and transferred, with the Farnese Collection, to the Capodimonte Royal Palace near Naples: P. Moreno, Il Farnese ritrovato e altri tipi di Eracle in riposo, Mélanges Ecole Française de Rome, Archéologie (MEFRA) 94, 1982, pages 379-526.
[43] The wife of Duke Nicola Giovane of Girasole, born Giuliana von Mundersbach, Baroness of Redewitz (1766-1805). In 1785, she became a dame at the court of Queen Maria Carolina and lived in the Royal Palace. In 1791, she moved to the court of Vienna, where she died: B. Croce, Volfango Goethe a Napoli, in Aneddoti e profili settecenteschi, Palermo, 1914, pages 97-162.
[44] This eruption lasted from 27 May to 21 December 1787.

My host – and I must say I could not have wished for a more convivial occasion – placed candles at the opposite end of the room; and the attractive woman, lit by the moonlight standing in the foreground of this marvellous "painting", seemed all the more beautiful to me: it was all the more enchanting for me, since I was delighted to hear a German dialect spoken in this southern paradise.

Since we had forgotten how late it already was, she reminded me saying that she was sorry to see me leave but the time was close when the galleries would be closed as if in a monastery. I therefore left with painful hesitation what was far from me and what was close to me, blessing my good fortune that such an evening had so well compensated the boring visits of the morning. Once in the fresh air, I told myself that had I gone to see the great lava flow I would actually only have seen a repetition of the smaller event and that this panorama, this farewell to Naples was everything I could ever have desired …

The Eruption of Vesuvius in 1781, seen from Ponte della Maddalena, Naples, in a painting by Jacques Volaire. Naples, Capodimonte National Museum.

Last days in Naples

From two letters to Carlotta von Stein respectively from Naples (1 June) and Rome (8 June 1787): *… if I am pleased to leave Naples, it is because, in the end, there is nothing more to be done here and lazy living does not suit me … I left Naples alone and happily; one is never fully aware here and it takes a particular state of mind and more time to get used to it all. I spent three and a half days happily travelling. Sitting alone in the coach, I let myself be transported, enjoying the landscape, drew a few sketches and summed up my time in Naples and Sicily. I have every reason to be happy about my travels, during which I put together many fine and lasting treasures.*

Return to Germany

Goethe kept himself informed about excavations in Italy and collected in his Weimar studio copies of Pompeian works of art. He was a friend of Johann Karl Wilhelm Zahn, who was later one of the founders of the *Archäologische Gesellschaft* in Berlin. Zahn was involved in excavations in Pompeii in 1824-1827 and, on his proposal, in 1832 one of the houses (discovered on 7 October 1830 in the presence of Goethe's son, Augustus, who died a few days later in Rome) was named "The House of Goethe"; today it is known as the "House of the Faun". A few days before his death, Goethe exhibited a drawing sent to him by Zahn of a mosaic found there – the famous "Mosaic of Alexander", discovered in 1831. On 10 March 1832 he noted: "*People today and in the future will not be able to comment on such a masterpiece correctly and will be obliged to return – even after careful investigation – to pure and simple admiration*". Goethe died at Weimar only twelve days later on 22 March 1832.

Photography credits

All the pictures are from Luciano Pedicini, Archivio Pedicini, Napoli, except of:
- Archivio Fotografico Musei Vaticani, Città del Vaticano: p. 24.
- Mark E. Smith: pp. 14-15, 19, 20-21, 30, 39, 41.

For the pictures of Ercolano, Oplontis, Pompei and Stabia permission requested to Ministero per i Beni e le Attività Culturali, Soprintendenza per i Beni Archeologici di Pompei.

For the pictures of Capri, Campi Flegrei, Cuma, Ischia, Napoli and Sorrento permission requested to Ministero per i Beni e le Attività Culturali, Soprintendenza per i Beni Archeologici di Napoli e Caserta.

For the pictures of Benevento, Velia and Paestum permission requested to Ministero per i Beni e le Attività Culturali, Soprintendenza per i Beni Archeologici di Salerno, Avellino e Benevento.

For the pictures on pp. 6-27-70-90-97-105-106-107 permission requested to Biblioteca Nazionale Vittorio Emanuele III.

For the pictures on pp. 6-27-70-90-97-105-106-107 permission requested to Soprintendenza Speciale per il Polo Museale di Napoli.

For the pictures on pp. 114-121 permission requested to Museo Campano di Capua.

The publisher should be excused if, for causes independent from his will, he has omitted or erroneously cited a source.

Bibliography

About Campania in general

AA.VV., *I culti della Campania Antica*. Atti Convegno Internazionale in onore di N. Valenza Mele, Napoli 15-17.V.1995, Roma 1998.

AA.VV., *La Campania fra il VI ed il III secolo a.C.* Atti XIV Convegno di Studi Etruschi e Italici, Galatina 1992.

AA.VV., *La presenza etrusca nella Campania meridionale*, Firenze 1994.

AA.VV., *Storia del Mezzogiorno*, vol. 1, 1-2, Napoli 1991.

S. DE CARO, A. GRECO PONTRANDOLFO, *Campania* (Guide Archeologiche Laterza), Roma-Bari 1981.

E. GRECO, *Magna Grecia* (Guide Archeologiche Laterza), Roma-Bari 1981.

W. JOHANNOWSKY, *Materiali di età arcaica dalla Campania*, Napoli 1983.

A. MAIURI, *Passeggiate Campane*, Firenze 1982.

G. NENCI, G. VALLET (edited by), *Bibliografia Topografica delle Colonie Greche e delle Isole Tirreniche* (= BTGCI), Pisa-Roma 1981.

G. PUGLIESE CARRATELLI *et al.*, *Megale Hellas. Storia e civiltà della Magna Grecia*, Milano 1983.

Soprintendenza Archeologica di Roma, *Studi sull'Italia dei Sanniti*, Milano 2000.

The Greeks and Greek colonisation

AA.VV., *I Greci in Occidente*, Napoli 1996.

L. CERCHIAI, *I Campani*, Milano 1995.

L. CERCHIAI, L. JANNELLI, F. LONGO, *Città greche della Magna Grecia e della Sicilia*, Verona 2002.

S. DE CARO, A. GRECO, *Campania*, Bari 1981.

E. GRECO, *Magna Grecia*, Bari 1993.

G. PUGLIESE CARRATELLI (edited by), *I Greci in Occidente*, Milano 1996.

G. PUGLIESE CARRATELLI (edited by), *Storia e Civiltà della Campania. L'Evo Antico*, Napoli 1991.

S. SETTIS, C. PARRA (edited by), *Magna Grecia. Archeologia di un sapere*, Milano 2005.

Ischia

G. BUCHNER, *Pithekoùssai*, vol. I, Monumenti Antichi dei Lincei, Roma 1993.

G. BUCHNER, C. GIALANELLA, *Guida al Museo di Ischia*, Napoli 1995.

Cuma

P. CAPUTO, R. MORICHI, R. PAONE, P. RISPOLI, *Cuma e il suo parco archeologico. Un territorio e le sue testimonianze*, Roma 1996.

G. GALASSO, *L'altra Europa. Per un'antropologia storica del Mezzogiorno d'Italia*, Milano 1982, in particular pp. 13-63.

M. PAGANO, *Considerazioni sull'antro della Sibilla a Cuma*, Rendiconti dell'Accademia di Archeologia, Lettere e Belle Arti di Napoli, n.s. 60, 1985, pp. 69-91.

The Cumaean Sibyl

L. BREGLIA PULCI DORIA, *Oracoli sibillini tra rituali e propaganda*, Napoli 1983.

S. DAKARIS, *Antichità dell'Epiro. II Necromanteion dell'Acheronte*, Atene s.d.

A. MAIURI in: Itinerario Flegreo, Napoli 1983: "*Come ho scoperto l'antro della Sibilla a Cuma*", pp. 195-203; "*Horrendae secreta Sibyllae. Scoperta dell'antro cumano*", pp.205-212.

D. REDIG DE CAMPOS, *Cappella Sistina*, Novara 1959.

G. ROUX, *Delphes, son oracles et ses dieux*, Paris 1976.

Paestum

AA.VV., *Il Museo di Paestum*, Agropoli 1986.

E. GRECO, *Il Pittore di Afrodite*, Roma 1970.

E. GRECO, I. D'AMBROSIO, D. THEODORESCU, *Guida archeologica e storica agli Scavi, al Museo ed alle Antichità di Posidonia-Paestum*, Taranto 1996.

E. GRECO, F. LONGO, *Paestum. La visita della città*, Roma 2002.

E. GRECO, F. LONGO, *Paestum. Scavi, studi ricerche. Bilancio di un decennio (1988-1999)*, Salerno 2000.

E. GRECO, D. THEODORESCU (edited by), *Poseidonia-Paestum*, 1, 1980; 2, 1983; 3, 1987; 4, 1999.

G. GRECO, *Il santuario di Hera alla Foce del Sele*, Salerno 2001.

A. MELE, *Storia di Poseidonia tra VI e V secolo a.C.*, in: Poseidonia e i Lucani, Napoli 1996.

M. NAPOLI, *Il Museo di Paestum*, Cava de' Tirreni 1969.

A. PONTRANDOLFO, *Le tombe dipinte di Paestum*, Paestum 1998.

J. RASPI SERRA (edited by), *La fortuna di Paestum e la memoria moderna del dorico 1750-1830*. Mostra Roma, Palazzo Braschi, 7.X.-23.XI.1986, Firenze 1986.

J. Raspi Serra, P. Mascilli Migliorini, M. Platania, *Paestum idea e immagine. Antologia di testi critici e di immagini di Paestum 1750-1836*, Modena 1990.
M. Taliercio, *Aspetti e problemi della monetazione di Poseidonia* in: Atti del XXVII Convegno di Studi sulla Magna Grecia, Taranto 1987, Napoli 1992, pp. 133-183.
M. Torelli, *Paestum Romana*, Roma 1999.
A.D. Trendall, *The Red-Figured Vases from Paestum*, Roma 1987.
P. Zancani Montuoro, U. Zanotti Bianco, *L' Heraion alla Foce del Sele*, Roma 1, 1951; 2, 1954.
F. Zevi (edited by), *Paestum*, Napoli 1990.

Velia
L. Cerchiai, L. Jannelli, F. Longo, *Città greche della Magna Grecia e della Sicilia*, Verona 2002, pp. 82-89.
C.A. Fiammenghi, *Le necropoli di Elea-Velia: qualche osservazione preliminare* in: G. Greco (edited by), *Le nuove ricerche*. Atti Convegno Studi Napoli 14.XII.2001, Napoli 2003, pp. 49-61, in particular p. 53, tav. 17, 2 (funerar y building in Velian bricks).
G. Greco, *Velia. La visita alla città*, Pozzuoli 2002.
G. Greco, F. Krinzinger, *Velia. Studi e ricerche*, Modena 1994.
M. Napoli, *Guida degli scavi di Velia*, Cava dei Tirreni 1972.

The Romans and Campania Felix
AA.VV., *La Magna Grecia nell'età romana*. Atti del XV Convegno di Studi sulla Magna Grecia, Taranto 5-10.X.1975, Napoli 1976.
AA.VV., *La romanisation du Samnium au IIme et Ier siècles av. J.C.*, Napoli 1991.
G. Galasso, *Passato e presente del meridionalismo*, Napoli 1978.
L.A. Thompson, *On Development and Underdevelopment in the Early Roman Empire*, Klio 64, 1982, pp. 383-401.
A. Varvaro, *Bilancio degli studi sulla storia linguistica meridionale* in: P. Giannantonio (edited by), *Cultura meridionale e letteratura italiana*, Napoli 1985, pp. 25-37.

Naples
AA.VV, *Napoli antica*, Napoli 1985.
AA.VV, *Neapolis*, Atti del XXV Convegno di Studi sulla Magna Grecia, Taranto 1986.
E. Lepore, *La vita politica e sociale* in: Storia di Napoli, vol. 1, Napoli 1967, pp. 41-212.
E. Lepore, *Origini e strutture della Campania antica*, Bologna 1989.
G. Vecchio, *La grotta di Seiano e il parco archeologico del Pausilypon*, Napoli1999.
F. Zevi (edited by), *Neapolis*, Napoli 1994.

Virgil the Seer
D. Comparetti, *Virgilio nel medioevo*, Firenze 1896.
B. Croce, *Storie e leggende napoletane*, Napoli 1919; reprint: Milano 1999.
A.W. Martin, *Janus von Neapel*, Frauenfeld 1966; Italian translation: Giano di Napoli, Capri 2005.
M. Serao, *Leggende napoletane*, Napoli 1890; reprint: Napoli 1994.

The National Archaeological Museum of Naples
AA.VV., *Le Collezioni del Museo Nazionale di Napoli*. Pictures from Archivio Fotografico Pedicini, vol. 1, Roma 1986: I mosaici, le pitture, gli oggetti di uso quotidiano, gli argenti, le terrecotte invetriate, i vetri, i cristalli, gli avori; vol. 2, Roma 1989: La scultura greco-romana, le sculture antiche della collezione Farnese, le collezioni monetali, le oreficerie, la collezione glittica.
F. Baratte, *Le trésor d'orfèvrerie romaine de Boscoreale*, Paris 1986.
S. De Caro, *Il Museo Archeologico Nazionale di Napoli*, Napoli 1994.
K. Fittschen, *Zum Figurenfries von Boscoreale*, in: B. Andreae, H. Kyrieleis (edited by), *Neue Forschungen in Pompeji*, Recklinghausen 1975, p. 93-100.
V. Franciosi, *Il Doriforo di Policleto* (with preface by P. Themelis), Napoli 2003.
C. Gasparri (edited by), *Le Gemme Farnese*, Napoli 1994.
E. La Rocca, *L'eta d'oro di Cleopatra. Indagine Sulla Tazza Farnese*, Roma 1984.
P. Moreno, *Vita e arte di Lisippo*, Milano 1997.
U. Pannuti, *La Tazza Farnese. Datazione, interpretazione e trasmissione del cimelio*, PACT 23, 1989, p. 205ss.
U. Pappalardo, *Il ritratto romano dipinto*, Rivista Studi Pompeiani 2007. (in print)
U. Pappalardo, *Le argenterie* in: G. Stefani (edited by), *Menander. La Casa del Menandro di Pompei*, Milano 2003, pp. 90-107.
E. Pozzi *et al.*, *Il Toro Farnese. La "montagna di marmo" tra Roma e Napoli*, Napoli 1991.
W.H. Schuchhardt, *Stauenkopien der Tyrannenmörder-Gruppe. Die Gruppe der Tyrannenmörder in Neapel*, Jahrbuch des Instituts 101, 1986, pp. 85-110.
Soprintendenza Archeologica di Pompei, *Il tesoro di Boscoreale. Una collezione di argenti da mensa tra cultura ellenistica e mondo romano*, Milano 1988.
F. Zevi, *I mosaici della Casa del Fauno a Pompei*, Napoli 1998.

Sir William Hamilton: the birth of volcanology and archaeology

J.G. HERDER, *Bloss für Dich geschrieben*, Berlin 1980, p. 234ss. (in particular 238s.), lettera a Karoline Herder "Rom 21. Febr. 1789".
CH. HIBBERT, *The Grand Tour*, London 1969.
I. JENKINS, K. SLOAN (edited by), *Vases and Volcanoes. Sir William Hamilton and his Collection*, London 1996.
C. KNIGHT, *Hamilton a Napoli. Cultura, svaghi, civiltà di una grande capitale europea*, Napoli 1990; revised edition: Napoli 2003.
R. MORRIS, *HMS Colossus. The Story of the Salvage of the Hamilton Treasures*, London 1979.

The Phlegrean Fields

AA.VV., *I Campi Flegrei nell'archeologia e nella storia*. Atti Convegni Lincei num. 33, Roma 1977.
AA.VV., *Rione Terra. Percorso archeologico*, Napoli 2002.
P. AMALFITANO, G. CAMODECA, M. MEDRI, *I Campi Flegrei. Un itinerario archeologico*, Venezia 1990.
M. BORRIELLO, A. D'AMBROSIO, *Baiae, Misenum*, Forma Italiae, Regio I, 14, Firenze 1979.
F. MANISCALCO, *Ninfei ed edifici marittimi severiani del Palatium imperiale di Baia*, Napoli 1997.
P. MINIERO (edited by), *I Campi Flegrei dal vedutismo alla foto aerea*, Napoli s.d.
P. MINIERO, *Il Museo Archeologico dei Campi Flegrei nel Castello di Baia*, Napoli 2000.
P. MINIERO (edited by), *Il Sacello degli Augustali di Miseno*, Napoli 2000.
G. TOCCO SCIARELLI (edited by), *Baia. Il ninfeo imperiale sommerso di Punta Epitaffio*, Napoli 1983.
F. ZEVI (edited by), *Puteoli*, 2 voll., Napoli 1993.

Bradyseism of the Phlegrean Fields

G. DE NATALE, G. MASTROLORENZO, F. PINGUE, R. SCARPA, *I Campi Flegrei e i fenomeni bradisismici*, Le Scienze 306, Febbr. 1994, pp. 32-43.
CH. MORANGE *et al.*, *New Data on Historical Sea-Level Movements in Pozzuoli*, Phys. Chem. Earth 24, 4, 1999, pp. 349-354.
U. PAPPALARDO, F. RUSSO, *Il bradisismo dei Campi Flegrei: dati geomorfologici ed evidenze archeologiche* in: P. GIANFROTTA, F. MANISCALCO (Editors), Forma Maris. Forum Internazionale di Archeologia Subacquea, Pozzuoli 22-24.IX.1998, Napoli 2001, pp. 107-119.
A. PARASCANDOLA, *I fenomeni bradisismici del Serapeo di Pozzuoli*, Bollettino Società Naturalisti di Napoli 56, 1947.
F. STARACE, *De balneis puteolanis* in: G. GALASSO, G. VALLET (edited by), *Storia del Mezzogiorno*, vol. I, 2: Storia di Napoli, del Mezzogiorno continentale e della Sicilia, Napoli 1991, p. 277 e fig. 9.
I. VARRIALE, *Costa flegrea e attività bradisismica dall'antichità ad oggi* in: L. DE MARIA and R. TURCHETTI (edited by), *Rotte e porti del Mediterraneo dopo la caduta dell'Impero Romano d'Occidente: continuità e innovazioni tecnologiche e funzionali*, Atti del IV seminario ANSER. Genova 18-19.VI.2004, Soveria Mannelli 2004, pp. 291-310.

Capua

A. ADRIANI, *Cataloghi illustrati del Museo Campano*. vol. I: Le sculture in tufo, Alessandria d'Egitto 1939.
F. ALVINO, *L'Anfiteatro campano ristaurato e illustrato*, Napoli 1833.
M. BEDELLO, *Capua preromana*. Catalogo del Museo Provinciale Campano. Terrecotte votive. Vol. III: Testine e busti, Firenze 1975.
M. BONGHI JOVINO, *Capua preromana*. Catalogo del Museo Provinciale Campano. Terrecotte votive. Vol. I: Teste isolate e mezze teste, Firenze 1965.
M. BONGHI JOVINO, *Capua preromana*. Catalogo del Museo Provinciale Campano. Terrecotte votive. Vol. II: Le statue, Firenze 1971.
M. BONGHI JOVINO, s.v. "Capua" in: G. NENCI, G. VALLET (edited by), Bibliografia Topografica della Colonizzazione Greca in Italia (=BTCGI), vol. IV, Pisa-Roma 1985, pp. 455-476.
S. DE CARO (edited by), *Matres Matutae dal Museo di Capua*, Milano 1991.
A. DE FRANCISCIS, *Templum Dianae Tifatinae*, Napoli 1989.
A. DE FRANCISCIS, R. PANE, *Mausolei romani in Campania*, Napoli 1957.
O. DELLA TORRE, S. CIAGHI, *Terrecotte figurate ed architettoniche nel Museo Nazionale di Napoli*. I: Terrecotte figurate da Capua, Napoli 1980.
J. HEURGON, *Recherches sur l'histoire, la religion et la civilisation de Capoue préromaine*, Paris 1942.
W. JOHANNOWSKY, *Capua antica*, Napoli 1989.
H. KOCH, *Hellenistische Architekturstücke in Capua*, RömMitt 22, 1907, p. 381ss.
H. KOCH, *Studien zu den kampanischen Dachterrakotten*, RömMitt 30, 1915, p.1ss.
U. PAPPALARDO, s.v. "Capua", in: Der Neue Pauly. Reallexikon der Antike, Stuttgart, vol. 2, 1997, col. 977-980.
F. PARISE BADONI, *Capua preromana. Ceramica campana a figure nere*, Firenze 1968.
V. SAMPAOLO, *Il Museo Archeologico dell'Antica Capua*, Napoli 1995.
J. VERMASEREN, *The Mithraeum at S. Maria Capua Vetere*, Leiden 1971.

Benevento

S. ADAMO MUSCETTOLA (edited by), *Benevento: l'arco e la città*, Napoli, 1985.
E. GALASSO, *Iside, madonna e strega di Benevento* in: E. ARSLAN (edited by) *Iside. Il mito, il mistero, la magia.*

Catalogo Mostra, Milano 1997, pp. 592-595.

H.W. Müller, *Der Isiskult im antiken Benevent und Katalog der Sculpturen im Museo del Sannio zu Benevent*, Berlin 1969; Italian translation: *Il culto di Iside nell'antica Benevento*. Catalogo delle sculture provenienti dai santuari egiziani dell'antica Benevento nel Museo del Sannio, Benevento 1971.

R. Pirelli, *L'Iseo di Benevento* in: E. Arslan (edited by) *Iside. Il mito, il mistero, la magia*. Catalogo Mostra, Milano 1997, pp. 376-713.

M. Rotili, *Il Museo del Sannio*, Benevento 1963.

M. Rotili, *Il Museo del Sannio nell'Abbazia di Santa Sofia e nella Rocca dei Rettori di Benevento*, Roma 1967.

Pompeii

F. Coarelli *et al.*, *Pompei. La vita ritrovata*, Udine 2002.

E. La Rocca, M. De Vos, *Guida archeologica di Pompei*, Verona 1994.

A. Maiuri, *La Villa dei Misteri*, Roma 1930.

U. Pappalardo, *Il fregio con eroti fra girali nella Sala dei Misteri a Pompei*, Jahrbuch des Instituts 97, 1982, pp. 251-280.

U. Pappalardo, *Pompeji*, Mainz 2006 (on press).

P. Zanker, *Pompei*, Einaudi, Torino 1993.

F. Zevi (edited by), *Pompei*, Napoli vol. 1, 1991; vol. 2, 1992.

Mozart in Pompeii: "I saw neither scorpions nor spiders!"

F.L. Bastet, *Mozart in Pompeji*, Mitteilungen Internationaler Stiftung Mozarteum 34, 1-4, 1986, pp. 50-59.

W.A. Bauer, O.E. Deutsch, *Mozart. Briefe und Aufzeichnungen*. Gesamtausgabe, voll. 1-7, Kassel 1962-1975.

D.A. D'Alessandro, *Mozart a Napoli in una testimonianza pittorica*, Napoli 2006 (on press).

F. Latapie, *Description des fouilles de Pompéi* (1776), with Introduction by P. Barriere and notes by A. Maiuri, Rendiconti Accademia di Archeologia Napoli n.s., 28, 1953.

P. Scialò, *Mozart a Napoli nelle lettere di Wolfgang e Leopold*, Napoli 2001.

Ercolano

S. Adamo Muscettola, *La Villa dei Papiri a Ercolano*, Napoli 2000.

S. Bisel, *The Secrets of Vesuvius*, Toronto 1990.

R. Ciardiello, *Die Villa der Papyri in Herculaneum*, Antike Welt 2006 (on press).

D. Comparetti, G. De Petra, *La villa ercolanese dei Pisoni, i suoi monumenti e la sua biblioteca*, Torino 1883; reprint with s note by A. De Franciscis, Napoli 1972.

A. De Simone, F. Ruffo, *Ercolano e la Villa dei Papiri alla luce dei nuovi scavi* in: "Cronache Ercolanesi" 33, 2003, pp. 279-311.

M. Gigante (edited by), *La Villa dei Papiri*, Napoli 1983.

M. Gigante, *La brigata virgiliana ad Ercolano* in: Virgilio e gli augustei, Napoli 1990, pp. 9-22.

A. Maiuri, *Ercolano. I nuovi scavi (1927-1958)*, vol. I, Roma, 1958, in particular pp. 57-62.

J. Mühlenbrock, D. Richter (edited by), *Die letzten Stunden von Herculaneum*, Mainz 2005.

M. Pagano, *Ercolano. Itinerario archeologico ragionato*, Torre del Greco 1997.

M. Pagano (edited by), *Gli antichi Ercolanesi. Antropologia, società, economia*, Napoli 2000.

U. Pappalardo, *Ercolano. Scavi e ricerche nell'ultimo trentennio (con bibliografia dal 1970 al 1998)*, Opuscula Pompeiana 8, Kyoto 1998, pp. 1-35

P.P. Petrone, F. Fedele, *Vesuvio 79 A.D. Vita e morte ad Ercolano*, Napoli 2002.

M.E.A. Pirozzi, *Ercolano, la storia, il territorio: gli scavi*, Napoli 2003.

M. Pagano, *La Villa dei Papiri* in: "Storie da un'eruzione. Pompei, Ercolano, Oplontis", Milano 2003, pp. 98-101.

M.R. Wojcik, *La Villa dei Papiri*, Roma 1986.

Oplontis

A. D'Ambrosio, *Gli ori di Oplontis. Gioielli romani dal suburbio pompeiano*. Mostra Roma, Castel Sant'Angelo 14-28.IV.1987, Napoli 1987.

S. De Caro, *The Sculptures of the Villa of Poppaea at Oplontis: A Preliminary Report* in: Ancient Roman Villa Gardens, Dumbarton Oaks Research Library and Collection, Washington D.C., 1987, pp. 79-133.

A. De Franciscis, *La villa romana di Oplontis* in: B. Andreae, H. Kyrieleis (*editores*), *Neue Forschungen in Pompeji und den anderen vom Vesuvausbruch 79 n.Chr. verschütteten Städten*, Recklinghausen 1975, pp. 9-38.

P.G. Guzzo, L. Fergola, *Oplontis. La Villa di Poppea*, Milano 2000.

Stabia

AA.VV., *In Stabiano. Cultura e archeologia da Stabiae: la città e il territorio tra l'età arcaica e l'età romana*, Castellammare 2001.

AA.VV., *Stabiae. Storia e Architettura 1749-1999*. Atti del Convegno Internazionale per il 250mo Anniversario degli Scavi di Stabiae, Roma 2002.

A. Barbet, P. Miniero (edited by), *La Villa di San Marco a Stabia*, Napoli-Roma-Pompei 1999.

G. Bonifacio, A.M. Sodo, *Stabiae. Guida archeologica alle ville*, 2001.

D. CAMARDO, A. FERRARA (edited by), *Stabiae dai Borboni alle ultime scoperte*, Castellammare di Stabia 2001.
D. CAMARDO, A. FERRARA, *Stabiae: le ville*, Castellammare di Stabia 1989.
D. CAMARDO, A. FERRARA, *Stabiae risorge*, Castellammare di Stabia 1991.
D. CAMARDO, A. FERRARA (edited by), *Tesori di Stabiae. Treasure of Stabiae*, Castellammare 2004 (in Italian and English).
O. ELIA, *Pitture di Stabia*, Napoli 1957.
P. MINIERO, *Stabiae. Pitture e stucchi dalle ville romane*, Napoli 1989.
M. RUGGIERO, *Degli scavi di Stabia dal 1744 al 1782*, Napoli 1881; reprint: Castellammare 1997.

Vesuvius
A. CINQUE, F. RUSSO, *La linea di costa del 79 d.C. fra Oplontis e Stabiae nel quadro della evoluzione olocenica della piana del Sarno*, Bollettino Società Geologica Italiana, 105, Roma 1986.
G. LUONGO (edited by), *Mons Vesuvius. Sfide e catastrofi tra paura e scienza*, Napoli 1997.
A. NAZZARO, *Vesuvio. Storia eruttiva e teorie vulcanologiche*, Napoli 2001, in particular pp. 60-64 ("*Bicipite o monocipite?*").
U. PAPPALARDO, *Vesuvius. Grosse Ausbrüche und Wiederbesiedlungen* in: E. OLSHAUSEN, H. SONNABEND (edited by), *Naturkatastrophen in der antiken Welt*. Akten des 6. Stuttgarter Kolloquium zur historischen Geographie des Altertums, Stuttgart 1996 (= Geographia Historica 10), Stuttgart 1998, pp. 267-274.
H. PICHLER, *Italienische Vulkan-Gebiete* I: Somma-Vesuv, Latium, Toscana, Berlin - Stuttgart 1990.
R. SANTACROCE (a cura di), Somma-Vesuv (= Quaderni della Ricerca Scientifica Consiglio Nazionale delle Ricerche, num. 114, Roma 1987 (with the official geological map).
A. SCHERILLO, *Il Vesuvio prima e dopo Plinio*, Atti Convengno La Regione Sotterrata dal Vesuvio, Napoli 1982, pp. 945-955.
H. SIGURDSSON *et al.*, *The Eruption of Vesuvius in A.D. 79*, National Geographic Research 1, 3, 1985.

Capri
E. FEDERICO, E. MIRANDA (edited by), *Capri antica. Dalla preistoria alla fine dell'eta romana*, Capri 1998.
A. HEDVALL, *San Michele di Axel Munthe*, Stoccolma 1980.
C. KRAUSE, *Villa Jovis. Die Residenz des Tiberius auf Capri*, Mainz 2003.
A. MAIURI, *Capri: storia e monumenti*, Roma 1978.
A. MAIURI, *Breviario di Capri*, Napoli 1988.

Sorrento
C. ALBORE LIVADIE (edited by), *Archeologia a Piano di Sorrento. Ricerche di Preistoria e Protostoria nella Penisola Sorrentina*, Piano di Sorrento 1990.
T. BUDETTA (edited by), *Il Museo archeologico territoriale della Penisola Sorrentina "Georges Vallet"*, Salerno 1999.
C. CECAMORE, *Apollo e Vesta sul Palatino fra Augusto e Vespasiano*, Bullettino Commissione Archeologica Comunale di Roma 96, 1994-1995, pp. 9-32.
S. DE CARO, *Il ninfeo di Massalubrense*, in: AA.VV., *Pompei. Abitare sotto il Vesuvio*. Catalogo della Mostra, Ferrara 1996, pp. 143-162.
S. DE CARO, T. BUDETTA, *Surrentum: venti anni di ricerche archeologiche nella Penisola sorrentino-amalfitana*, Sorrento 1994.
N. DEGRASSI, *La dimora di Augusto sul Palatino e la base di Sorrento*, Rendiconti Pontificia Accademia Romana di Archeologia 39, 1966-1967.
P. MINGAZZINI, F. PFISTER, *Surrentum* (Forma Italiae, Reg. 1, 2), Roma 1946.
U. PAPPALARDO *et al.*, *Statua colossale femminile da Surrentum*, Mitteilungen des Deutschen Archäologischen Instituts, Römische Abteilung 107, 2000, pp. 469-486.
M. RUSSO *et al.* (a cura di P. ZANCANI MONTUORO), *Punta della Campanella. Epigrafe rupestre osca e reperti vari dall'Athenaion*, Monumenti Antichi dei Lincei 8, 3, 1990.
M. RUSSO, *Sorrento. Archeologia tra l'Hotel Vittoria e Capo Circe. Scavi e rinvenimenti dal Settecento a oggi*, Sorrento 1997.

Goethe, Vesuvius and the antiquities of Campania: "Et in Arcadia ego!"
A. ALLROGGEN BEDEL, *Goethe und die antike Kunst* in: AA.VV., *Eine Reise nach Weimar*, Bad Ems 1996, pp. 5-12.
B. ANDREAE, *Goethes Betrachtung antiker Kunst* in: AA.VV. *Goethe in Rom*, 2 voll., Mainz 1997, vol. 1, pp. 132-139.
W. GOETHE, *Lettere da Napoli*, translated by G. FORTUNATO, Introduction and edited by M. ROSSI DORIA, Napoli 1989.
J. GÖRES (edited by), *Goethe in Italien*. Catalogo Mostra Goethe-Museums Düsseldorf, Mainz 1986.
CH. MICHEL, H.G. DEWITZ (edited by), *J.W. Goethe, Italienische Reise*, 2 Bände (= Goethe, Sämtliche Werke, Bd.15, 1-2) Frankfurt 1993. Italian translations: *J.W. Goethe, Viaggio in Italia (1786-1788)*, translated by E. ZANIBONI, Firenze 1980; *J.W. Goethe, Viaggio in Italia*, translated by E. CASTELLANI, Milano 1983.
A. PORZIO, M. CAUSA PICONE, *Goethe e i suoi interlocutori*, Napoli 1983.
D. RICHTER, *Neapel. Biographie einer Stadt*, Berlin 2005.
G. ROVERETO, *Volfango Goethe geologo in Italia*, Memorie della Reale Accademia d'Italia, Classe di Scienze Fisiche, Matematiche e Naturali 13, 6, 1942, pp. 709-729, figg. 1-10.